The Emergence of Malaysia

By the same author

This Was Singapore
Proud Echo
The Heroes

THE EMERGENCE OF
MALAYSIA

by Ronald McKie

Harcourt, Brace & World, Inc., New York

first American edition

Originally published in Australia under the title *Malaysia in Focus*
Library of Congress Catalog Card Number: 63-13504
Printed in the United States of America

For Anne

Acknowledgments

I wish to thank the following:
Paul Abisheganaden, Dorothy Atherton, Norman Bartlett,
William Belton, Alan Blades, R. J. Brooks, Chan You Seek,
Neville Fakes, Charles Gamba, Peter Golding, Bruce Grant,
Oswald Henry, Les Hoffman, Martin Hutton, Eric Jennings,
Alex Josey, R. B. Kelley, Charles Letts, Hugh Mabbett,
Jean Marshall, Gillian Mills, Alastair Morrison, V. T. Sambandan,
Frank Sullivan, George Thompson, and others who,
though nameless, will know whom I mean.

And special thanks to:
Mr. and Mrs. Len Bardsdell, Mr. and Mrs. Harald Brokenshire,
Mr. and Mrs. Robert Dunhauser, Mr. and Mrs. John Shaw,
Mr. and Mrs. Ronald Stead.

Contents

The Emergence of Malaysia

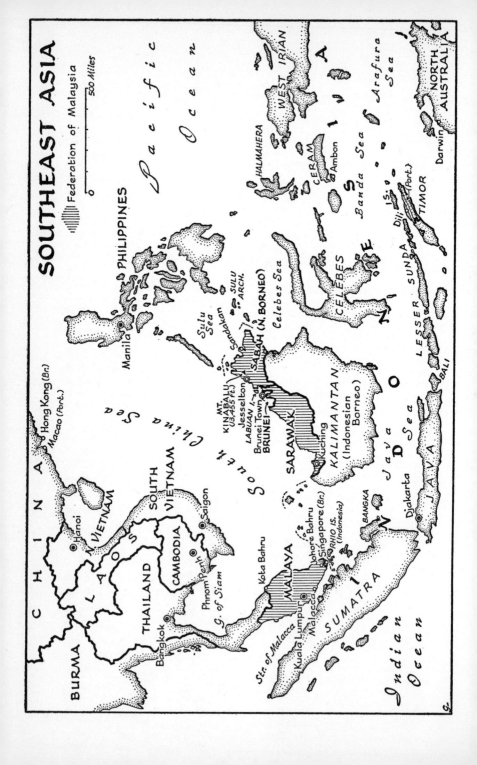

An End—and a Beginning

The thunderheads were lifting in grey folds above the rain trees, and the stained tile roofs of the white barracks. The temperature was in the eighties, humidity higher still, a heat which pressed down with damp hands on this cricket field in Singapore not a hundred miles north of the Equator. Across the turf a Malay boy slept under a banana clump weighted with purple flowers, and at the pavilion, near where the road embraced the outfield, players sagged in cane chairs or lay under the trees, their boots small tombstones rising from the grass.

At the brown matting strip pegged on red earth the game was being played with guile and sweat, and presiding over this tribal rite, his silk shirt sticking to his thin shoulders, was Lord Selkirk, British Commissioner General for Southeast Asia, a wide straw hat decorated with a red paisley pugaree shading his lined, humorously cynical face.

Lord Selkirk was keeping wickets, and keeping them skillfully for a man of more than sixty on a tropical afternoon when any sensible person should have been, if not asleep, then at least inert and in the shade. Crouched behind the stumps, he failed to catch few of the balls which General Ivan Harris, the opposing captain, missed, for this was a challenge game be-

tween the Army and the Commissioner General's team within
the shrinking little England of Far East Land Forces Headquarters at Phoenix Park.

The sun began to dip toward the trees. The dancing air
smelled of scorched grass, curled leaves, curdled bitumen from
the road along which an Indian girl in a rose sari was riding
her Lambretta. But on the field cricket was still being worshipped with that casual but passionate concentration which
the British reserve for sport, beer, and warfare.

A six had just been hit, a faultless arc right out of the ground,
and Lord Selkirk was getting down on his hams again to watch
the next fast ball when a car pulled in behind the pavilion and
a senior official from the British High Commission got out
carrying a black dispatch case.

I saw no sign, no signal, pass between the newcomer and the
field, but the game stopped halfway through an over as though
a sergeant-major had bawled an order. Lord Selkirk went to
the pavilion, put on a short crimson sweat jacket and, still wearing his straw and now smoking a cigarette in a long black
holder, sauntered with the official to another part of the ground
where, joined by a playing member of his staff, the three sat
under a tree.

As any cricketer knows, only the most urgent news, war or
revolution, can stop a cricket match, and particularly one between a Commissioner General and a General Officer Com-
manding. But the black dispatch case was already open and
papers of state spread on the grass, so that the other players had
no alternative but to wipe their faces and gather at the marquee
on the far side of the field—as far away as possible from the
cabinet meeting—and have afternoon tea.

For half an hour nothing moved except one bird which settled in a tree near the pavilion, put its head under its wing,
and went to sleep. Then a Chinese boy in white carried a tray
around the boundary and placed it almost reverently on the
grass beside the Commissioner General. His Lordship soured,
sipped, and ate iced cucumber sandwiches while the official

scribbled on a pad on his knee what was probably the most uncomfortably conceived dispatch in the history of Britain's colonial empire.

The scribbling continued. More papers littered the grass. The High Commissioner fitted yet another cigarette to his long holder. The players came from the marquee, gathered in groups, began to stroll back to the field, aimlessly flicking the ball among them. Another fifteen minutes of that heated afternoon dribbled away before the cabinet meeting ended.

The papers were returned to the black dispatch case. The official hurried to his car. Lord Selkirk returned to the pavilion, removed his crimson jacket, put on his batting pads, since the other team had been forced by the delay to close its innings, and went to the wicket to break every rule of batsmanship in the next few minutes.

But those dispatches? They were from No. 10 Downing Street, from Prime Minister Macmillan. They welcomed the concept of Greater Malaysia, suggested that the father of the plan, the Prime Minister of the Federation of Malaya, Tunku Abdul Rahman, should confer with Mr. Macmillan in London, and set in motion the negotiations designed to end Britain's colonial era in Southeast Asia and in time to create a new and independent nation, the union of Malaya, Singapore, and the Borneo territories—the Crown Colonies of Sarawak and North Borneo and the British Protectorate of Brunei—and to begin one of the most fascinating political and social experiments of our time.

I know that May 27, 1961, will be more acceptable to history as the genesis of the idea to link these five territories in a political union, for that was the date when Tunku Abdul Rahman almost casually suggested the new federation at a luncheon given by the Foreign Correspondents' Association in Singapore, but I shall always feel that Greater Malaysia began traditionally with tea and iced cucumber sandwiches beside that cricket field on a drowsy Singapore afternoon in the gathering twilight of British rule, as a Malay boy slept under a banana tree.

Singapore I

1

A high-castled junk from Kelantan, perhaps from Thailand, was making in toward the Roads, the last of the sun splashing her russet sails and the blue-and-white eyes painted on her hand-shaped bows.

For more than two decades I had not seen junk sails against the distant Thousand Islands or the sun going to bed behind the squalor and luxury of Singapore. Now, in a frangipani-scented garden along the coast, I was about to begin an old journey of new discovery, an experiment in time among people and places I once knew.

I first saw Singapore before World War II after flying from Australia in three and a half days in a biplane you will find only in aviation-history books. Singapore then was at its colonial peak, a small provincial port and base dominated by traders, colonial servants, and barrack-minded soldiers who lived a twilight existence as far apart as possible from half a million Asiatics, mostly Chinese, who did not count.

Now I was back, in eight jet hours, in a city which had sprawled but where other changes were less obvious though more significant. This was the last phase of British rule in Southeast Asia, the final months of endemic rejection of white supremacy, the climax of yet another revolution more of our own making than Asian—a revolution we had helped create by providing Asians with their own historical dissatisfactions, through our own eagerness over the generations to take but to give little, except superficially, to command but not to understand, to rule but not to join, to be just when justice was not enough.

I had no detailed plan, except that people would play an important part in this journey of rediscovery. Knowing a little of the Southeast Asian past, I would try to assess, though in no authoritative way, the patterns of change and the forces which had shaped that change. I would look, with sympathy I hoped, at the world's newest country-to-be, Malaysia, at its genesis. I would wander with a notebook, seeing, listening, and remembering.

The junk is turning the point. The light is changing. The palms step closer, reach higher into a sky of mother-of-pearl. The starlings stop their frantic circling and blacken the fronds. A sarong smolders at the end of the long garden.

For perhaps a minute, when colors are more brilliant, sounds more distinct, shapes more defined, the flare lasts. Then the blue light drains away and for the first time the air is cool ahead of the night sea mist as a light splutters on a fishing pagar a mile offshore to give the day its ultimate perspective.

Night comes quickly. It sweeps a last smear of rose toward Sumatra, dissolves a cloud, paints out the Plimsolls and the rust of anchored ships. A dark palm trunk reappears in another place. The dusk is almost suffocating. The garden stretches, stretches, and is lost in the sea.

From the past I still wonder, as the dark dust settles, at this miracle of night and day, still feel the sudden pressure of unspoken things, unknown forces, in the incomparable Malayan night. Even when light spills on the terrace and the Chinese boy brings gin and fresh limes I feel, as I did the first time, the night's presence around the house, in the garden shadows above the little beach where monsoon and tide have played for

years with the concrete machine-gun nest—nostalgic monument
to the thinking of men who faced the wrong way.

This vague uneasiness is peculiar to this place, or perhaps
only to me in this place. It is part of the transformation from
light to dark, a change so violent and yet so gentle that the
mind has no time to adjust to another dimension.

It is linked with an awareness of jungle, although there is no
real jungle for miles, of the menace of wild things. It has something to do with the original inhabitants of this small island
and area, the Malays themselves and their brooding spirits of
earth and water and fire, of their hantus, who speak from the
sea and perch in trees and ride the clouds of this still animistic
world of red earth clothed in green fur. Even *malam*, Malay for
"night," is an ominous word of restless scatterings, of furtive unseen things which have no place in the thinking of men whose
race memory goes back to Celtic crosses on bare hillsides and
beyond.

Perhaps this is why you feel in this place, among the gods and
spirits which have shaped Asia, that at any moment something
will happen to you that has never happened before, that you
will be influenced by forces over which you have no control. It
is a feeling almost indefinable and so illogical that you know it
could be true.

Then I hear the cooling earth breathing and relax, drenched
in night, and watch the stars arranging themselves and a flying
fox like the Chinese symbol of happiness flap in the moon's
peasant face. I listen for old familiar sounds. . . .

Flute and drums and brass . . .

Plaint of cart wheels passing slowly and the song of the Tamil
driver, broken with pauses, like a man muttering in his
sleep . . .

Padding of a rickshaw puller, steady as a pulse, the high
clamor of his bell or his half-shouted, half-grunted warning as
he swerves and pads on, his oil lamp dwindling . . .

But all I hear from the road beyond the trees is the swish,
swish of tires.

.   .   .

The manager repeated the legend that his hotel had been built last century by an English duke. A nineteenth-century duke could have been responsible for decorating the lounge bar in woodland scenes from deepest England, complete with prints of hunting and highwaymanship, but only a contemporary duke would have nailed four Chinese characters to the wall above the dusty Bols bottles—characters which resembled a house, a man running, a bush, and a head of a Sioux—and supplied the simple translation below, "Terms Cash."

My Chinese hotel was a house of surprise. Swing doors opened, a little reluctantly, to another time, for in what had once been the original reception hall was a double staircase of carved teak with mirrors painted with Chinese birds and flowers let into the woodwork under the stairs. Even the carved posts supporting the central landing of the staircase were faced with mirrors, and enormous mirrors in carved frames with faded gold leaf were set beside historical scrolls, now rotting and stained, that were once masterpieces of Chinese embroidery art.

At the top of the grand staircase was an open hall, with rooms on either side and each room distinguished by columns supporting a doorway arch. The high roof of this hall was domed, narrowing upward into a glassed turret thirty feet above the floor, and below the dome was a musicians' gallery, where no musician had ever played, enclosed by a fragile double rail.

Below again, and behind the staircase, was the dining room, where tables were set between sweeping white arches supporting a beamed blue roof. This room was open to gardens on either side, and to the flap of washing, and from one end was dominated by the largest mirror in the house, ten feet high and five feet wide, a collector's piece topped with carved gold flowers and filigree held together by the talons of golden eagles.

It was here among the reflected ghosts of the nineteenth-century colonial era, among Chinese scrolls, Siamese teak, Greek arches, and abominable cooking, that I settled into a bedroom where an ancient air-conditioning unit thumped and wheezed all night and where Foo Wee Suan, the room boy, looked after me like a favorite aunt.

Foo was a Hailam from Hainan Island, tall and thin with elegant hands and a stretched face. When he smiled he looked at the world with gentle irony, or perhaps he was observing just another foreign devil. He had natural dignity, and he moved as positively and silently as a good safe-breaker.

With that unique bush telegraph of the Chinese he knew when I came in and when I went out, when to fill the thermos or bring tea, when the laundry was needed, whether I preferred bananas or papaya. Foo also saw that the tub was always full, since the bathroom was primitive—an old washtub on a stand and a metal dipper, and much the same as many other bathrooms I had known in Singapore, except that in place of the tub I missed the big decorative Shanghai jar. Some of these jars, which kept water almost ice cold, were so large that you could get into them, and the story used to be told of the woman who did and became stuck and had to call her house-boy. After much shouted persuasion the boy brought a hammer and smashed the jar, and the woman never recovered from the shock of a "native" seeing her, white, flabby, and glistening, awash on the bathroom tiles among the broken crockery.

It was in this hotel that I began to discover other more significant echoes of twenty years before. My fellow guests in the blue-roofed dining room were Chinese, English, Eurasian, Hindu, Dutch, American, a collection which, even in a non-European hotel, was unknown in the Singapore of the past, where segregation between white and other racial colors, and between the different colors themselves, was, except for a few rare nonconformists, rigidly practiced. This multi-racial and religious mixing, even in an impersonal dining room, suggested the breaking down of old taboos, old prejudices, the development of new thought and attitudes, and of a new and healthy toleration. If this was only a rare beginning, then here was a revolutionary room where a new society in microcosm broke bread.

Here was the source of endless speculation and inquiry. And I was still wondering what other changes I would find when from above the grand staircase a child began to play scales, but softly, so that when he or she stopped, the notes did not cease but seemed to drift among the rooms, into the building itself, into the teak carving, into the stained spaces behind the old mirrors whose eyes were long blurred with the seeing of too many things.

Then surer fingers played Chopin as a bat, no bigger than a matchbox, came in from the garden, circled near the ceiling, and flicked into the flowering shrubs on the other side. I waited, hoping it would return. Then I followed it into the night.

2

The wise warn us never to go back. The wise are probably right, but the cave urge is strong in most of us to take another look, even though the romantic garden has shrunk to an untidy back yard by the time we arrive.

On a steaming morning, under a sifted sky, I returned to Orchard Road, which used to dissect an area of almost rural peace between the city and the main residential suburbs. Flame of the Forests still opened their scarlet umbrellas along its way, but now over traffic like Chicago's, and shops and flats and bars covered once-open grassland where a herd of milking goats, wearing pink and blue and white brassières, grazed in the late afternoons watched by a crippled Indian herdsman and stray startled tourists.

The old Chinese cemetery, where monsoon rain flattened the long grass around the womb graves, and where relatives brought rice and fruit and baskets of frangipani, had disappeared, and in its place was a block of flats and a wasteland behind and beside it—a bulldozed hillside the color of orange peel above which still hovered the outraged spirits of the Chinese dead.

A Chinese duster man passed, his familiar bicycle a nodding, swaying mass of brown feathers. A drink seller languidly shook his bell and spat betel juice at the cars. The sweating pedicab riders, who had replaced the rickshaw pullers, allegedly on humanitarian grounds, pedaled their heavy clumsy vehicles with three times the effort that any despised rickshaw boy ever pulled.

I came at last to one of the objects of my search—a long low building which, in the time I had known it as Café Wien, was painted green and looked like a tired bordello. Now it was Prince's Restaurant, where you need an expense account to eat, and although redesigned and redecorated, probably many times, and air-conditioned with Antarctic thoroughness, there still lingered behind the paneling of its darker corners the small echoes of conspiracy, for Café Wien had been a café–rooming house and a gathering center of the local German Nazi party in those days when Adolf Hitler was advancing to Munich and beyond and to the death of millions.

It was here, where the Nazi manager terrorized his assistant with party threats, and where the assistant was servile and arrogant by turns to his guests, that I had spent my first uncomfortable weeks in prewar Singapore amid the weary smell of sauerkraut. It was here, too, that I listened interminably to advice on tropical living and colonial taboos from my fellow English Tuans.

White society in those days was not unlike a geological chart. At the top were the important white masters, the Tuan Besars, who ruled political and commercial Singapore like grandmothers in a traditional Chinese home and who tolerated no deviations from colonial norms. In the middle were the secondary but still important Tuan Ketchils or Small Tuans, the down-the-line executives, and at the bottom of the chart were the young or otherwise unimportant underpaid Tuans like myself. But even to be a Tuan, the lowliest member of the ruling class, conferred special privileges, including the right to shout at servants and to be rude to Asians in general.

A Tuan, I was warned, did not mix with Asiatics or Eurasians, although it was permissible to sleep with them, or travel in public transport, or sit in the same seats at any entertainment, but he must wear a coat and tie, except at weekends, must soon after arrival in the colony drop his visiting cards in the private letter boxes of his company's Tuan Besars, and must not wear a sarong instead of pajamas because that was an early sign of going native. He should also sleep with a sheet or light blanket across his middle, a ritual under the ever-clicking ceiling fans which discouraged the fever, a word which even Somerset Maugham could not resist, though it did not protect me from the mosquito which gave me dengue or the melancholia of that fever's convalescence. A Tuan also had a duty to himself and to society to take as much exercise as possible because this was good for health and white morale and a good example to Asiatics, who lacked all sporting instincts. Avoidance of games was regarded as almost a new form of perversion.

This was the time, and long before the air-conditioner had turned Singapore nights into autumn, when a few old European hands still slept the traditional way—on a hard wood Chinese bed covered with a thin mat and with a wood block, curved to fit the head and neck, as pillow. With this went the Dutch Wife, on every bed when I first knew Singapore, and still used by a few—a tight sausage-shaped bolster in a white slip over which you cocked one leg for comfort and added coolness.

From Café Wien four of us had moved to a crumbling Dutch colonial bungalow where we lived in decaying splendor with a garden full of orchids, the common variety, a tennis court, an ancient Portuguese cannon which we dug up from a flower bed and mounted near the front steps, and staff of four servants.

But when I searched for the house, with its four bathrooms equipped with huge Shanghai jars and the walls of its big veranda room crawling with copulating chichaks, the small pink-tongued house lizards which keep down the flies, new bungalows covered the area.

It was a happy place, an amusing and curious place. The

ghost, wearing a white topee, picking orchids in the garden, but seen only by one of my messmates after he had finished most of a bottle of whisky. The hypnotist who put a whole party to sleep and later hypnotized an American girl tourist by remote control—by going into the garden, facing the house, and willing her to sleep where she sat on the veranda. The party which bet hundreds of dollars on the toctoc, that night bird with a sense of humor whose monotonous call is like bamboo sticks being beaten together but who never makes the same number of calls twice running. The Indian Hatha Yogi who ate a double handful of tacks, a thick saucer, the head of a snake which he bit off while it was still alive and chewed to bloody pulp, a bowl of concentrated nitric acid in which a copper coin had been dissolved, and who then stood in a fire pit for five minutes and walked out—unharmed.

A time of youth and magic and boredom and excitement and loneliness. The muttering of kampong drums at night. The trunks of rubber trees silver-etched in the moonlight. The thrashing of a Sumatra, that demented wind which sweeps Singapore. The sour-mice smell of mildew in the wet season. The bleached monotony of white clothes, white buildings, white minds. The boredom of repetition in a society of sameness. The frustrations, anxieties, aches of youth among strangers.

But I had other calls that were part of the nostalgia of return, and I had to move on from the bungalow whose reality was as frail as a faded photograph.

I went to Bukit Larangan, the Forbidden Hill and the heart of Singapore, a climb which took me through crumbling gates and up a walled slope under great trees to the place where Singapore's oldest Europeans lie.

The large monuments were unbroken and strong, determined never to accept the inevitable; the smaller stones swayed, reclined, the struggle over, the grass encroaching. Many of the original inscriptions had been lifted to make patterns in marble and stone on the handmade brick walls around this ancient graveyard, where empire builders unaware that empires could crumble—sailors and clergymen, merchants and soldiers, wives and children—were detained forever as they passed this way.

Jane Elizabeth, beloved wife of John Fleming Martin Reid, Esquire, of the Bengal Civil Service, who died in 1838. Paula Tereipa, died four years earlier. Seph Harvey Weed, who was only thirty-two and who came from Rockingham, Vermont, to die in 1848. His memorial, one of the sturdy ones, was erected to his memory by friends in the United States. But who was Seph Weed, and how did he come to die so young and so far from home?

Up old stone steps through the Chinese tea smell of grass hand-cut by a Malay with circling parang, up to the top of the Forbidden Hill and the origins of this city of gardens and tree-lined roads and hedge-bordered lanes, of Christian spires and temple roofs, of aseptic mansions and the sores of Chinatown, of flats and kampongs, of modern traffic roundabouts and road-steads packed with ships, of a sea of emerald, of sapphire, set in filigree haze, of wealth and ostentation and dejection and poverty, of monuments and nostalgic words and names and memories bittersweet. Genesis of this island of stained beach sand, mud flat, swamp and low hills, of palm and jungle and the grey huddles of kampong thatch, of nearly two million people, a racial spectrum in a diamond-shaped area only twenty-six miles long and fourteen wide off the tip of thrusting Asia, a place of gathering tension in the sweat of endless summer.

The ancient Greeks knew Malaya as the Golden Chersonese, the Golden Peninsula, and a Greek geographer called it "The last inhabited land beneath the rising sun itself." Tumasek—Sea Town—was the name the ancient Javanese and Chinese gave this city, and later it was known as the City of the Lion, from the Sanskrit *singa pura*. This was six hundred years ago, when the Lion City was ruled by Hindu kings and when a moated palace was on Bukit Larangan and its spring, where the royal harem bathed, was the Forbidden Place. But in the four-teenth century, twenty years before Agincourt, the warlike power of Mejapahit in Java sacked Singapore, and the Malays still say that the red clay of Singapore Island takes its color from the blood of that massacre. Centuries later the white bungalow of Sir Stamford Raffles, the founder of modern Singapore in 1819, was built on Government Hill, as the Forbidden Hill was then named, and later still the hill became Fort Canning and military headquarters. It was Canning when Yamashita's Japanese captured Singapore in 1942 and renamed the city and island Shonan, which meant Bright South.

I climbed Bukit Larangan to speak again to Mohamad Noor, but the big, bearded, soft-voiced Moslem was long dead, and his son, Mohamad Abas, was now the custodian of the tomb of Sultan Iskandar Shah. Historians say that Iskandar Shah, last of the Lion City kings, died years later in Malacca after the city was sacked by the Javanese, and that he could not have been buried on Singapore's Forbidden Hill. They say that the man in the tomb could be a prince of Palembang in Sumatra, Sri Tri Buana, founder of the Singapore dynasty, who was said to have been buried on the "hill of Singapore." Whoever is buried there is still well cared for and much revered, for the tomb and its adjoining prayer house have been sacred ground to the Malays, to all Moslems, since well before British times, and the family of Mohamad Abas claim to have been traditional guardians of the shrine for at least one hundred and thirty-five years.

This is such sacred ground that on the day the Japanese occupied Singapore and hoisted their flag on the Forbidden Hill, the Malays shook their heads and muttered, "This is a bad omen for the invaders." The Malays were also quick to notice that the Japanese flag rotted quickly and had often to be replaced. They still say that the Japanese heard of their prediction and in 1943 stopped flying their flag on the Forbidden Hill and even took down the flagstaff. The Japanese will have their own version.

Mohamad Abas, in a blue shirt outside his blue-and-white sarong and wearing a brown velvet songkok, or Malay cap, was glad to talk to anyone who had known Mohamad Noor, his father. Mohamad Abas is a bachelor, but by family arrangement his younger brother, who has children, will carry on the guardianship. Mohamad spends his days at the shrine, and often sleeps on a mat there, particularly if there are storms, so that he can make sure that the oil lamps, which have never gone out, are kept burning.

The shrine of Iskandar Shah, whom the Malays call the "Last King," is a small whitewashed compound, and from it tall trees race down the slope. The tomb is shaded by a white-and-yellow canopy which bears the star and crescent of Islam. The tomb itself is covered with a faded pink cloth draped to fit an almost bodylike shape, and on this cloth Mohamad daily sprinkles flowers and leaves and herbs. At the head of the tomb are two stone pillars, like ancient cannons firing at the sky, and on their mouths are the star and crescent and between the columns burn tapers of sandalwood and above them hang coconut-oil lamps with limp smoking wicks.

Devotees bring flowers and fruit and rice wrapped in the polished green of banana leaves. Some take the food away after they have prayed, but most leave it for Mohamad Abas and his family so that, even if money is not dropped into the little box beside the shrine, he is never in need. Just-married couples come to squat on the mats in the open prayer house and to hang stones and lumps of charcoal on the gold-painted iron fence which surrounds the tomb, and to ask the spirit of Iskandar Shah for children. And others just come to stand before the Last King and then go on their way.

At night the oil lamps flicker above the muttering neon city, and once, in Mohamad Noor's time, so he told me himself, a white tiger crawled from the tomb and went down the slopes of the Forbidden Hill toward the roofs of the city.

I said good-by at last to Sultan Iskandar Shah and his guardian and on the way down patted the headstone of Seph Harvey Weed. Then I drove miles along the island's coast to Pasir

Panjang to make another call, but although the Coconut Grove had, like Mohamad Noor, disappeared, tracks led back to a narrow street of Chinese shop-houses off Orchard Road and to a mansion of Victorian Singapore at its end.

The rain-stained walls of the old house had not been painted for decades. Its double iron gates, pushed back to expose a short curving drive, had not moved in fifty years. Bamboo in front of the entrance steps had been there so long that a hundred people could have stood in its shade. A fishpond held dead leaves, a faded cigarette pack, and dust printed with the feet of sparrows.

In what was once the ballroom cane chairs and tables had been pushed against the walls and stacked in alcoves and side rooms. Mirrors gazed at the shabbiness with blurred eyes. On one side was a circular bar and even it seemed to have been nailed together in a hurry. Inside the bar was a refrigerator and a beer barrel marked "Old Faithful 1946-1957 (retired)," and around the top of the bar were grinning "shrunken" heads, with beards and glass eyes, made from coconut husks.

This was the Coconut Grove, or what was left of it, and the old man with soft white hair and wasted arms whose bare feet made no sound as he crossed the dance floor was American Bill Bailey, last of the old-time troopers of the Southeast Asian entertainment world.

"Be with you in a minute . . . Got a bit of cleaning up to do."

His accent was an amalgam of Californian and Australian. His voice was tired, like his eyes.

I perched on a stool as he rinsed a cloth and began to wash down the bar. He wore white cotton slacks. His silky hair looked powdered. I remembered him as medium height and heavy with a rubber face, the face of a clown, for this man could stand for minutes before an audience and not say a word and still they laughed and didn't know why. Now he was frail and shrunken, the damp skin of his chest in folds and wrinkles. And beneath, deep inside, I sensed a lethal weariness of the spirit.

"You don't remember me."

"Seen you before sometime. But I've seen a million faces."
He didn't look up.

"It's more than twenty years since I last heard you sing—
and tell stories."

"I always did have a dirty mind. Where was that?"

"Out Pasir Panjang way—back in the thirties."

"So you knew the Grove?"

"We bachelors helped keep you and Cowan in business."

He asked my name.

"I know your face now. You and the boys used to sit on the
far side of the floor from the entrance. One was a Kiwi, a big
fellow who did a Haka."

"Right. The dance floor built over the sea. The curving palm
above the floor, or was it two palms? The lights of the fishermen netting in the shallow water . . . It's a long time."

"My son of a bitch it's a long time."

Bill rubbed away at an ashtray, and even that made him
tired.

"It's twenty years since the Japs bombed out the old Grove.
Thirty since I lived in the States, where I was born. Forty since
I worked in Australia, except for one short visit. I was born in
eighty-six—January first. Too bloody right it's a long time. Now
I'm tired. I have blackouts. I want to die. But I'm not going
to do a Hemingway."

He rinsed the cloth and spread it on the top of the barrel and
turned almost fiercely.

"Not me."

He came from behind the bar and we went across the floor
and sat near a window which overlooked the garden of a Bud-
dhist nunnery. We talked about the Singapore of the past,
about the Grove and the people from every country who went
there, and all the time I was conscious of the sadness of this
meeting and of its finality.

"The Sultan of Johore was there one night with a gorgeous
Chinese girl," I deliberately recalled. "We couldn't take our
eyes off her."

Bill grinned. "I introduced Bourbon to the old son of a —— to His Royal Highness. He liked it."

"And the boys from the Iniskilling Fusiliers."

"The mad Irishmen. They nearly wrecked the place one night."

On and on we went.

"Bill," I said at last, "There's something I want to ask you. I've heard it said you're the original of that song. . . ."

He rubbed his beaked nose, spread his arms and sang:

"Won't you come home, Bill Bailey,
Won't you come home, Bill Bailey,
Won't you please come home."

He shook his silver head. "It's not true, and what's more I've never claimed to be the original. Some American magazines have run small pieces about me, but the truth about that song is that Bill Bailey never existed. There never was one. Bill Bailey is just like Old Black Joe and Uncle Tom all over again. Customers even say to me, 'Bill Bailey, why don't you go home?' and I say, 'Hell, I like it here.' "

Bill was born in Maxwell, Iowa, but he isn't even sure whether Maxwell still exists. His real name isn't Bailey, but that is a personal secret he won't discuss. His father, David, took the name Bailey—and that's all that can be said. Bill's grandmother helped look after him as a child. A long way back in his ancestry, which is basically Welsh, was an Indian squaw from Quebec.

"My old man, who was a medicine man, looked like Pawnee Bill with a pointed beard and a five-gallon hat. He called himself a doctor but he was a wandering patent-medicine hawker who made his own corn moonshine and colored it with burnt sugar. The result was awful. He labeled it 'Bailey's Gypsy Liniment' and sold the stuff to farmers, if their wives didn't catch him first and beat him up. The Liniment was so strong that if you put it on your leg the leg fell off. That Liniment wasn't healthy. Perhaps that's why we were always on the move—in summer. In winter we laid up in stalls and bars. I never went to school—never had the chance. I worked from the time I was eight—sweeping stables, odd jobs, helping Father sell his Liniment, learning song-and-dance routines from passing shows and using them as part of the sales act. Every time my father and mother separated—and that was often—Father would drink all the liquor he couldn't sell, and that was a powerful lot of liquor. Whenever my parents separated, Grandmother took me. She had black hair, beady eyes, and high cheekbones. You could see the Indian in her. I never knew much about Grandfather. He drove a stagecoach."

Bill Bailey has been everything in this world except a pimp. His own words. Actor, salesman, shop assistant, circus hand, rancher, gold miner, street cleaner, and many more. At fourteen he worked in a hotel in Seattle, Washington, where he was known as the Musical Bellboy who played a one-string fiddle he made from a cigar box and a harp made from a bicycle frame—two of the fourteen instruments he finally learned to play. He prospected in Alaska, worked a gold mine in Mexico until he was given twenty-four hours to leave the country—and got out in six. As an actor he even performed in an asylum in Los Angeles, where, to the delight of the inmates, who knew that he was crazier than they were, he ate a bowl of goldfish made from raw carrot.

He first went into vaudeville when he joined Dave Hodges, who changed his name to Barnum, and as Bailey and Barnum they performed in many parts of the world and lasted until the mid-twenties, with a break for World War I, when Bill served with the American Army in France as a sergeant instructor and expert on the water-cooled Browning machine-gun. On one short leave in Paris Bill spent eight hundred dollars and was drunk for eight days. What he calls the most glorious week in his seventy-six years.

Bill appeared with his partner in Fred and Adele Astaire's *Lady Be Good* and claims, with complete lack of reticence, that because they stopped the show the pit musicians charged overtime. He toured Asia with Betty Compson, who had a "beautiful body, played the fiddle, was having husband trouble, and could drape herself round a coconut tree and send sane men mad." He played the cello with his shoe, helped by Marion Davies and George Gershwin, at one of William Randolph Hearst's birthday parties. He knew Cary Grant when he was Archie Leach, the Bristol Boy stilt walker, who lived in Greenwich Village with Orry Kelly. He was a friend of Charles Chick Sale and W. C. Fields and John McCormick and Mae West and even Houdini.

Bill tells stories with many rude words and with complete disregard for dates or sequence, so that one moment you're with him in Shanghai, the next getting drunk in London, the next being booked by Joseph Schenck for one show a day at Palisades Park, and the next in Atlantic City while Samuel Gompers nurses a girl on his knees and holds a furled umbrella in his right hand. You need to be an authority on the American theater, with a memory back to Edwardian times, to hope to keep track of Bill's career.

"I've even been in Pago Pago, where Somerset Maugham wrote *Rain*. And I'm the only son-of-a-bitch actor in the world who has never played the sex-starved Rev. Davidson."

Bill Bailey toured South Africa in 1921 and then spent three years in vaudeville in Australia, where he was a friend of comedians like Roy Rene and Jim Gerald, poets like Banjo Patterson and C. J. Dennis, and even gangsters like Squizzy Taylor—"A little Jew in a bowler hat who used to visit me in my dressing room at the Tivoli in Sydney to give me the latest racing tips."

Bill married Jean Marsh, who played in *The Birth of a Nation*.

"We lived scrappily for forty years and she saved every cent she could get her hands on. She was wonderful. The biggest lump of money I ever had in my life was one hundred and ninety thousand U.S. dollars, and it was all due to her. She was a crazy bird lover, and when we landed back in San Francisco from Australia in 1924, we had four hundred African and Australian birds, including a white cockatoo which whistled 'Yes, we have no bananas.' They cost me fifty cents' duty a bird to land, and for a couple of days we had to keep the lot in our hotel bathroom. I thought the birds would go mad."

Scenting depression in 1929 Bill Bailey left the United States to tour again and has never returned. He was in Australia, briefly, in 1931, and five years later he and Lynn Cowan, a civil engineer turned entertainer whom he had known for years and worked with in California and with the Betty Compson company, opened the Coconut Grove in Singapore.

It was a gay place, thanks to the antics and humor of thin Cowan and fat Bailey. But the Grove lasted only a few years. The Japanese bombed it during their attack on Singapore, and after the war Mrs. Bailey could find only one piece of marble tile from the front hall to keep as a paperweight souvenir of the original cabaret.

Bill, who was fifty-six when Singapore surrendered, used his years as a prisoner of war to learn to read and write. And this is what he wrote one day in 1945 when the Japanese handed out postcards to be filled in by prisoners:

Mr. William Randolph Hearst,
c/o San Francisco Chronicle,
Market Street,
San Francisco.

Dear Bill,
    Having a good time. Wish you were here instead of me.

                                        Bill Bailey.

When the Pacific war ended, Bill and his wife began again in the present old mansion in the street of Chinese houses. It was once the British Army Paymaster's Office, but the Japanese

Kempeitai first occupied it after the British surrender and only partly painted out the British Army signs, which can still be seen, and later the Japanese Navy took it over.

As Bill says: "The Coconut Grove reopened on Christmas Day, 1945, with fifty tables and twenty-five Chinese thieves as cooks and waiters. I had the greatest difficulty finding musical instruments to get a band started and was forced to buy a full band on the black market to get one bass viol."

But that was nearly twenty years ago. Today, Lynn Cowan lives in Okinawa. Mrs. Bailey, who played in *The Birth of a Nation*, saved money, and loved birds, is dead. The Coconut Grove has withered to a bar. And frail Bill Bailey, last of the troopers, is on his way to eighty.

Some years ago a newspaper owner from Ohio, who had known Bill for a long time, was visiting Singapore. He told Bill a home was always waiting in Ohio and asked him to come back and live with him and his wife for the rest of his days. Bill refused. Ever since, at midnight on Bill's birthday, January 1, this friend has telephoned and pleaded with Bill to change his mind and come home. These annual calls have come from the United States and from many world capitals. But the answer has always been the same.

"I'm never going back," Bill said as we shook hands on the entrance steps. "I want to die, in my sleep, here, soon. I know why Hemingway did it. I can understand. A man reaches the stage when he knows he is tired and can't go on."

> Won't you come home, Bill Bailey,
> Won't you please come home.

3

From Stevens Road, where the trees genuflect over stately homes, wide stairs lift into Tanglin, but the act of climbing to this club, where the city's white Establishment has so long presided, brings closer the clamor of Asian Singapore and the end of an era.

Waiting in an oasis of indoor plants I watch members of one of the last exclusive white clubs in Asia move in and out. Businessmen in dark suits or dark trousers and light coats, for the traditional all-white tropical uniform is now as outmoded as the topee was in my time. Mems in summer dresses carrying novels and shopping baskets and the weight of social responsibilities. Diplomats, doctors, travelers, servicemen. Even an aging general in jungle green, bright decorations, and knee dimples winking below his wide shorts. And all white, for despite lip service to social equality which allows non-Europeans to be associates—and a few brave souls are—only Europeans can be members.

My charming host showed me around—the blue swimming pool, the squash courts, the elegant carpeted lounge where, if a lady lost a safety pin, she would never hear it fall. The club had contracted here, expanded there, and, in keeping with the

political climate of Singapore, the ceiling of the open lounge-
ballroom was pinker than I remembered it through the haze
of a far-distant New Year's Eve.

We drank gimlets at an air-conditioned bar among accents
from London to Dundee, and in a cool dining room, where the
conversation as well as the décor was hushed, and where it was
impossible to imagine a shout of "Boy"—a call for service
which, like white prestige, has also disappeared into history—
the chilled soup, the lobster, and the tinned lichee were delicious.

But I had an uncomfortable feeling that I had seen it all
before. The clothes were different, but nothing else seemed to
have changed, except that the food had improved and the
temperature had dropped. Thinking back, I could not help
wondering whether lessons taught in blood not so many years
ago had ever been learned.

Deep in colonial times, when a few Englishmen lived in
Singapore or Kuala Lumpur, the club was an island of privacy
where they could relax after a day's ruling or trading. It was a
common meeting place for them and for people who lived isolated from each other. Even a generation ago clubs like Tanglin
were still historically understandable, although they had long
outlived their purpose and had become, what the British would
never face, centers of political and social disaster, even centers
of hate. It was what they represented, not what they were.

By the act of coming ashore at Singapore, ordinary white
people became Tuans and Mems, Masters and Mistresses, automatically confirmed in the certainty of their own position and
superiority. However uneducated or insignificant, they were the
rulers and all others the ruled. They represented, at their worst,
the narrowness and ignorance, and at times the arrogance, of a
small, intellectually limited society with a monopoly of position and power, and their most successful members in government, in commerce, and in the armed services gravitated, under
certain rigid conditions, to membership in the Tanglin Club.

Some of these people, who lacked qualities essential to hold a job in any competitive society, were the source of the old but not always accurate definition of Singapore-Malaya as a first-class country for third-rate people, for there were intelligent, thoughtful, liberal citizens and members who, knowing that the colonial inheritance from the nineteenth century and earlier had long reached its peak and could not survive, unchanged and unchanging, were still bedeviled by the system itself, by their inability to change or influence the thinking from the past, and, never far below the surface, by their own brooding sense of impermanence, the knowledge that the Island of Singapore, or the mainland of Malaya, was not their own, that the people they ruled or worked with were, however much they liked or disliked them, strangers, and that eventually they would return "home," after a lifetime in the tropics, on a pension, to die within a year of so, as many did, from cold and smog-inspired respiratory diseases.

British colonial rule in Singapore and Malaya, even a generation ago, was still nineteenth century in its thinking, attitude, and methods, but although it jailed or deported if the Establishment considered ideas too liberal, and even though it made sure that wages were at bedrock to give British investment a handsome profit, it was not corrupt or vicious as the twentieth-century colonial powers, Russia and China, would now like the world, and particularly the Afro-Asian world, to believe. The only disgraceful official act I know of in two years I lived in Singapore was not directed against Asians but against British people. This was a secret round-up of male homosexuals before World War II and their deportation, without any charge being laid against them, without inquiry or appeal, back to England. That to me was a brutal act, but not a word was ever published about that round-up by newspapers, which, though not censored, appeared virtually at the Governor's pleasure.

Where the British failed, and it was the failure of most colonial societies, was that although they gave material things, which were also part of their own control and development of foreign territory, they ignored one important fact—that the people they ruled and employed were human beings with intelligence, fears, hopes, pride. Perhaps above all, pride. The one rule in Asia the British consistently broke was "Face," for to make a Malay or a Chinese or an Indian lose face was to make him despise and hate. Women, by their own example, the futile lives they led, and their attitude to Asians, were more responsible for this than their menfolk. Transplanted to a society where they became overnight queens, where many, though by no means all, led an indolent existence, and where they often lacked the elementary education and background to understand the people and forces around them, they lived apart, self-segregated from Asia, despising or indifferent to everything outside their little Englands under the palms. If any one collective group presided over the decline of the British Empire, it was those English women, the Mems of Asia.

Years ago a club like Tanglin was anachronistic, but since World War II it has been a historical curiosity which has survived despite Japanese conquest, the Emergency, as the Communist civil war in Malaya was naïvely named, and even internal self-rule in 1959, when Singapore became a city-state governed not by its minority whites but its majority Chinese.

The Tanglin mentality, for here gathered the rule makers of an ultra-conservative society, contributed to the surrender to Japan, but Tanglin was not then, nor is it now, the only club group which still ignores the lessons of the past. In an era of revolutionary change in Asia, where the European still exists not because he is wanted but because he represents capital and technical knowledge and is temporarily needed for specialist work, the all-white Singapore Swimming Club graciously allows its members to invite Asian guests, in an Asian city about to become independent, on guest nights. It is not surprising that the Chinese staff of this club, who give the worst service in Singapore, have perfected a form of dumb insolence unsurpassed anywhere. It is also not surprising that the Queen's portrait, since local self-government was achieved, has disappeared from government and public buildings—though it is still in the Tanglin Club—and has been replaced by the sad Mischa Auer–like face of a local-born Malay journalist, Inche Yusof bin Ishak, the Yang di-Pertuan Negara, or Head of State.

Singapore is still British, but only for a few months more as it moves to its federation with Malaya and the Borneo territories and the creation of Greater Malaysia. The powers the British still have, over defense, foreign affairs, and security, are running out, and after nearly one hundred and fifty years the British, under the pressure of history and their own failure to settle Malaya instead of colonizing it and, perhaps more important, to identify themselves with its people, are getting out. Under local self-government the white civil service has already gone—replaced by Chinese, Indians, Malays, Eurasians—except for a few individuals who remain in key administrative positions and who will soon be handing over to Asians and heading "home." The civilian whites of Singapore, and not only the British, are rapidly becoming almost exclusively commercial and professional—businessmen mostly operating in a Chinese-governed island which will soon be British no longer.

It is therefore one of the paradoxes of Singapore that white clubs like Tanglin and the Swimming can still exist, or that foreign businessmen who assess the future with critical eyes can afford to be identified with these small segregated white islands adrift in an Asian sea. It is also paradoxical that while members of curiosities like Tanglin have become the real aliens of the Malaysian world, many Europeans, and especially younger Europeans, don't segregate themselves but mix with refreshing freedom with the local Asian community.

In the Singapore I knew, mixing, though possible, was discouraged, mostly by subtle social pressures. The young man who was seen out with an Asian or Eurasian girl was already a marked young man. If he worked for any of the major

British firms, and was reported for breaking the unwritten taboos of white society, he would be paraded by his company chief and warned that the meetings must stop. If he ignored this fatherly advice he was handed his ticket and put on the next ship to England. The young "rebel" had no say in his departure. He was quietly deported and never allowed back. To his fellows with contracts uncompleted or who liked the place and wanted to stay, he was a living though permanently absent example that the rulers demanded and could enforce conformity.

Some firms even dictated the dress of their employees, one brokerage company insisting that all should wear the Tutup, a starched white close-fitting coat with a high suffocating neck-band clamped with white studs. Tutup in Malay means "closed," but more closed than those Tutups were the minds which prescribed them.

It is not difficult to trace the origins of this new mixing, this new freedom between the races. The old colonial English have departed or perhaps they never appeared in force after the war. There are Expatriates, the postwar term for prewar white Malayans, but they are now fairly thin on the ground and getting thinner. Among the new generation who have appeared are many who are less conformist, less past-bound, more cosmopolitan, more enlightened toward race and color and religion. More conscious, too, of the social and political changes that are shaping and shaking the world.

There was a time, not so distant, when many Europeans, and not only the English, spent lifetimes without real contact with any Asian except their servants and a few shopkeepers. Some were even proud, in a curiously inverted way, that they had been able to escape any such contamination and looked down on the less fortunate who showed a preference, however slight, for fraternization with the local people. Their lives were an insulated monotony between bungalow, office, and club. They looked at history through a mosquito net and were sure it would continue in mathematically divided squares forever.

In a city where even a plain European girl could be booked up for months ahead—bachelors outnumbered spinsters by about twenty to one—attractive girls today are often dateless because many young men prefer to take out Asians, especially those lovely girls, the Chinese. I was not prepared for the social revolution, of which this is a symptom, that has taken place in comparatively few years, or the extraordinary vitality of this city which reflects that revolution.

Singapore was a mid-Victorian serving wench who had been overworked and kept belowstairs for so long that all the personality and spirit had been kicked out of her. Singapore today is youth, perhaps a student who is conscious of his growing power and place in society. He is alert, impatient, a trifle arrogant now he has rejected the restraints of his parents. He is still unsure of many things, but he at least knows that if he makes mistakes they will be his own and that he alone is at last free to create or destroy.

When the Tuan Besar was still unchallenged, to be non-white was to know humiliation and discrimination, though not necessarily directly, for many whites behaved with sympathy and understanding toward Asians among whom they worked and lived. Prejudice was inherent in the system itself, as it was and is in any monolithic system where autocratic power is exerted by few over many.

Among first impressions I felt the surge and sweep of this changed Singapore, where shadows are short and black and memories long, as the memories of Asia are long. I felt the new vitality and assertiveness of a people already free in their minds and no longer forced to walk with lowered eyes. It was good to come back to find these things, to feel that Singapore, for all the faults I would discover, all the criticisms I would hear, all the problems it is facing, was a better place for people to live in than it was a generation ago when I was a Tuan.

4

This is a city that never sleeps. Day and night the traffic sweeps past the white cathedral, under lichen-covered trees which enclose the sports fields of the Padang, and on across Anderson Bridge to Collyer Quay and its Roadstead rocking like a bathful of toy ships. Day and night bicycle tires whine across the thin suspension bridge just upriver from Anderson and shoes and sandals argue on the boarded way and bare feet, black, brown, amber, endlessly pass.

Rowing sampans, tethered below the grey mass of the Fullerton Building where a fort once guarded the river mouth, rock in propeller wash as heavily loaded tongkangs from anchored ships move inland like weary animals toward upriver godowns, and motor sampans with eyes painted on their red and green and blue bows chase each other up and down the crowded waterway.

The heated air is honey thick and a fluffy wind which brings the smell of open sea rattles the black pods on the trees along the river and shakes Flame petals onto the leaves, powdered by restless feet, which gild the sloping bank.

A Malay with oiled hair lies on his back and catches drifting petals. An Indian in a white dhoti edged with blue rests

against a tree and stares at the water, thinking in another
dimension. A Chinese in singlet and loose pants squats and
spits. Along the bank three Malays in black songkoks eat
steaming curry and tease the woman who runs the food stall
under faded canvas. Her sarong spreads a garden of red and
black flowers across her ample bottom, her dark green kebaya
is loose and comfortable, her hair is scraped back into a bird's-
nest bun, her silver bangles sing. She blends with this morning
hour along the river. She is part of the mesmeric hum of
marine motors, exhausts, bicycle bells, stray words, pad of
bare feet, rattle of pods among the leaves.

A Hindu woman in a sari of wine and gold floats among
the stream of white shirts on the silver bridge, and beyond
the bridge trees toss shade at wavelet tips playing in the sunlight, and beyond again, as the river curves, massed sampans
huddle like frightened bugs—hundreds, thousands of them,
gunwhale to gunwhale, upward-curving pointed bow nuzzling
square-cut stern, a mat of boats on a floor of churned water
and mud and human refuse.

The Orang Laut, the Malay Gypsies of the Sea, tied up here
in the long past when the river wandered through malarial
swamp in the time of the city's foundation by Stamford
Raffles. Now this bend is the permanent home of the Water
Chinese, for on the sampans children are born, mature, wrinkle,
and die, rocked by passing boats, by the changing tide, by monsoon winds which sweep in from the China Sea.

Beyond the sampans the river changes its shape, its character,
and its nationality. As it narrows to a camel-back bridge,
twists and twists again to other bridges, moves on aimlessly
into the island, Europe rapidly merges into China. The air-
conditioned banks and office blocks along the sea front are a
thin façade, a pretense, for at their backs and all along the
river the streets and homes and shops and warehouses are all
Chinese—a rash of weather-stained tile roofs, balconies of
faded green and celestial blue, red peeling shutters open to
the winding water.

Here is China on the Equator, stinking, noisy, never still, a close-packed area of opulence and hunger and pity, an ant city within a city, scurrying, vital. Shopkeepers, pimps, salesmen, prostitutes, clerks, gangsters, importers, tailors, gold beaters, coffin makers, carvers, jewel cutters, cake makers . . . Here, too, upstream beyond the Forbidden Hill, behind rice mills and rubber godowns, Chinese craftsmen still make boats as their ancestors did a thousand years ago, beautiful junks and other craft which grow from hand-hewn keels laid on sunbaked mud and red wood shavings. These boats, and the near naked men who build them with primitive tools and rough hands, are enduring symbols of the patience, artistry, and determination of one of the most talented races of mankind.

Singapore, although British for six generations, is a Chinese city, and the world's biggest outside China. Its Prime Minister is Chinese, its governing Cabinet is largely Chinese. Two thirds of its fifty members in the Legislative Assembly are Chinese, and that parliament is unique because it is the only one in existence where British parliamentary practices have been adopted intact by Chinese.

Most of Singapore's labor and shops and few factories are Chinese, and much of its wealth as an entrepôt is in Chinese hands. Nearly eighty per cent of its one million seven hundred thousand people, packed into a city and island only twenty-six miles by fourteen, are Chinese. About half of them were not born in Singapore and about two thirds of them speak only their own southern Chinese dialects, mainly Hokkien, Cantonese, Hakka, Hailam.

Because the Chinese are among the fastest-breeding people on earth, of the eight babies born every hour in Singapore about seven are Chinese, which means that, of the fifty to sixty thousand extra people who have to be found work each year, most of them are Chinese.

Singapore is unique among cities because of the extreme youth of its population. Half of its people are under eighteen years of age, more than forty per cent are under fifteen—and most of these children and young people are Chinese. It is this youth which injects into the city its tremendous vitality, which gives it a brash adventurous probing purpose. Its youth, too, is the source of some of its most significant problems of today and tomorrow.

Old people were once conspicuous. A Chinese street contained many aged. You were aware of them, sitting in the evening in front of shop-houses, minding children, working. The tightly bound feet and stilted hobbling walk, so sexually exciting to the Chinese of earlier centuries and so physically restricting, told more poignantly than their faces and bodies their age and how close they were to the ancient customs of the China past. And so did the long sparse straggling beards grown by the old men from another more venerable time.

There are old people today, many of them, but they have to be sought in a population which is so young that age is almost a curiosity. The Chinese schools alone, where thousands of children, including boys in brilliant blue shirts who turn playgrounds into fields of swaying cornflowers, tell their own story of a city where every second person is a child or still in his teens, yet still a place where one person in three is forced to work so that the others may live.

It is also a city where the Chinese have the lowest literacy rate, particularly among the women, a rate so low that is is lower than the average for all other races on the island. Literacy is a pretty meaningless yardstick. Its significance has always been overrated, and the word, parrot-repeated from generation to generation, has been given an almost mystic importance beyond its true worth. For what does literacy really mean? In Singapore it is the ability to read and write a simple letter in any one language, but its real meaning is that the majority Chinese are, as a community, at the bottom of the elementary-education list, yet in this same society, where the Government is spending about a quarter of its annual revenue on education, young Singapore is on the way to becoming perhaps the best mass-educated people in Asia, and most of those youngsters are Chinese.

Education has become almost a public obsession in Singapore. The aim is to get all children into school, even if there are not enough schools, if classrooms are grossly overcrowded, if teachers are overworked, undertrained, and there are not enough of them, and if the general teaching and educational standard is low. But the Singapore Government is doing a remarkable job and has already made an advance of far-reaching significance in this part of the world. The contrast with what is being done and what was never attempted in any serious way is staggering. In the colonial Singapore I knew, only a small percentage of children received any education, and that education was largely designed to produce a cheap-clerk class, with a basic knowledge of English, to serve the Government and business. Under this system there were exceptions, the brilliant, the fortunate, the wealthy, who were able to move on to higher English education, but the mass of Asian children received little or no education under colonial rule.

The Chinese, who even in those days outnumbered all other races many times, were virtually ignored, and the Chinese community, particularly its wealthier members, was forced, so that they could give their children even elementary training, to start and finance their own Chinese schools, and later still their own Chinese university, as we shall see. The standard of some of those schools was reasonably high. The standard of most was low. A few provided little more than a crude appreciation of a few of the Chinese classics. But even the worst provided more education than the British were prepared to give.

If the British had shown long-range vision, they would have made certain of the English education of the Chinese mass. This would have given Singapore at least a form of cohesion it has never possessed, and in time one language on which to build social and political change. They failed to look ahead and thus developed, through the deliberate exclusion of the

Chinese, not only two distinct educational streams, the English and the Chinese, but two streams which, through language, knowledge, and tradition, separated and kept apart in one community the mass of the majority Chinese.

If the British decades ago had deliberately planned the end of their colonial rule and their own exodus, they could not have achieved it more efficiently than by turning many of the Chinese, who have been good citizens of Singapore, into white-disliking aliens on an island where some Chinese families have lived for generations. For it was the Chinese who, learning from their old enemies the Japanese, forced self-government, and the Chinese who rule Singapore today, just as it is the Chinese, characterized by their strong clannishness, political consciousness, religious conservatism, fecundity, and ability to survive on a bowl of rice a day and under the most appalling living conditions, who give this city and island its distinctive color and background and personality and its modern questing spirit. It is also the Chinese who provide it with some of its gravest problems and dangers.

The Chinese are not newcomers to Singapore. They have been there since the beginning or before. Chinese gambier and pepper planters farmed Pearl's Hill, south of the Forbidden Hill, before 1819, and more than five thousand Chinese were already living on the island not long after Raffles came. "My city of Singapore," he said, soon after the foundation, "is already attracting the peaceable, industrious, thrifty Chinese."

They came almost entirely from South China, and especially from Canton and Fukien Province, ancestral home of the Hokkien community, to escape famine, poverty, war lords, and all the other pests, the whites not excluded, who have bled China for centuries. They were mostly peasants, fishermen, poor artisans, and they brought with them their local customs, superstitions, festivals, food, feudal class structure, gods, temples.

They established clan and family associations for their common protection and for trade and business reasons, and provident and secret and other clannish societies. They transplanted their China intact to Nanyang, the South Seas, as they call it, and established, as the Chinese did in many parts of the world, a little China on the Equator.

In time, as even their powerful feudal structure was penetrated by the West and by day-to-day contact with other races like the indigenous Malays and the immigrant Indians, some of their customs changed or new customs evolved, and they became no longer completely the Chinese of South China. If they had been isolated from China, they would probably have taken another road of transplanted evolution. But steady immigration from the area of their origins, constant movement back and forth between China and Singapore, their own education system, the power of their mighty language, weakened the effect of the alien influences to which they as a community, and an island community, were exposed.

It is often said that, of all races in Singapore, there has been most mixing between the European and the Chinese. This is true, but if mixing means not only contact but also real understanding, appreciation, then it is a negative blend except among individuals at the wealthy level or among a few intellectuals.

After a century and a half the transplanted Chinese, living in a tropical climate among half a dozen major races and cultures, are in superficial ways a little different from their ancestors. But they are still basically Chinese in thought and habit—and Chinese who are not only facing a new penetration from their ancestral homeland but who also will have to make up their minds who they are, Chinese first, and all that implies, or people who are no longer "Chinese," but citizens of something new and different, not of Singapore or even Malaya but of Greater Malaysia, the new state which is about to be established. This, however, is part of the wider political story.

Pagoda, Sago, Mosque, Nankin, Fish, Chin Chew, Kreta Ayer, Ann Shang—a double abacus of streets and lanes on what was once a tidal swamp between the Forbidden Hill and Pearl's Hill and the sea, a steaming area exclusively Chinese where a thousand people and more exist in the inhuman clutter of every acre.

In a special study of six adjacent two-story shop-houses in one street, Upper Nankin, a sociologist counted three hundred and thirty-eight people—tailors, hawkers, plumbers, rubber workers, and their wives, children, and relations. That was an average of about fifty-six to each house, but in twenty-four cubicles in one shop-house lived seventy-eight people. There were also in this house five other "spaces"—four fixed and one movable. A fixed space is one bunk, or the smallest house in the world, and a movable space is just big enough to hold the smallest-size camp bed. Another house contained thirteen cubicles and eighteen spaces, few with any direct light or air. Some of the cubicles in these buildings held eight or nine people, but the majority held four or five. Lavatory space was generally part of a veranda and near the kitchen, and lavatory equipment open buckets—forty people to one bucket on some floors. In all these shop-houses food was cooked over open fire buckets, and on wet days the kitchens, which were partly open to verandas or passageways, were awash.

This study was made some time ago, but conditions like this are still common—whole families living in one room, people with no daytime homes, only night space, because the corner of a room or balcony they rent is used for working or cooking or sleeping by someone else during the day. One Chinese wife told the Divorce Court that she wanted to leave her husband because his mother slept under their bed—the only space available for the old lady in the family's one-room home already packed with children and other relatives.

Half of the ten thousand flats built by the Government in the past two years are one-bedroom places, and cheap to rent, and in the next three years the Government plans to build another forty thousand. By 1965 one in four of Singapore's three hundred thousand families will live in Government-built housing, against one in ten now. This will make a dent in the overcrowding of Chinatown, but it won't abolish the stinking tenements, the hunger, or the dirt. Many Chinese prefer the friendly pungent atmosphere of Chinatown's streets and lanes and tenements to the impersonality of the new apartment blocks where life fifty feet above the ground may be hygienic and quiet, but can be drab.

Chinatown is a face of orange against a green shutter, water stains and dirt congealed into monstrous penicillin on walls suffering from the pox, filth like thick soy sauce welling between restless toes, a taper burning in the gloom of a shophouse, the thin nasal wail of a Cantonese love song, all mixed up with the smell of food, stale urine, and smoldering sandalwood, clash of brass from a screaming radio like the heads of giants meeting, tearing of wet linen as an old man clears his throat and spits, the monotonous argument of metal beaten behind crimson doors, a pigtailed girl trailing a rose umbrella, a grandmother in black holding her widdling granddaughter over a gutter choked with fish heads and cabbage leaves, paper garlands like blood splashes over a doorway, a man on a bicycle dangling three gutted fish on a string, eyes watching from balconies, coffee shops, food stalls, and saying nothing, rice steaming in huge pots beside platters of chopped vegetables, iced lollywater the color of crème de menthe, a boy with the face of a golden angel playing with a green paper flower, a near naked man clasping his majestic belly as he laughs at his naked son crawling among squashed fruit, a silver chain round a little girl's left ankle, chaining her to life and frustrating the prowling demons of the outer world.

Chinatown is characters almost as numerous as its hurrying, lounging, squatting, busy thousands—red and amber and gold set on panels of blue, lime, white, turquoise, ideographs which shout, scream, plead, pontificate even if you don't understand one of them, characters like explosions, apes, horses, trees, tents, girls, playing and prancing up and down the sides of buildings, on shop fronts, balconies, placards, trucks, characters even making speeches in the sky.

Chinatown is washing—arms and legs and necks impaled by long bamboo poles, from windows and balconies, which almost meet above the center of gravity of streets. Fluttering blues and reds and whites, dripping, dry, slapping, cracking in the heated air above the noise and dust and smells and shouts and calls and laughter of a Chinatown where every day is Monday.

Near the mouth of Temple Street roasted ducks hang by their beaks among beef rolled in oil, like human fingers, and enigmatic chunks and blobs of meat that could be pieces of puppy and probably are. The flies, thick as tar, hardly glance up as you pass this streetside butchery wide open to petrol fumes and dust and spittle. But what is bacteria to the indestructible Chinese?

A cup mender pushes his tool boxes on wheels under a vermilion awning and wipes his face with a filthy rag. He has a thin tired face. The struggle to survive is endless; the pressure of that struggle would break anyone but a Chinese. He fans himself with his old felt hat and rattles a small brass box, not unlike a Georgian snuffbox, to proclaim his trade.

Just inside Sago Street a brown goat stands on frail hind legs to reach for a cake, but the stallholder sees just in time and almost breaks its back with a kick in the belly. I sympathized with that thieving goat, for Chinese cakes are wondrous things to make a cake lover drool. On the stall were X cakes made from flour and sugar and looking like mounds of powder puffs. There were Green cakes and Prince cakes in Technicolor and Nut Sticks like crisp curled golden-brown paper. You feel like buying a basketful and eating the lot, all by yourself. But so do the flies.

Baskets of nuts, yellow, black, wine, heaps of plaited palm-leaf baskets, cabbages sold in quarters under a beach umbrella, brown hens in wire coops, patient and panting, their combs adroop, dried fish like old soles, and withered fish heads which stare and comprehend, months-old eggs encased in black and khaki mud, and eggs in half shell, strong flavoring for fish dishes, disclosing yolks as angry as diseased eyes.

An ancient totters by, fumbling his way among the stalls which now close the street to traffic. His pantaloons and blouse are black. His head is bald and the blood vessels wriggle down his temples. Gripping the end of his nose are steel-rimmed spectacles he could have bought for a few cents at the barrow loaded with tenth-hand spectacles just across the way. His beard is seven yellow strands which reach his middle, and he holds them in one hand as he walks.

Near Sago Lane, where up to eight people share cubicles not as large as bachelor-flat kitchens, and where sleeping bunks are hired by the hour and never have time to cool, little fish make olive pyramids on trestles draped with cloth as shocking pink as the ribbons on the Chinese wedding car which has just inched through, horn bellowing.

Here life is beginning and life is ending, for outside a shop are bundles of scarlet incense sticks, some gold tipped, some blue, and wads of blue and gold paper money to offer to the spirits, and inside the shop a candle is burning, a pale lemon flame beside a flickering body in the Dead House of Sago Street opposite the workshops of the coffin makers, where men stripped to shorts hew logs with ancient adzes to take the bodies of the still living.

The air shudders with cymbals and drums, the cries of hawkers, the scrape of sandals, the steady chopping of the adzes, as an old woman, her hair so thin that her scalp stares through, works on hands and knees on the roadway, spreading wood shavings and chips from the coffin shops to dry so that in the morning she will be able to boil her first hot water and add to it, if she is lucky, one leaf of tea.

Beyond her and near a corner a mother with a child on hip brings a cut-down fruit tin to the man milking an almond cow in the gutter while the calf tries to nuzzle from the other side—a sight that is becoming rarer as the Chinese, who were never milk drinkers, gradually accept alien bottled milk, and as the elements of hygiene begin to penetrate the proletarian Asian mind. As she waits, and the cow tongues a vegetable stall, black characters on a red board proclaim that Kong Chay Son is the keeper of a rooming house, and outside her door on the filthy concrete five-foot-way, as sidewalks are called in this part of Asia, is a large stone rounded and smoothed by generations of restless bottoms. This is Kong's sit-down stone for use in the evening when the heat of the day has faded.

Chilies like betel spit on a brown mat, soap which resembles dried cow dung for cleaning hats, red paper boats to be burned in the temple flicker of red and white candles, lovely hanging contraptions to make Dali envious, flowers and paper and tassels twined and hung on frames to delight children or adults whose eyes have not been dulled by the endless shoddy of a five-and-ten world.

Outside a teashop, where the spittoons are gay with painted flowers like women's hats turned upside down, and near the little Monkey God shrine which keeps away the bad spirits, a hawker who looks like a stained Danny Kaye slices pineapple with a small parang. He wears red rubber household gloves but still blows his nose with his hand.

Metal shops, key makers, gold beaters, carpenters, tailors. Stench of bad meat, rotting fish, ancient fruit, pepper, sweaty clothes, wood smoke. Multi-colored awnings below a street of flapping washing. Oranges, cool limes, green bananas, the smooth clean paleness of Japanese pears.

And in a window, near a door where a mirror faces outward to reflect away the demons, a large glass bowl filled with green water snakes coiled in a liquid that could be diluted claret. It's snake whisky, and one tablespoon three times a day after meals is guaranteed to make the weakest hot and strong at night.

Later, sitting in a food shop drinking bowls of jasmine tea, the ever-moving faces of a Chinese street crowd slide, drift, halt, fade. There is a medieval face with a fine cruel nose and bone formation to delight a sculptor and large proud eyes and the palest lemon skin. There is the face of a clown with a skin almost as dark as a Malay. There is a girl in floral blouse and trousers, carrying a live fowl under one arm, an exquisite doll with a button nose, a permanent, pouting lips, and gently undulating bottom.

Chinese faces vary so much in shape and texture and color that I never weary watching them. I am tired of anemic Western faces. I am tired of expressionless Western faces—faces as ruddy as steak, as pale as rubbish-tin paper. The Chinese are a handsome race, a humorous race, and if you know them well you know that the inscrutable Chinese is a myth handed down from other centuries, when the all-powerful occupying Europeans didn't speak their language, didn't want to, showed little interest in them as human beings, and sometimes treated them abominably.

I finished my tea and crossed the street to the man on a stool beside a table covered with a red cloth. He pointed to a wood block. We inspected each other. Wu Tack Seng was not a fortuneteller, as I had thought, but a physiognomist who interpreted character and temperament by studying facial characteristics. He was Cantonese with a remote face and fine hands with long pointed nails—clean nails. He was a little deaf. His table, which held small wooden boxes, black sticks in bamboo containers, cards and books, was backed by gold characters the size of meat plates on long strips of red paper stuck to the building wall with adhesive tape, and a framed double life-size line drawing of a Chinese face with small characters and animal and other symbols superimposed on the drawing.

To the Chinese who believe that a map of your life already exists before you were born, there is nothing unusual about a physiognomist having his consulting room opposite a coffee shop and between an apothecary's displaying bottles of colored water, jars of herbs and potions, and bronze mortars and pestles, and a five-foot-way barber, dressed in underpants, dry-shaving a man's head with an old Bengal cutthroat razor.

A physiognomist is one of a traditional group which ranges from astrologers to palmists, from fortunetellers to bone feelers who, for a consideration, will advise and help you bypass the traps which wait for you along your predestined way. They will interpret simple abnormalities like eyelid fluttering, which my grandmother insisted was the sign of a disturbed liver. They will tell you the meaning of your sneezes, which are much more important than you think, because if you are in love and you wake up sneezing in the small hours of the morning it means that your beloved is thinking of you when the foolish girl would be far better occupied getting her beauty sleep. They will explain your dreams and why frogs mean good luck and dark clouds mean bad luck. They will even examine your moles, if you have any, and in the most intimate places, and tell you among other things to beware the man with a small mole on his cheek near his left ear.

Wu Tack Seng was a face specialist and much consulted, as I learned from the inevitable group which had gathered to hear the bad character of the foreign devil, particularly by girls wanting to marry and not having much success and businessmen planning doubtful deals.

The consultation began when Mr. Wu suggested fifty cents. With equal firmness I suggested thirty cents. Mr. Wu considered this and mentioned forty-five. I said thirty-five. Mr. Wu sighed and said he might be able to accept forty. I closed the deal.

He asked my age—his only question—then for minutes he studied my face until it began to itch—behind one ear, in the corner of my left eye—under his cold scrutiny. He bent forward and examined my chin and my ears, consulted his face chart, referred to one of his cards, touched my chin with one fingertip and seemed to probe the depths of my slight, high cleft. Then he lit a candle and took a flat bamboo stick from one of his containers and noted the characters carved at one end. At last he was ready.

I was reserved, shy at times. I looked for and found music in the stars—his own words. I preferred the company of women to men. My chin cleft indicated loyalty to friends, but if it had been slightly lower and deeper that would have been a sign of a pretty despicable character. My eyes were the best eyes, whatever that meant, because of their spacing and their shape. I had five extremely lucky years ahead of me, but only five.

He had asked one question, so I asked only one. Without hesitation he said I would die at seventy-eight—and then refused to speak again. Which made me wonder if, for another ten cents, I might not have lived to my century.

Two Samsui women pass, barefoot, magnificent, like characters from the Middle Ages, and I watch them admiringly until they are out of sight. The Samsuis are female Chinese laborers, mostly builders' laborers, who wear a distinctive work uniform of half-mast blue pants, loose blue shirtlike blouse, and a wide, flat, folded medieval headdress of thick red or blue cloth which helps to shade their faces. They are women the Brueghels would have liked to paint. Before World War II their characteristic headgear was always red, but some of them are said to have changed to blue or blue with white spots or even red with white spots during the Pacific war because they believed the red hats attracted the Japanese bombers. To anyone with knowledge of bombers this is ridiculous, but if a Chinese, and a Samsui Chinese, believed that her red headdress was a green light to a high and busy bomb aimer, then she was sensible to change the color of her hat. The bomber story could be correct, but I prefer to believe in a much simpler explanation—that even the strict Samsuis decided on a small fashion change.

The Samsui women are a celibate sisterhood who came originally from rural areas of South China. They are not a religious sisterhood, nor does religion in any form seem to influence them. Some of them have been married and even had children, but most are single. Few of them can read or write and their general knowledge is sparse. They are women who scorn domestic jobs of any kind to seek personal and group salvation through hard outdoor physical work. They band together in Kongsis, or associations, live in community houses, pool their resources, and help each other in sickness or unemployment. If Lesbianism exists among them, it is extremely rare. Celibacy is practiced in the Kongsi houses with almost religious austerity, and although a few Samsui women break the Kongsi rules—one I know to have a baby so that she could sell it on the open child market in Singapore to get money to help relatives in China—many of these women are virgin from birth to death.

Many of the Samsuis are handsome, even without the aid of the cheapest cosmetics. Some have broad rounded faces with smooth peach-bloom skins and strong, beautiful hands and legs, although their large almost prehensile feet probably explain why they are the world's most skillful scaffold acrobats. A Samsui walking a narrow plank well above street level, and carrying two baskets of cement slung on a shoulder pole, is an admirable but frightening sight.

They are accustomed to the hardest laboring work in all weathers and are in perfect physical condition. I've seen them lift weights few white men would attempt and they will do more work in a week than a white laborer will do in three. It is not surprising that these tough skillful women are regularly employed by Chinese contractors on all forms of building and heavy construction work.

Although their headdress helps keep cement dust and dirt out of their hair, the main purpose of this unique covering is to shade their faces, for the Samsui has an almost pathological dislike of sun tan. In the extreme heat of the day some will even further protect their skins by tying large handkerchiefs over their heads and under their chins, so that all you can see of their sweating faces, as they carry timber or bricks, is the tip of a nose and bright eyes.

This desire to have a pale skin is not uncommon in Asia. Perhaps it is due to long European influence, a desire developed over centuries to copy the white overlords, though that seems too simple an explanation. Perhaps it has something to do with the caste and class systems, for in India the Brahman is generally paler skinned and northern Chinese have beautiful fair skins and rosy cheeks. It may even go back to the times when paler races overran and enslaved darker aboriginal tribes and strong pigment was a symbol of subjection. Whatever the reason, this strong urge for a lighter skin still exists, even though it does not make sense today.

The domestic, baby-minding Amahs of Singapore are, like the Samsui women, members of another curious sisterhood. Once again there is no religious motivation. They, too, live together, for economic reasons, in Kongsi houses, helping each other in any way they can, including saving to send money to needy relatives in Communist China.

Many of these Amahs take a vow never to marry. Among these women are rice winners whose family responsibilities prevent them marrying, and also the marital failures, the sexual deviates, and probably those who just don't like men. But some Amahs are married and have children before they join, or marry while members of the sisterhood, so that the rules are not so strict as in the Samsui Kongsis.

Most of the Amahs are Cantonese, of urban rather than rural origin, and many of them come from the old Chinese equivalent of lower-middle-class homes. They wear while on duty white jackets, wide-cut trousers of shiny black cotton, which used to be called "Amah cloth," and their oiled hair is combed top and sides into a tight coiled bun. Different Amah Kongsis can be distinguished by the way the hair is worn, particularly the bun or its comb adornments, or the design and color of their working slippers. Their work uniform, and it is a uniform today, has no significance in the sisterhood. Nor did they originally design it. One story says that it was imposed by a European Mem when the first members of the sisterhood migrated from Hong Kong and Canton forty to fifty years ago, and that it was rapidly adopted as a suitable, easy-to-clean domestic uniform.

Although there have been examples in the past of Amahs giving children opium to make them sleep, or even masturbating them, few will disagree that most Amahs are fine women—so intelligent, hard working, and loyal that many homes in Singapore, both European and Asian, could not operate without them. Children long grown up remember the warmth and love they received from their Amahs, and many hungry families in China today are grateful when food parcels and money arrive each month from these selfless daughters.

Nobody knows how much the Amahs contribute to their relatives in China, but there are thousands of Amahs working in Malaya and it must be a fair percentage of the thirteen million Malayan dollars which Singapore Chinese send to Red China each year. The Amah of one European family told me that one of her sister's children had died of starvation near Canton and that she had been keeping the rest of the family alive with her food parcels and money.

With its electric-light bills Chinese Singapore received a booklet so revolutionary that mothers were horrified and grandmothers thought the end of the world had come.

The booklet, in comic-strip form and four colors and issued by the Ministry of Health, was on birth control, an almost unmentionable subject, particularly among the Chinese-educated Chinese. The cover showed a Chinese wife sitting up in bed weeping while her pajama-clad husband scowled through thick cigarette smoke.

"I just can't go on in this way," she says. "Oh, darling, don't you see how this fear is tearing us to pieces. We tried everything we know—and failed."

The eight-page picture story, of a wife frightened of yet another pregnancy, told how Ah Chong and his wife consulted a doctor, learned about contraception, and how their marriage was saved.

Escape from Fear, as the booklet was called, jolted many of Singapore's inhabitants, for free discussion about sex is quite alien to the Chinese family. But when school children went in thousands to a family-planning exhibition where clinically precise drawings and diagrams displayed the innermost privacies of male and female kind, and birth-control devices were distributed at the door, the older people shuddered. Nothing like it in Singapore, where a Chinese baby is born every seven minutes, had ever been seen before.

Birth control is winning converts, but desperately slowly in a city which is breeding itself out of land and work, where ignorance and superstition is still twelfth century, and where the mother-in-law still dominates family life.

In many a Singapore home even elementary biology is still a mystery. If you use contraceptives, the old women say, your husband will go blind or get cancer, or at least you will lose weight or come out in a rash. Some mothers-in-law still direct their married daughters when and when not to have sexual relations, and the daughters obey, as they always have, and some still won't allow their daughters to limit their families.

It is normal for women in Singapore, especially the Chinese, to have ten to a dozen children. One woman had eleven girls, and because of the insults of her mother-in-law that she could not produce a son, was determined to continue until she did. Another Chinese of thirty-six had a record of twenty-five pregnancies, twelve aborted with herbs. Yet another, married eight years, had fifteen pregnancies.

Every month in Singapore more than a hundred babies are given away. One woman with seventeen children gave away eight. And every month babies are sold on this island which has no resources of its own except its frightening supply of children. This city's most desperate need is a new kind of mother-in-law.

5

The call came at midnight, and at 1:00 A.M. I reported to the Cecil Street Charge Room of the Criminal Investigation Department in Chinatown, where a Malay constable in light grey shirt, dark shorts, and black boots too big for him led me along a corridor of the big grey building to a room bare of furniture except for two small tables and a wall blackboard chalked with rough street diagrams.

Twelve detectives, ten Chinese and two Malay, were waiting. They wore gay open-neck shirts hung outside their trousers and could have come direct from a day at the beach, except that they were checking their palm-size automatics as they listened almost casually to the final briefing from Inspector Cecil Cheng, Head of the Cantonese Section of the C.I.D.

The Inspector, rotund and jovial with high brushed hair and rimless glasses, wore dark trousers, a cream silk shirt, and well-polished black shoes. He looked more like a Chinese version of an American chartered accountant than a policeman. He switched from Chinese to Malay and then to English to explain to me that we were to raid hideouts of members of the 108 Chinese Secret Society and why the raids were being launched.

"In raids a few days ago we brought in six secret-society members of the 24 Group. Some of these men talked and gave us information about 108 Group membership we did not already know. A war had developed between the two groups over the burial of the father of a 108 man. The local Dead House was inside 24 territory and 24 Group demanded money to allow the body in. Group 108 refused and began raiding and beating up their enemies."

The Inspector smiled amiably as he polished his glasses.

"I always believe that prevention is better than cure. That is why we hope to catch some of the 108 Group fighting men tonight."

We went out to two cars and two motorcycles. I traveled with the Inspector, who drove his own sedan, and even a light coat would have been uncomfortable as we drove deep into Chinatown through the smoke of cooking fires, for many eating houses and food stalls were still open and the streets were full of people.

We cruised, weaving through the traffic in the red-and-amber glow of neon signs. Then the other car and one of the cycles left us. We continued on for a few hundred yards, swung a corner, squealed into another street. As we advanced I could see at the far end the lights of another car coming toward us. The other car was ours. The trap was closing in Pagoda Street.

The Inspector slowed and braked, and before the car had stopped, the four detectives were out of the back seat and running toward a corner house while men from the other car converged on its rear.

"All these warrens are interconnected," Cecil Cheng said as he opened the door. "Follow me—and look out."

I ran after him and up a steep and narrow stairway to the first floor of the shop-house. For a man of his bulk he moved quickly and silently. The detectives were already moving through the building, kicking open doors, flicking screens aside, checking the inhabitants in this ant bed of thinly partitioned cubicles and sleep spaces.

The walls were unpainted and covered with water stains and filth. In places where the ceilings had collapsed, sagging plaster and boards seemed about to fall into the rooms. In the probing light of torches I counted dozens of people in a few cubicles, lying, squatting, standing, and there were dozens more in other parts of the house. The place smelled of ancient cooking, urine, dirty clothes, age-old damp and dirt.

The Inspector called in Cantonese. A detective turned and shrugged.

"Nothing here," Cheng said, making for the stairs. "We're wasting time."

Pagoda Street had been almost deserted when we arrived. Now Chinese, many stripped to the waist, had gathered in tight groups. They stood in the dim light from open doorways, behind posts, in the shadows of balconies, beside the wooden skeletons of daytime stalls. They watched the police come from the building and from behind the building. They were silent, motionless. Their very passivity was ominous. I shall never forget the insolent menacing stillness of that street—a stillness that was clamorous and frightening.

"Stay close to me. I don't want you to be hit with an acid bomb or something. They often throw things. Men have been hurt before."

The Inspector almost whispered, but the words seemed to be much too loud in the too-quiet quiet of Pagoda Street.

"If you got hurt there would be explanations. I don't want that."

The Chinese watched as we moved back to the car, as some of the detectives walked slowly backward, as the motors came to life. The watchers didn't move as we accelerated past them.

Again we circled, but only for a minute or two. Then the cars closed part of another street—sealed it with practiced skill.

This time I was just behind Cecil Cheng as we almost dragged our way up stairs so steep that they were nearly vertical and so rotten that the boards crunched under our weight.

Twelve people were in two cubicles near the head of the

stairs, and many more were on this floor. Two frail Chinese women with lank hair rose from the bare boards and stared without blinking into the torchlight. They were fully dressed in black jackets and pantaloons. A detective prodded a young Chinese, asleep or pretending, in a low bunk. The man slowly opened his eyes.

"Identity card."

When the stained card was produced the policeman compared the photograph on it with a collection he carried. He swung the torch for the Inspector to see. Cheng nodded. Handcuffs clicked on.

"Wanted for illegal lottery," Cheng said. "Not very serious. But he's a 108—we know that. We've been looking for him."

A detective found a switch and one fly-specked bulb gave enough light to examine the cubicles and the communal kitchen. This place was even filthier and more chaotic than the first we had raided. The walls were streaked and blotched with green-black damp. The floors were littered with paper, old tins, baskets, clothes, dirty rags. A little boy fully dressed slept on a heap of rubbish below a cheap God of Happiness and a roll of lavatory paper in a wall alcove. Gold characters on a scarlet strip split down a partition. In one corner was a broken bowl, a broken red lantern, an old car battery, and some scattered rice. On the floor, on benches, under tables, men, women, and children were asleep or half awake, peering, blinking, muttering, cursing.

We moved to the communal kitchen which served the entire building. Here among the pots and pans were heaps of firewood, food, old tins, rags, a clothesline. Fat cockroaches waved their whiskers from every hole and crack or scuttled with dry rasping of legs among the pots and rubbish. The kitchen was half open to the weather. The water-black ceiling had collapsed and was prevented from falling by one roughly nailed board. The whole place stank.

After the arrest the detectives searched for arms. Two in the kitchen worked unhurriedly, yet in a few minutes they found two short and ugly parangs, freshly sharpened, hidden in a corner, then five knives, two sheathed, and a plastic toy pistol. One of the daggers, wrapped in brown paper, was in a bamboo sheath among dirty chopsticks and could easily have been missed.

The Inspector showed me the pistol. "This comes under the definition of arms. A man found carrying a toy like this faces the same charge as a man armed with a genuine pistol." He handed the toy back to the detective who had found it. "We have to be tough because the secret-society boys are tough. They often fight—acid, knives, bicycle chains, anything—and we have to be prepared for the worst on these raids. It's not easy to pick them up quickly in these places. This house holds about two hundred people."

But this was our second house and I had not seen any of the police produce a warrant. I pointed this out as we went down the stairs to the street.

"If I don't come along, search warrants have to be carried and produced. But when I come, I'm a walking warrant. As an Inspector I represent in my person and title a warrant to enter and search any building."

The third place we raided that night housed two hundred and fifty people. That was a quick estimate of the experienced detectives. We found no weapons but arrested three Chinese, all under twenty and all, I noticed, wearing their oiled hair in a curious high-brushed, curled style.

"All members of 108," one of the policemen told me. "We can pick them by their hair. Other gangs have different styles."

One man was dragged from a cubicle not much bigger than a large dog kennel. The others were asleep on the top of a double bunk. Living in the same room, if you could call it either living or a room, was another man, his wife, their three children, and yet another man. So that in this cubicle, which measured about eight feet by six, were eight people.

The children, aged four to eight, did not even wake. They lay on the bare floor, clothed, just as they had fallen asleep.

The youngest, a beautiful little girl already far too thin for her age, clutched a rag doll. But it was the mother who worried me most. She squatted in one corner with a long thin hand resting on one of the sleeping children. Her fact was gaunt; her tight high cheekbones accentuated the deep hollowness of her cheeks. Motionless she watched the police. She did not answer even when they spoke to her. Her eyes had reached beyond suffering. They were the most hopeless eyes I have ever seen.

The Inspector was moving back from the kitchen when one of the arrested men leaped from the cubicle and made for the stairs. A detective shouted and dived. Another grabbed. In seconds they had the man on the floor and handcuffed. He stopped struggling.

They lifted him to his feet. He wore black underpants and a filthy sweat shirt. He was not much over five feet, with a thin, sullenly handsome face. He was seventeen.

"This one doesn't live here," the Inspector explained. "He was hiding out with his friends and these are the only clothes he has. Tomorrow, if we hadn't caught him, he would have moved on, collected some of his clothes, and found another hideout. He's 108 Group and a real find. Wanted for knifing."

The lane was empty as the three handcuffed men were brought out, but from every shop-house eyes were watching. Just above our car a shutter moved and a detective reached for his gun. From the raided house a woman watched from the balcony. I could just see the top of her head and the shadows that were her eyes.

"Stay close," Cheng said, "and dive for the road if you see anything coming."

It was nearly 4:00 A.M. when we returned to the briefing room at the C.I.D., and the questioning began.

The Inspector took me aside. "They seldom talk under a couple of hours, but we hope to learn a lot tonight. . . . I've arranged transport for you."

The night was obviously over, for me, but it was only just starting for the 108 boys.

Cecil Cheng took me out to my car and held out his hand.

"Just a routine night, but I hope you found it interesting."

He took off his glasses, polished them, smiled his accountant's smile.

"I'm glad nobody threw an acid bomb. . . . Unpleasant things."

At the Secret Societies Section of the C.I.D. I was later shown an acid bomb by Mr. Ong Kian Tiong, the Officer in Charge. An electric-light bulb drilled, filled with concentrated sulphuric, and plugged to become, in accurate hands, a fearsome weapon. I was also shown its equally deadly and often-used brother, an acid container stolen from a fire extinguisher.

From Mr. Ong and others I brought myself up to date with these strange and ancient societies and of the crime which makes the outwardly peaceful Singapore the visitor sees such a violent city. That taxi driver who takes you to Raffles or Goodwood Park—the grinning or sullen Chinese who drives his worn-out Morris with one foot on the accelerator, one big toe on the brake, one finger on the wheel, and one elbow on the horn. That hawker in Orchard Road, coolie at the docks, cobbler stitching on the five-foot-way, waiter in that coffee shop. That harmless pleading beggar . . . Any of these and many more could be members of a secret society—even a fighting member of 108 or 24 or 36—for between five and seven thousand men in Singapore are members of these gangs, apart from a thousand or so under direct police supervision and about seven hundred in jail for secret-society crimes.

Although Chinese secret societies have operated in Singapore, and Malaya, for more than a century, their histories and rules are still fairly obscure. This is understandable, for the member who broke his initiation oath and talked did not repeat his offense. He died violently.

The origins of the secret societies are deep in Chinese history, probably as deep as Han times or even earlier, but Malayan societies are generally conceded to be in direct descent from the Triad Society, or Hung League, as it is sometimes called, of South China, which was formed in the seventeenth century to help "overthrow the Ch'ing and restore the Ming."

When the invading Manchus from the north overthrew the nearly three-hundred-year-old rule of the Mings and established the Ch'ing Dynasty in Peking in 1644, it was not a popular occupation among the Chinese, and especially the southern Chinese. The Manchus were not only despised northerners but also hated foreigners, and Robin Hood groups like the Triad Society were formed to fight a guerrilla war against the Ch'ings and to push them out of China. They did not succeed, for the Ch'ing Dynasty lasted until early this century, yet indirectly the powerful Triad achieved its aim when it supported Sun Yat-sen and helped to destroy the Ch'ings and established the Chinese Republic in 1911. So members of the Triad did play a part in "overthrowing the Ch'ings," but instead of "restoring the Mings," they helped set in motion the forces of even more significant revolutions which led in time to the defeat of Chiang Kai-shek and the Kuomintang and the rise of Communist China.

When, through migration from South China, the secret societies were established in Singapore and the mainland of Malaya, they were first regarded as organizations of social benefit to the community. They were, at least in their purest form, akin to an Asian version of Freemasonry among the immigrant Chinese, and in many ways they were a combined government and police force of their own transplanted society. Only later, when the British realized that the societies, or at least many of their members, had no intention of kowtowing to even reasonable authority, were they outlawed.

The organization and inner strength of these curious groups has always been so marked that even today, when they are degenerate branches of a sturdy trunk, authority is still trying to suppress them—and not succeeding. Perhaps most revealing is that the secret societies still exist in Red China despite every effort by the Communist Chinese to destroy them.

Forty to fifty years ago there were three main secret-society groups in Singapore. These were the Gi Hin, Gi Hok, and Goan Seng. They were all in direct line from the Triad or Hung League, with strict Triad organization, symbols, and initiation. Then, in the mid-1920's, and after much inter-gang warfare, they splintered and from that splintering evolved the six main secret-society groups of Singapore today.

These are Groups 108, 18, 24, 36, 8, and Independents, but each Group consists of between thirty to forty distinct secret societies, and in each society active membership ranges from ten to thirty, with an average of perhaps fifteen to twenty.

The four main Groups, especially 108 and 24, are criminal gangs, but members of Group 8 are mostly water-front laborers whose societies resemble clubs, and many of the Independents are also non-criminal and are found mostly among pineapple workers.

The Group numbers are pure Triad and have symbolic meaning, which has never been completely understood. Group 108 could almost be defined as a blend of Heaven and Earth, for Heaven to many Chinese is divided into thirty-six equal parts and Earth is inhabited by seventy-two special spirits, so that if you add those sections and those spirits you get the mystical 108. Again, one of the best-known secret societies in Group 24 today is 969. Add those three numbers and you have 24.

The societies themselves have numbers or names. Sea Land Society, Two Tiger Mountain, Old Soldiers, Faithful Golden Mountain. But because of constant police pressure and arrests, numbers and names are frequently changed in an attempt to preserve secrecy and frustrate the police.

The societies include older men, but most active members are between sixteen and twenty-five. Many are from the unemployed or unemployable. They include school truants, boys from broken homes, deserted boys, youths influenced by American gangster films or pulp magazines, the hero worshipper, the bored, the mentally unbalanced. Many, too, have been forced into the gangs by threats, blackmail, physical violence and, once in, remain members because they know too much about society activities or have broken the law and have no choice between the gang and the police.

Each secret-society Group has its own signs and recognition signals, its own idiom and slang, its own rules and methods, its own territory to exploit and defend. Members of societies within a Group know each other by finger and hand signals, by the position of common articles—bowls, chopsticks, matches, cigarettes—and by special words and phrases. If a man from one Group enters another Group's territory, he will if discovered be asked, "Where do you play?" and if he doesn't give the correct answer, and give it quickly, or doesn't start running, he will be beaten up, or worse. "Wind" is a common term for the police—"The wind is coming," or "There is no wind tonight." "Water" means reinforcements—"send for more water." "Dog" is a pistol. "Brother" is a member of the same society or group. "Wash" is to raid—"We will wash his house." And, among all the societies, "No. 7" has only one meaning, a traitor—and a traitor sooner or later will die by the knife or by strangulation.

Not many years ago the secret societies were organized and operated with military rigidity under an almost regimental tradition. They had their own fighting men under "Tiger Generals"—still have—and even their own official executioners. They had strict rules of membership, behavior, customs, attack, initiation. They used badges, and some members even carried special society or Group visiting cards. They had distinguishing tattoo marks—snakes, butterflies, dragons, tigers, bats, and countless others.

The marks of Group 108 include a dragon tattooed on one shoulder and a tiger tattooed on the other, or two dragons fighting for a pearl. Group 36 has a dagger and a rose or a sitting Buddha or a warrior carrying a spear. Group 24 signs include, for reasons nobody could explain, Christ on the Cross, an American Indian's head, cobras, a kissing couple, a panther (the Black Panther Society). The Independents have among their marks a stork in a tree and a human-faced bat.

Secret-society marks are still found today, but they are getting rare as the old Triad-indoctrinated members are killed or die naturally, at home or in jail, as police methods improve and police pressure against the gangs increases, and as the secret societies degenerate into stand-over groups of thugs and protection racketeers.

Secret-society members now avoid any easily found distinguishing marks like cards or badges or special belt buckles, and if a man has a tattoo mark he tries to get rid of it, by surgery or by defacing it with another mark, or, more crudely, by destroying it with acid. And some of the wounds of acid obliteration are not pretty.

Perhaps the most dramatic ceremony of a secret society is the initiation of a new member, a solemn, tradition-inspired event and an example of the deeply embedded symbolism of Triad rules and ritual.

The police told me that, so far as they know, the last authentic initiation ceremony took place in Singapore in 1957 and that it involved the entry of a new recruit to Group 108. But Chinese friends insisted that Triad initiation ceremonies still take place, although they admitted that these were becoming rare and would probably disappear within this decade.

Initiation, when the ceremonies were common, began in the headquarters house of a society and then moved the same night to a secret outdoor place—coconut plantation, small rubber estate, deserted beach—where the real ceremony took place. There is no initiation in a headquarters house today because a secret-society house would be an invitation to a police raid.

There are many versions of initiation ceremonies, but most seem to agree on basic details and their meaning. The ceremony is held in the open, at night, and the area is closely guarded. The Master of Ceremonies is an authority on society history and ritual, though he does not necessarily belong to any particular society. He has been likened to an Army commander in chief. He is in complete command of a ceremony and receives a fee for each initiation This fee, though real money, is always in symbolic amounts which vary according to the ability of the recruit to pay. The amounts must be, in Malayan dollars, 1.80, 3.60, 7.20, 10.80, 36.00, 72.00, or 108.00, and each mystic Triad number is a multiple of three.

The ceremony starts with the construction with sticks of a symbolic Chinese city. The sticks represent walls, gates, buildings. The central building is generally called the Red Flower Pavilion, and on its symbolic altar are placed candles and red paper marked in black with the names of traditional Triad objects—the ruler, the fan, and others. The symbolic gates are called the Hung Gates and each gate during the ceremony is guarded by a society member. The Master of Ceremonies stands in the middle of the city and orders the new member or members, since more than one recruit can be initiated at the same time, to approach.

The initiate, who must dress only in shirt and trousers, and must carry only his fee, is brought to the main Hung Gate, where he is challenged and forced to kneel before being questioned. He is asked what he wants, where he comes from, and whether he is prepared to keep the rules and secrets of the society. In some ceremonies he answers that he wants to join the Hung Army, that he comes from the east, and that he will obey all rules, but in other ceremonies the guard recites the questions and answers for him in verse form.

After this formal questioning the recruit is tapped on the back, given a stick, and passed on from gate to gate until he reaches the Red Flower Pavilion, where the Master stands holding a scepter like a notched ruler to symbolize the fusion of Earth, Heaven, and Man. His assistant carries a white silk fan and wears sandals to show that he is a Hung soldier.

Then, as a white cock is killed and the blood run into a white bowl of Chinese wine, the kneeling man swears an oath to the society and an oath of death to traitors. A stick is broken or a taper is extinguished as he swears. The meaning is obvious. The middle finger of his left hand is then pricked and a drop of blood squeezed into the chicken blood and wine, and with his fingers in the wine, he drinks, thus showing that he has mingled his blood with the blood of the society brotherhood.

The final part of the ceremony is when the Master hands to the new recruit three copper coins and red thread for good luck. The recruit is then known as the "New Born One" and his career as a secret-society member begins. In the old ceremonies he was given as a final gesture a written diploma or receipt and the society's rules and punishments. But today secrecy from the police is so essential that no document records his entry and no written copies of society rules exist, or if they do they are kept hidden.

Although it is true that the secret societies of today are losing their mystic background and degenerating into gangs, they are still extremely active, lawless, and dangerous. They are responsible for every form of crime, from murder to petty theft, from illegal gambling to kidnapping, from smuggling to piracy. They control protection rackets of all kinds, and with intimidation and brutality squeeze the hawker, the shop owner, the taxi driver, the prostitute.

The societies have a nominal leader or Head Man, but he does not necessarily physically lead them. Sometimes a senior fighting member will take charge and direct an operation or plan some new piece of gang skulduggery. There are also "protected members" of a gang, people who pay squeeze and generally under threat. They are acknowledged as members of the gang, but may not regard themselves as members, a distinction they keep to themselves if they are wise and wish to survive.

Some gangs also have a few women members, though not formally initiated members. They are nearly always prostitutes who are used for society intelligence, as decoys and as weapon carriers. During a raid one of these women will carry a weapon, hand it to a fighting man at the last minute, and even collect it from him after the attack. This reduces the chance, if the police pounce, of a gang member being arrested while armed.

These days the gangs seldom use guns. Not more than two per cent of crime in Singapore involves firearms. This isn't because members dislike guns or can't get them but because of the heavy penalties for carrying a "dog"—even a toy one— and the availability and silence of so many other simple, highly efficient weapons. Scout knives and shortened razor-sharp parangs are most popular, though some prefer bicycle chains, water pipe, bearing scrapers, broken bottles, or acid bombs. These are much better weapons than police-attracting pistols in a night attack on a teashop where members of an enemy secret society are meeting or on a house where a gang drinking party is being held. Although individual fighting men are brave, and will fight to the death if cornered, as the police readily admit, gang members are generally not overcourageous unless they have superiority in numbers.

The societies make most of their revenue, which is shared equally among fighting members, from their stand-over protection rackets, and they always increase these activities in special months, largely to bring in additional money to finance their own entertainment. At Chinese New Year, which is in February, and the Seventh Moon Festival, in August, they move into many parts of their own territory and extort extra money from frightened shopkeepers and hawkers. The societies are also financed by smugglers, who use them mainly as intelligence agents, contact men, and guards when a consignment of tobacco or opium is coming ashore.

Citizens, including men whose names would make news, hire society fighting men to blackmail or beat up business competitors and political enemies, and even to murder them. And political groups also pay the gangs to vote at elections and to "persuade" others how to vote.

Ninety-five per cent of all secret-society gangs are Chinese, and all of these, even the most debased, have a background of

Triad history. The five per cent are a few mixed gangs of Indians, Malays, and Eurasians. There is only one all-Malay gang. They call themselves the Red and the White and are such expert burglars that other gangs hire them when they want to raid a house and find it difficult to get in.

In Singapore most murderers are Chinese, which is reasonable in a predominantly Chinese city. And Singapore averages a murder a week. But at least one quarter of Singapore's murders are committed by secret-society fighting men, which explains the open warfare between the gangs and the police.

Most secret-society murders are with knives, bearing scrapers, or by strangulation. Most murders by Indians are with parangs and are because of woman trouble. And most murders by Sikhs are with heavy sticks and are directly traceable to drink. Poison, contrary to all the Asian thrillers you have read, is practically unknown as a murder weapon in Singapore.

One of the most fascinating sidelights on serious crime in Singapore is that the urge to murder seems to be directly influenced by the climate. Singapore has a uniform temperature in the eighties and high humidity, though never as unpleasant as weeks in New York or Washington in midsummer. There are seasonal changes, but they're so slight that the newcomer can't tell the difference. After living in Singapore for a couple of years you begin to surprise yourself by reaching for a light pullover at night in the cool season.

The cool or wet season is during the northeast monsoon, about September-January, and the hot or dry season is during the southwest monsoon, about April-August. But hot and cool are little more than nominal definitions, for it is hot all the time and it can rain almost as much during the dry season, and in between, as in the wet. Only an Irishman would properly understand Singapore's climate, but it is also true that the local born notice even the slight seasonal changes much more than the visitor or the comparatively new resident and, as statistics show, react to them.

The worst months for murder are always in the hot dry sea-

:son between April and August when the climate is generally a little more enervating and when, presumably, this is sufficient to build tensions to danger point. And September-January, the months when there are fewer murders than at any other period during the year, are in the cool wet season when the climate is least exacting on human flesh and emotions.

The month for maximum murder is May—perhaps the hottest month of the hot season. Of the fifty-odd murders in 1961, eleven were in May. Of the fifty murders in 1960, ten were in May. And this pattern repeats itself as you trace back along the years. The month when murder almost disappears from the police charts is December—one of the coolest months of the cool season—and this again is a regular phenomenon.

Why should Singapore murderers be most active in May and exercise almost virtuous abstinence in December? This interested me, primarily because of an odd book in my library, a stray discovery published by an English doctor about seventy years ago. He had studied the relationship between climate and crime and had come to the conclusion after long statistical analysis that the maximum number of murders, attacks, rapes, suicides, and even illegitimate births, occurred in the English summer and the minimum number in winter, and that these figures were constant on a population basis over a decade and more.

I can understand why murderers are less conscientious in the bitter cold of an English winter, and no central heating to make a delicate job of slitting a throat a little more congenial. But why should Singapore murderers, living ten thousand miles away, in an extreme tropical climate, and a climate whose seasonal change is never more than a few degrees, also hibernate in the cool season?

Why, too, should May be the peak month for murder in Singapore? The only possible explanation I could find, except for some close relationship between heat and tension, is that the Chinese All Souls celebration covers a fortnight in May-June and is a time of greatly stimulated racial emotion when, as many Chinese believe, the souls of their dead are liberated by the devil.

Liberated souls could be interesting or embarrassing, depending on their histories before they became souls, and could probably increase blood pressures among the susceptible, but murderers are still active in June, July, and August, when souls have gone where all souls go, when the atmosphere is free again of their wanderings, and when emotions have calmed.

Russian doctors have a theory that heart attacks are more frequent during periods of high sunspot activity, so perhaps some learned medical scientist can explain why tropical murderers prefer May.

The Chinese also monopolize kidnapping, but in 1960, when there were twenty "grabs," as the locals call them, kidnapping almost achieved the status of an industry.

In August that year, when no Chinese millionaire was safe, and when most of them did not move without their armed Chinese or Sikh guards, meetings at the Millionaires Club, along the coast near the Swimming Club, had the greatest difficulty even getting a quorum.

Kidnapping lacks the clear pattern of murder, but it is again mostly the work of secret-society men, and especially the more intelligent among them, though the societies are not exclusively involved. It is also a violent dramatization of the extremes of wealth and poverty in this city—a social comment on an Asian community where the vast majority subsists, six and eight to a cubicle in Chinatown, and a few live in extreme luxury.

I never got to the Millionaires Club, but I lunched with one of its members at the Garden Club above the Overseas Chinese Bank in Chinatown. He was Lee Kong Chian, or K. C. Lee, as he is generally called, though his more popular name is the Rubber Baron of Malaya. With interests in rubber estates and factories, banks, and businesses, he is so many times a millionaire in Malayan dollars that it is said he has lost count, although I would guess that he knows to a million or two whether he is worth two hundred million or only fifty.

We were eight at a circular table facing a central revolving platform holding a simple meal of pig's-stomach soup, sliced pork and chicken, bamboo shoots, diced egg, and sliced oranges and bananas. K. C. Lee, who ate sparingly and drank only water and who wore the simplest clothes, fawn trousers, tan shoes, and a shirt without a tie, would be the despair of any cartoonist who wanted to depict him as the bloated capitalist. He is small and slight with warm humorous eyes—extremely observant eyes behind glasses—prominent teeth, and greying brushed-back hair. He talked in an easy, friendly way, laughed a lot, and looked after three of his guests who did not speak English with the charm of an accomplished host. As he interpreted for them in his native Hokkien and kept them in the conversation, he explained that he could tell exactly where a Chinese came from in his own Fukien Province by his accent, including those whose families, originally northerners, had been driven south centuries ago by the Mongols.

K. C. Lee's story is, like the origins of most Singapore millionaires, the old rags to riches. He was born near Amoy of poor parents and came to Singapore in 1903, where he learned English at a Tamil school and earned a few coppers milking cows. But he was a careful boy, and the pennies accumulated, and by living on a bowl of rice a day with a little vegetable occasionally, he was able to save enough to return to China to study. He received his Imperial Degree in Peking in 1911 from the last Emperor, Pu Yi, and returned to Singapore, where he joined the Government service as a surveyor. But carrying a theodolite on Singapore Island, where he helped survey many of the built-up areas of today, lasted only a few years—just time to save enough money to buy his first small trading business. From then on he bought land, sold, saved, moved into rubber, and from those beginnings began to build a fortune and his title of the Rubber Baron. K. C. Lee is a man of intelligence, simplicity, and charm. His good works no doubt benefit many of his countrymen. But it is fortunes like his which are a gold-embossed encouragement to kidnappers, as recent history proves, and of course to the Communist party.

The Singapore Chinese did not have to learn kidnapping. The Chinese have been experts for centuries. They are careful planners and follow a strict, unspectacular routine. There is nothing "flash" about them. After selecting their millionaire, they watch him for days or weeks until they have a complete record of his movements and habits. They then decide where the "grab" will be made and for about a week, using two cars, practice dummy runs to get their timing perfect. They even follow the victim home, many times, or to the house of one of his girl friends. On the day or night of the grab, one car blocks the victim's, and armed men in the second car pick him up and take him to a prepared hideout—a house they own or have rented and generally outside the city in one of the rural areas. The actual kidnappers hand the victim over to another group, change the number plates of their car, or use another car, and disappear. The new group keeps the victim for days or weeks before contacting the family. They force him under threat of mutilation or death to write a letter, and they post with this, from a central city box, their own ransom note. They then follow the letter with phone calls—often made by a hired third person who is not a member of the gang—and will even haggle about the price before establishing a rendezvous with a representative of the family. At the appointed time and place this representative waits carrying agreed identification— a Chinese newspaper in one hand, a packet of Camel cigarettes in the other—and the money in old notes. The contact man produces a letter carrying a crude seal—one was the seal of the Blue Dragon Society—as his identification, the money is paid over, and, at an arranged time and place, the victim, after being driven blindfolded from the hideout, is released.

Singapore's kidnappers are the most cold-blooded of all the Island's killers. If anything goes wrong during a grab or in the waiting period, or the ransom is not paid, they will kill, but failure to release a prisoner after payment is extremely rare. Of the twenty kidnappings in 1960, three millionaires were killed. Two of these resisted, and one was shot and the other stabbed. The third man, found bound and gagged, had suffocated.

But Singapore kidnappers are just as ruthless with their own members. A member of one gang who squealed to the police was caught and systematically murdered. The leader of the gang, an expert on Koon-tow, the Chinese art of self-defense which specializes in the stiff-finger technique of attack, broke this man's ribs one by one and pulped his chest. The skilled Koon-tow exponent can strangle with two fingers, can kill with one stiff-finger hit over the heart.

The stone lions guarding the red-and-gold House of Tang from evil spirits did not prevent C. K. Tang, the Curio King, from being kidnapped. Even the old theory that the gangs won't touch a millionaire if he gives generously to charity did not help him. His family got him back—for about fifty thousand U.S. dollars. Ong Ching Siang, the bus-company millionaire, was kept bound and gagged for nine days in an underground cell, but was released after payment of a huge ransom, said to be about eighty thousand U.S. dollars. Biscuit King Lee Gee Chong was not so lucky. He was the man already described who was found knifed. The only non-Chinese to be kidnapped was an Indian millionaire—and the gang was Indian. They kept him for weeks in a wooden box about the size of a coffin, then let him go for a ransom of five thousand U.S. dollars.

But of all kidnapping stories, one stands out. Chia Yee Soh, a multimillionaire, was driving home from golf when a car blocked the road and four young Chinese grabbed him. They took him by motorboat to one of the small offshore islands and demanded one hundred and fifty thousand dollars—the biggest ransom demand known. Chia refused and lectured them, told them they should be ashamed of themselves. They continued to threaten and he continued to scold. And Chia wasn't the first to tire. After a week they brought him back to Singapore

Island and let him go. They even gave him his bus fare. But Chia Yee Soh was a multimillionaire and knew the value of money. He pocketed the fifty cents and hitchhiked home.

The worst year ever was 1960, when kidnapping flared and waned just like an epidemic. The law against kidnapping was lax and punishment too lenient, but the real carriers of the disease, as experience proved, were the families of the kidnapped. The main weakness in attempts to combat kidnapping was that, except in rare cases, the police heard of the grab only after the ransom had been paid and the man released. This drastically reduced police effectiveness. And so the law was strengthened—by death or life imprisonment and no trial by jury because of the almost certain danger that the gangs would attack the families of jurymen. But the real power in the law was not the death penalty, that archaic expression of social revenge which has never been a deterrent anywhere. It was punishment for the families who failed to report a kidnapping immediately or who paid ransom. The police were also given the power to freeze the bank accounts of involved families, to intercept their mail, and to tap their phones.

These were drastic and potentially dangerous powers to give any policeman, since there is nothing more certain than the old truism that power corrupts. But kidnapping had to be stopped and these new powers were directed at the kidnapper through the family. His only reason for kidnapping was easy money to be won at minimum risk, but under the new laws money became difficult to get and at greatly increased risk.

There will always be kidnappings, just as there will always be murder, death penalty or no death penalty. Human beings, as the author of *Lord of the Flies* so skillfully showed, are not social animals except under the restraints of law. Heredity, environment, mental capacity, mental abnormality, social inequality—they all play a part in violence or non-violence. But since the law began to operate in Singapore in 1961 the drop in kidnappings has been dramatic.

Today the millionaires still keep their armed guards, but in

Tanjong Rhu, where they have their ugly club, they now even have their meetings at night—and seldom fail to get a quorum.

The Chinese are masters of violent crime, but amateurs compared with the Malays and their cousins the Javanese at burglary. Burglary suits the Malay temperament, for good housebreaking is a subtle individualistic art which needs intelligence, planning, and a high degree of sensitivity. I have always admired the good unarmed burglar because he is a challenging spirit who is prepared to risk his liberty, and even his life, on a loose board or a housekeeper's insomnia or a child's toy left in the middle of the living-room carpet.

The Malays have all the characteristics which add up to good burglary. They are far superior to the Chinese because they lack their crudity, their arrogance. The Malay will climb a perpendicular wall with no more aid than commando holds. He will out-baboon any baboon on a drainpipe. He will drill a hole in a door and you won't hear a sound two yards away.

They are among the world's most ingenious fishing-rod burglars, and through an open window or a hole snipped in a wire screen will lift your wallet or watch from the far side of your room or your shirt from the floor where you usually drop it—and you won't miss your property until next morning. In unsewered areas where Chic Sale privies are part of houses, a Malay will remove the tin and enter that way. They have been known, when opposed by a nailed-down seat, to wriggle through the seat hole, rifle a house, and leave by the same entrance.

One of the city's most expert burglars was a rag-and-bone collector who carefully studied his houses by day, broke in at night, always cut the phone first, always stole the most valuable property, always hid his loot near the burgled house and never where he lived, and always made a special point of calling next day to ask for rags and bones.

The Orang Minyak, the Oily Men, are also mostly Malays. They wear swimming trunks, cover themselves with oil, and molest women in the streets and in houses. One who was caught had cut the breast out of the nightdress of a sleeping girl. Another climbed into a bedroom and lay down beside a sleeping woman and her husband. During the night the strong oil smell woke her and she turned on the light. The Oily Man dived through a window. Playing Oily Men is a favorite game among schoolboys. A group will stare at a balcony until pedestrians begin to stop. Then one of the boys will point and shout, "Look, an Oily Man." The boys of course soon disappear as a crowd gathers and stares at the empty balcony of an innocent house.

"Take a look at that," my Chinese friend said.

He handed me what looked like a lump of drying mud, about the size of a big cake, black flecked with dark brown. It weighed about two pounds and smelled of fresh-turned earth scented with chlorine. This was opium—raw opium—and although it was not ready to be smoked, it represented about seven thousand pipes or thirty-five thousand inhalations of opium fumes.

It was grown and prepared about fifteen hundred miles north of Singapore in a valley among jungle hills where China, Burma, Thailand, and Laos meet—a wild neutral zone between China and Southeast Asia where no country commands. It was carried on a woman's back, by mule, by elephant, and finally by native boat down to the muddy Menam and then to Bangkok, where it was repacked, and on again to the Gulf of Thailand. From there a fishing boat sailed it south until, far out at sea, off the east coast of Malaya, it was transshipped to a junk, and fifty miles from Singapore it was handed over once again, and at night, to a Chinese in a speedboat who put it aboard another fishing boat outside the Straits of Singapore. A week later, when that boat returned to Singapore, the opium was under five tons of fish and ice, and it would have remained there until safely moved ashore if a member of the anti-smuggling squad had not developed an illogical suspicion about that boat's innocent cargo of fish.

This large lump in my hand was part of a consignment of

eighteen hundred pounds of raw opium, packed in sealed tins, and worth nearly one hundred and twenty-five thousand U.S. dollars, intercepted at Singapore. Yet this consignment was only part of two to three tons of raw opium captured in Singapore and the Federation of Malaya in a year, and those two to three tons were in turn only a fraction of the opium which is coming out of the Burma-China-Thailand-Laos triangle through Rangoon, Bangkok, Singapore, Hong Kong, and Macao. Those who have studied the opium trade claim that up to four hundred tons of opium and opium derivatives come each year from the border areas, and that much of it moves through Chiengmai, in northern Thailand, and down to Bangkok and the world.

There is no doubt that some of this opium comes from areas of extreme southwest Communist China and that the trade is encouraged from realistic Peking not to foster drug addiction in the West, though the more opium which gets out inevitably helps this, but as a steady source of much-needed foreign exchange to help pay for the imported food China so desperately needs to feed her immense population.

Before World War II the Government's opium monopoly in Singapore—the profits from the sale of prepared opium to addicts in Singapore—was worth twenty-five million Straits dollars a year to the British. Opium was at the top of the Colony's revenue list. But in 1946 opium was at last prohibited and it became an offense for an addict—for anyone—to smoke. But the drive to stop the traffic is still going on.

In 1942 there were seventy thousand licensed opium smokers in Singapore, most of them Chinese, and even after opium and opium smoking were outlawed, thousands of dens, many with three or four sleeping racks and up to fifteen lamps, were still operating. Today there are still about ten thousand addicts and at least one thousand dens, but most of the dens today are small slum rooms with single lamps, and not dens at all except in the minds of romantics.

Smoking is declining and will eventually cease. The older

addicts are dying; the younger people, better educated, better informed, smoke little. There are too many other distractions, and opium represents the past, and particularly the white past. Most addicts today are fifty years or older, and most arrests for opium smoking, about thirteen hundred a year, are of people over forty.

But even with declining numbers, huge profits are still being made. Raw opium costs between forty and fifty U.S. dollars a pound in Singapore, but when it is cleaned of leaf, twigs, sand, and other impurities and prepared as smoking opium—the treacle-like Chandu, as it used to be called—the cost rises to one hundred and twenty-five U.S. dollars a pound. A packet of prepared opium—one fortieth of an ounce—costs the smoker today one Malayan dollar or about twenty-five cents U.S., and from that he gets about fifteen inhalations.

At least sixty per cent of the raw opium which reaches Singapore is exported, a little to Borneo, Indonesia, and Australia, but most of it to the United States to feed the hideous drug traffic, for heroin, which is thirty to eighty times as potent as opium, is a derivative of morphine, and morphine, six to ten times as potent as opium, is manufactured from opium. Morphine hydrochloride, the halfway stage between opium and heroin, is exported in small blocks like pink plaster of Paris.

Some heroin reaches Singapore, mainly from Bangkok or Hong Kong, and finds a steady sale, particularly among trishaw riders and heavy laborers. They take it by injection or they "chase the dragon" or smoke it. To chase the dragon you heat granules of heroin in folded tinfoil and inhale the fumes through a bamboo tube or rolled paper. The fumes flow up and down the tinfoil trough and resemble the undulating tail of a dragon of Chinese mythology. Another method is to put the heroin on the tip of a cigarette and to smoke it vertically so that few of the fumes escape.

The chief heroin ports, Bangkok and Hong Kong, have heroin refineries—where unemployed chemists find steady jobs —and cruder refineries also operate in the border areas. It is these ports which are the biggest distributing centers not only for this drug but also for morphine and opium. Although opium smoking and trafficking have been illegal in Thailand for several years, little is done to stop the traffic. Opium is money, and too many people, including officials, are involved, despite face-saving ceremonial burning of opium pipes collected by the police. Seized opium has left Bangkok on the next boat.

In Hong Kong, where heroin addiction, mostly among men, has been described as "horrifying," addicts have been conservatively estimated at between two and three hundred thousand, though the true figure is probably much higher. Statistics shown me in Singapore made grim reading, for of more than eighteen thousand people jailed in one year in Hong Kong, a recent year, nearly twelve thousand were drug addicts and more than seven thousand of these addicts used heroin.

The Chinese are the opium and heroin addicts in Singapore, but the Indians are almost exclusively the hashish smokers and chewers. Hashish, marihuana, ganja, bhang—they are all the same and come from Indian hemp or, more correctly, from the little brownish pods of this weedlike plant. I was given some of these pods and told that if I crushed them they would emit a distinctive smell. I followed instructions, but the hashish-marihuana in my palm was completely odorless.

The tall Indian hemp with its long narrow leaves and feathery tops grows wild in Thailand and Indonesia, and that is where it comes from to Singapore. About two hundred pounds are smuggled in each year to sell to Indian addicts, who smoke it in water pipes or in cigarettes, at about six U.S. dollars a pound, so that smugglers don't make fortunes from this trade. The real money is in the opium-heroin traffic, and that is why it is so difficult to stop.

6

In that splatter of streets where Serangoon Road rises and Little India begins, Christ gazes sadly from a mission building at a neon tiger which limps along a rooftop to advertise Tiger Balm.

Tiger Balm, which will cure anything from warts to embolism, was created by Aw Boon Haw, a Chinese peasant who amassed millions and who with his brother spent a million Malayan dollars just before World War II to build Haw Par Villa, or, as it is better known, the Tiger Balm Gardens, at Pasir Panjang on the west coast of Singapore Island.

One of Singapore's guides refers to this "fascinating, beautiful park" and adds, almost with reverence, that a visit to the Gardens "will never be forgotten." This is an understatement. It is impossible to forget Tiger Balm Gardens, which is one of the world's best examples of the fact that money can buy even a landscaped nightmare.

On lawns and slopes near the sea life-size figures and groups in Technicolor illustrate Chinese myths and fairy tales. White marble Buddhas pray among mythical animals, wolflike frogs, women with the talons of carrion birds. One group tells the story of a monk on pilgrimage and of the temptations which beset him, another shows torture and murder in a Chinese purgatory, with pints of synthetic blood to add realism. There are swimming pools and mermaids and dog creatures all mixed up with assassination and sadism. The million-dollar Gardens are an obscenity of ugliness. They would horrify the gentle Buddha so much that if the spirits of the departed Aw Boon Haw and his brother Aw Boon Par ever run into the Gautama's on the Tenth Plain they will have a lot of explaining to do.

The sign of the limping tiger is near the spot in Singapore where you leave China behind and cross an unseen border into the India of this multi-racial city beside the sea. There are Chinese in long-crowded Serangoon, plenty of them, but they are passing through or shopping or trading, and if they work here, as many do, they work for Indians:

Tamils from southern India, coolies or the descendants of coolies who came to Singapore and Malaya at the end of the last century to work on the first of the rubber estates. Thin-featured people, many with heads shaved far back from their foreheads and long greased hair, their skins black or near black brushed with the purplish bloom of fresh grapes. Tall, hand-some Sikhs with Greek faces stained like old coins, warrior people from the Punjab whose name itself means "Disciple" and who must wear the five K's—the Kes, or uncut hair worn coiled under the turban, the Kachh, or long drawers, the Kara, or iron bangle, the Kirpan, or sword, replaced today by the Khanda, or small dagger, and the Khanga, or hair comb. The Sikhs are small shopkeepers, watchmen, guards, police. Pale Parsees, followers of the Prophet Zoroaster, the Persian Christ, whose center of worship is the ever-flickering flame in their fire temples and whose life is supposed to be guided by Humata, or good thoughts, Hukhta, or good words, and Huvarashta, or good deeds. Muscular Pathans, Muslim tribesmen from the North-West Frontier; dull copper Bengalis from Calcutta, quick-witted, devious; Gurkhas from their Himalayan home-land of Nepal, small, sturdy, Mongoloid; charm sellers from Kashmir touting protection against the evil eye; even an oc-

casional Jain, who will not take life in any form and who, if
orthodox, wears a strip of gauze over the mouth to prevent
careless insects from committing suicide.

In Serangoon Road, where cyclists swerve and wobble among
hooting cars and where pedestrians stroll indifferent to the
curses of pedicab riders and the squealing of brakes, you pass
the shops of the gold workers where bangles wink from glass
cases, the shops of the jewel merchants, shops where birds
call sadly from gilt cages, shops where silks and cottons spill
amber, cobalt, tangerine, amethyst into the street near temple
gates painted rose and silver.

Serangoon Road is the smell of India—hot ghee and dal in
food-shop pans, curry, tarragon, rose water, oil, sweat, cow
dung, flowers, all mixed with cooking smoke and incense and
the bloody astringent splashes of the betel chewers.

The Indians and Pakistanis and the dozens of different peoples who come under the racial and religious umbrella of those
names, plus the Jews and Arabs and Persians and many more,
are shopkeepers, traders, moneylenders, taxi drivers, manual
workers, street cleaners, clerks, and even policemen and politicians. They range from the millionaire in sharkskin to coolies
in filthy dhotis and handkerchief headgear.

There are only about one hundred and seventy thousand
Indians and Pakistanis in Singapore, so that every dark-skinned
one is outbalanced by at least eight Chinese. But the races from
the Indian subcontinent stand out much more than the other
minorities. It is true that the wide variety of pigments, features,
hair styles, caste marks, and headgear attracts the eye, and so
do the white clothes of the men and the brilliant saris of the
women. But the real reason is that their religions, apart from
Islam, are more obvious, their temples more garish and numerous, and that if you turn your back you're almost certain to
miss some festival or procession.

At the Mariamman Temple butter-colored bulls gaze im-
potently down from the high narrow wall on white-clad Hindus
flowing through the gateway. Behind the walls every ledge and

cornice and column is violet, emerald, and crimson splashed and inhabited by sirens, elephants, gods with mustaches, mythical animals, weird birds, all intermingled with clusters of indigestible fruit hanging above the heads of warlike gods of the Hindu pantheon and fierce virgins scampering along galleries in the direction of a cornucopia of phallic symbols.

I reach the Temple roof by an iron stairway almost on the shoulders of the pushing crowd and, wedged between an animal like a dachshund with a satyr's face and a bull's behind, look down into the courtyard. The heat lifts in almost solid waves from a pit fifteen to twenty yards long where a fire has been burning for days and where the ash is grey and powdered. Sweat drips off my nose. My shirt grips me. The air hurts to breathe as I watch dark priests with steaming cloths over their heads rake the pit, then step back and pour buckets of water over their bodies. As they finish preparing the smoldering ash a trough at the far end of the fire pit is filled with milk, goat's milk, and a priest with cruel lips prays as he scatters pink and white flowers which wreathe, shrink, and disappear as they touch the ash.

Then, as two priests lead in a shaggy billy goat, a deep welling sound, a mass exhalation, flows from the spectators, and the Temple is silent as the goat sniggers at the heat, stamps, and tries to back away. One priest holds the animal's hindquarters, another his horns, as the man who had scattered the flowers advances carrying a curved scimitar, silver-white against his black wet shoulder. Those holding the goat pull against each other to steady the animal and stretch its neck. The priest grips the scimitar with both hands, spreads his feet, measures the distance. The blade flickers in a high sweep and a blunt neck pumps blood. The crowd roars, almost angrily, as the headless goat is dragged by the hind legs around the pit. Blood sprays into steam on the white-grey ash. The heated air smells of salt.

Now the devotees are dragged in. Their spittle is clotted around their screaming mouths, their haunted eyes float aimlessly in blood-red sockets. They resist, fight, maul each other, swing at the priests, but they are held, then pushed closer and closer to the pit. The devotees are wasted. Their ribs make bird cages of their chests. They have starved themselves for weeks in preparation for this ordeal by fire in expiation for sins, to help loved ones who are sick, or friends in trouble, and, above all, in devotion to the gods of Hinduism.

The crowd grumbles like a full stomach as the priests select a devotee, lash his wrists with rope ends to bring him momentarily from his walking coma, and push him forward. For a moment he stands, desperately alone, then he walks along the ash, walks slowly to the pool of goat's milk and through it, to be absorbed by the black arms and white clothing of his welcoming relatives. But the next man runs and is jeered and pelted with orange peel and goat's droppings. Others follow him along the pit. Some stumble and nearly fall. Some wander from side to side. One refuses to enter the pit, even under the "persuasion" of the priests. They lash him across the face, the shoulders. Only then does he stop resisting and walk forward, kicking disdainfully now at the ash as though it is cool beach sand.

If we had walked that fire pit, we would never have walked again, perhaps not have lived to remember an ordeal which witches and criminals were subjected to not many centuries ago. But none of those devotees was burned or even mildly blistered.

The sacred bo trees drip on the shoulders of other devotees who await their day of pain. They wait, shivering like puppies, snatching at their hair, their ears, their genitals, seeing but recording little with eyes dulled from lack of sleep, starvation, the throb of festering self-inflicted gashes on chests and legs and arms.

The priests come from the Temple, one stabbing at a drum of buffalo hide until the vibration seems to shake the leaves and fling big drops to the already warming ground. Another carries a brass dish filled with double-ended hooks of silver wire. Another holds a basket of small limes sprinkled with flower petals.

The devotees stagger forward. The priests advance. The crowd moves closer. Dirty tongues circle dark lips and eyes become stilled and cruel, for men enjoy the infliction of pain, yet deny it, as they enjoy their own frail immortality when looking at the dead.

A priest takes a silver hook from the bowl, clamps a devotee's nipple with thumb and first finger, and impales the hook. The devotee shudders but makes no sound. Another hook goes in, and another and another, until chest and arms are covered in a thin chain mail of silver wire. Then a priest hooks limes to the dangling barbs to weigh them down, to add to the pain, yet nowhere on this devotee, his skin pierced more than a hundred times, is there one speck of blood.

His relations lead him through the gates to the road and turn him to face the Subramaniar Temple, several miles away. The limes bounce on his chest as he vomits and tears at his hair and begins his shambling march of devotion in the early-morning sunlight. And as he disappears others are being impaled with the hooks, mostly on chest and arms and back, but some now have them through the ears, the cheeks, and even the tongue. One by one they start their journey, to the encouragement of the drum and the soft muttered words of their friends.

The kavadi carriers come next. The first sits on a stone and the priest places a kavadi, a metal contraption that could be a piece of contemporary sculpture, on his shoulders and "nails" it to his body with long steel spikes which slide through holes in the metal frame and into the skin of chest and back. When the spikes are in, without a whimper, without blood, the erect kavadi is decorated with flowers, fruit, garlands, bells, streamers, flags, an oil lamp or two, already smoking, and even small bowls of water which fit into rings. The man's cheeks are then pierced with a silver spear and onto this is screwed a silver plate which gags him. He is ready to go, and as he is helped to his feet, for the kavadi and its decorations are heavy, he sways and nearly falls from pain and exhaustion. His eyes look drugged. He dribbles. Urine trickles down his skinny legs. He takes his first steps, the kavadi swaying above his sweating head, the spikes straining at his impaled flesh to keep the kavadi upright. In the roadway he is stronger and begins his march. Soon he is almost running, a slow, stumbling progress which takes him, and all the other devotees, to the Temple and the end of his penance, for pain is part of the festival of Thaipusam, and through pain he seeks personal fulfillment in the eyes of the god, who, in the glare of torches and sitting on his golden peacock throne, is dragged by screaming thousands in his silver car to the Temple services.

The throaty plucking of the tambur, a lute grown too tall for its age, was the first sound. Then the violin came in, high and chill, and the drum, patted and stroked with purple palms, began to argue and plead and command until the other instruments ceased to have meaning except as servants to the voice of the drum.

Curtains split and the singer entered to sit cross-legged on the carpeted platform between the male tambur player in white and the violinist in apricot and sapphire. The singer draped a black-and-gold shawl over her strawberry-colored sari and began to beat time with a loose flat hand on her sturdy right knee. The diamond stud in the violinist's nose winked at the thousand light bulbs reflected in the Temple mirrors, a flicker of fire in her darkly beautiful face. The drum faltered and almost stopped, as though the drummer was turning a page of music, then continued with new vigor, with almost terrifying insistence, as the first long wailing cry of the singer reached the roof above thick blue pillars banded with gold and blood-red and lime.

This was a Tamil religious song, Manshenker explained. It would last a long time. He was right, because an hour later the song showed no sign of ending and the drummer's hands were still rippling over the sweat-stained skins, caressing them, slapping them, beating out a broken rhythm that seemed to tell of suffering and tears.

I liked the drum and the husky tambur and the lament in another tongue, but my bottom, with only a thin rush mat between it and hard tiles, was aching, my shoulders were aching, my back was aching. I had been designed for a chair. I glanced at Manshenker, who squatted beside me, spotless in his handwoven cream silk jhabba, like a long Western shirt with full sleeves and no collar, and his white dhoti. His black eyes were far away, following this Indian corroboree. I glanced to my right. An old Tamil, white haired and wearing glasses fashionable fifty years ago, was reading a religious book, page after page of the curling dotted right-leaning script of the Tamil language. There was no help on that side either and nothing to do, for I was the only non-Indian guest at the Nine Nights of the Goddess ceremony, except to listen and watch.

The men around me sit in uneven rows between the blue columns. They face the singer, their feet tucked under them. They are all in white or cream and their skin colors vary from honey to copper to blue-black. Smooth, watchful faces with only the very old among them showing the first signs of sagging and wrinkling. They reminded me, sitting on the Temple floor and reflected in a huge mirror behind the musicians, of a colony of sea lions in fancy dress.

The women sit apart from the men, bunches of dark-faced flowers with the red forehead dots of the married just discernible among saris and shawls of every color. The women gossip and show white teeth, and their gold and silver ornaments sparkle, and some have flowers in their tight-brushed hair. They are less reserved, more human, than their menfolk. I like the look of the girls and smile at one immense lump of womanhood with arms almost covered in bangles. She is so surprised— in the Temple, too—that she giggles, and in no time all the women in her group are giggling and assessing the infidel. The large lady's forehead lacks a red dot. She is a widow, and widows, even among Indians, never lose that desire for repetition.

The children are restless, bored. The little ones run about and play hide-and-seek behind their mothers, around the pillars. They are too young to wear the sari and are in Western clothes. Their pigtails are black snakes. Their faces have that wondrous eagerness of the young, the beauty of all small growing things, but their eyes carry latent rebellion against the main source of all their problems, their elders.

I squirm to ease the aches. I stray from the singer to watch the young priest, naked to the waist, his hair tight-combed and oiled, shred leaves and drop them on the black-and-white tiles before the alcove where a god, in the glare of a dozen naked bulbs, sits in splendor, his many ropes of diamonds winking and splashing. I think the god is Vishnu, but it doesn't really matter. I'm more interested in the living as they advance, making the joined-hands sign of devotion, under the spreading chandelier of pale-rose-and-blue grass. Some bow deeply, some go on their knees, then take a pinch of the holy ash, made from sandalwood and offered by the priest on a silver platter, and smear their foreheads and down their noses, and then select a petal from another tray and arrange it—in the hair for girls, behind the left ear for the men.

The drum renews its argument but the devout don't seem to hear as they move on, deeper into the Temple, to other alcoves, other altars, where incense spirals plait themselves to the painted ceiling and oil lamps, like the floating wick lamps of medieval times, wave their flames and blow their smoke against carved brass doors which lead to the sanctum of the god Subramanin. Here the smoke is a transparent blind between the altar and the rest of the Temple, and the air is sticky with incense and bodies and oiled hair and fresh flowers. Devotion is here, wordless and silent. It is simple personal worship, as unself-conscious as breathing, and conducted apart and yet part of the activities of a community, within reach of women gossiping, religious music, children playing, an old man reading. I feel more religion here than at many a planned bloodless service in many a vaulted cathedral.

But the singer had reached her final words and the last drum beats were echoing faintly in the recesses of the Temple, beyond the altar, beyond the smoking lamps and the carved brass doors.

Come, Manshenker said.

We went outside, put on our shoes, walked to one end of the Temple, and took off our shoes at an open door. In the eating room of the priests we sat on a bare concrete floor, and fresh banana leaves were laid in front of us. On them were placed white rice cakes, fried rice, chili, and sweet sauces. We ate with our right hands, for the left is the body-cleaning hand and taboo, breaking the rice cake and molding it with the rice and hot sauces with the tips of our thumb and first two fingers. We ate until the banana leaf showed through, sipped coffee, thanked our hosts, and went out to lace our shoes under a warm sky weighted with stars.

As we walked toward the gates the Temple was silent and its heavy studded doors were closed, but on the covered benches in front of the entrance some of the men who had sat on the floor listening to the singer and the drum and the tambur were reclining on the blue tiles, their shawls about their shoulders. Now they looked just like Roman senators.

Nicoll Highway, which leads in a roundabout way to the Orang Melayu, goes through Kallang, where heraldic lions try to convince those who pass that they are guarding Merdeka Bridge.

Here all is changed. Kallang Airport terminal, which travelers once stared at in admiration, since it was the most modern in the world, now looks like a thinly patronized public lavatory and is the headquarters of the People's Association. The ex-airport's swamp-reclaimed runways are the tree-lined avenues of Kallang Park. The planes which landed there are now in picture books, to be smiled at with grandfather's whiskers or mother's hats.

Only nearby Boat Port is the same, backwater acres where junks and prahus and other sailing craft from Thailand, Borneo, Sumatra, from the Sulu and Celebes Seas, rest from their journeying. Here hulls are tight-packed as crews unload, sort gear, make repairs. Here, too, masts and spars and trailing ropes are, from a distance, fields of drying weeds, and patched sails, up to dry, are stray leaves hoisted by the wind.

Beyond the bridge and Boat Port the new multi-story apartment buildings cover what was once a tidal swamp where wading fishermen searched at night with lamp and net. Blue, white, brick, glass, the flats are the homes of Chinese who have escaped from Chinatown and other crowded areas. But these people, despite tiled bathrooms and hot water, have not forgotten their Chinatown life or the ways of their parents, for the bamboo washing poles which touch ends above slum streets reach out here from every window and every balcony, so that apartment buildings and groups of such buildings, draped with the drying washing of thousands, seem to be dressed for some gay and everlasting festival. This transplanted custom, which derives from the lack of space in crowded Chinese cities, has become accepted practice because the architects of the most recent apartment buildings in Singapore have even included a special balcony attachment to take and hold the bamboo washing poles.

On to Geylang and the city limit between gardens where oleander and bougainvillaea make mosaics against white walls and buttercup trees are golden waves curling among jacaranda. This is Chinese suburbia, where gilded tigers guard wealthy gates and animals of legend crouch beside red front doors. But soon the Chinese surrender to the Malays, to the thatch and squalor of kampongs or the remains of kampongs where flimsy stilted houses stand in mud to the knees when it rains and scraggy chickens scratch dust when it's dry.

Descendants of the Island's original inhabitants, the Malays, live in these parts. They outnumber the Indians in Singapore, but are still heavily outnumbered by the majority Chinese. For every Malay on the Island there are at least five Chinese, and just as the Chinese include sub-races like the Hokkien, the Cantonese, the Hakka, and others, so the Malay population is a mixture of many people and many bloods—Javanese, Bugis, Sumatran, Bornean, and many others from the islands of Southeast Asia.

But a great-grandson of a Bugis pirate, the daughter of a sultan, the nephew of a Singapore sais, or chauffeur, all have one thing in common, their religion. They are Muslim and through their religion are linked with the Islamic world which sweeps from Indonesia, Singapore, and Malaya through Pakistan to the Middle East, southern Russia, the Mediterranean, and much of Africa. This is an almost unbroken belt of common faith, but also a civilization and a culture which, after centuries of Western intrusion and domination, has become bemused and uncertain in the face of Western technology and ideas, which the conservatives of Islam have always resisted. But independence from the West, instead of stopping or at least retarding Westernization, has accelerated it, and the impact on social life, customs, and thought from Djakarta to Casablanca is almost catastrophic. Islam today, and the Malays are very much part of it, is facing a tremendous social, political, and spiritual crisis which could destroy or rejuvenate it. The only certainty, as it emerges to face what is left of this scientific and technological century, is that it can never be the same again.

The Malays of Singapore and Malaya are only a tiny minority in the total sprawl of Islam, but they are facing the destructive and creative forces of Westernization just as much as the millions of Pakistan or of Egypt or Islamic Africa. There is a parallel between the story of the Malays and the story of Islamic civilization in the last century and a half.

A popular definition in the Singapore I once knew was that Malaya was owned by the British for the protection of the Malays and the benefit of the Chinese. Like many such dinner-table definitions, it had some truth in it. The British ruled

Singapore, and Malaya, and made as much money as they could out of it. The Chinese, who didn't need protecting, also made millions. But the Malays, who were just emerging from semi-feudalism, hadn't a chance of more than an existence against the competition of two professionals like the British and the Chinese, and needed British arms and law to physically survive in the same society.

The Malays were, and most still are, basically simple peasants and fishermen, still centuries back but living in what was their country, dominated politically and commercially by two extremely sagacious people, who were joined by a third and equally materialistic trading race, the Indians. And so developed the story that the Malay was a charming, happy, lazy, no-good, useless playboy, and for generations the British, Chinese, Indians, and others who would sell you at an outrageous price a genuine Bokhara rug copied in Manchester or a Tang horse made in Hong Kong, have repeated the story, and still repeat it.

It is not entirely a myth but: You occupy much of a man's land, buy his produce at your price, sell the goods he needs in your shops, control the labor market in your own interest, develop his country's resources, bully him economically, and dominate him politically, and then accuse him of being a lazy good-for-nothing who won't work. This is precisely what has happened to the Malays and why, in a society designed to produce millionaires, the slums of Chinatown, and big dividends for absentee landlords, the Malays have been given few opportunities to rise above clerks, office boys, chauffeurs, gardeners, grass cutters, and policemen, and all among the lowest paid in the community.

The extraordinary thing is that the Malays, while facing the deadly impact of at least three dominant foreign races and cultures on their society, while adjusting themselves physically and mentally from the kampong to the jet, while suffering the spiritual malaise of Western intrusion on their religion, life, and thought, have survived into the twentieth century at all. But they have survived and they are showing, particularly in

Malaya, that they are not the indolent, ineffectual, lazy people they have been labeled for years.

It is easy to find fault with the Malays to divert attention from your own rapacity. The Malays have been a convenient scapegoat to explain why foreigners in the land of the Malays own land, shops, rubber, tin, and most other things. The Malay is not perfect. He has his weaknesses. But to treat him as a retarded child, as many still do, is to ignore the real qualities of a sensitive, intelligent people who have never been allowed the opportunity, until the last few years, to develop their talents and show their quality. In a world of growing crudity and declining ideas, the Malay may yet prove a man who has been seriously underestimated.

The short, brown-skinned, soft-voiced Malays are among the most attractive and delightful of all races. Even the poorest peasants have good manners, the courtesy of men who know instinctively how to behave. They may be technically backward, but against them many advanced people are barbarous. They are wise and humorous. They find love in a flower, beauty in a reed. And from the violin they took from the Portuguese three centuries ago they can make music of gaiety and tears. Their still-little-known fables are among the most enchanting in all literature—stories of sultans and peasants and lovely ladies and animals all blended with history and myth and nonsense and deep wisdom. These fables come from the ancient Malay Annals, whose author is unknown, which perhaps adds in some way to their elusive charm, for adults just as much as children love miracles and mystery and find some deeply embedded emotional consolation in the absurd. Ann Parkinson has published a fine collection of these fables, but omits one of my favorites, the story of Pelandok, the mouse deer, and how he crossed the river. The mouse deer, the Malay Br'er Rabbit, is not much more than fifteen inches high, an elegant little fellow whose smallness, speed, and intelligence aid his survival. He is the symbol of superiority of brains over brawn, of reason over the brute. . . .

When Pelandok reached the stream it was too wide for him

to jump, too dangerous for him to swim. So he called the crocodiles and told them what delightful fellows they were and how misjudged by all other inhabitants of the jungle. The crocodiles gathered. Tiny Pelandok told them how superior they were to Gajah the elephant, how graceful they were compared with Rimau the tiger. The crocodiles had never heard such adulation before, and from upstream and downstream they swam to listen to the golden words until hardly room was left in the water for one more. Then, on their hard and scaly backs, which formed a perfect bridge, Pelandok crossed the stream and had disappeared in the jungle before the crocodiles realized that the mouse deer had tricked them.

Again, Malay wisdom and sensitivity is no better illustrated than in their pantuns, pronounced "pun-tone," four-line versicles from their literature which comment on life, reflect their history and customs, explore the emotions, deflate the pompous, advise the lovelorn. They are crooned or spoken, quoted or sung during the dance, when participants use them in a form of musical repartee, capping other verses like Regency wits or Elizabethan clowns. And always many words and phrases have unbroken traditional meaning—a flower for a young girl, a peacock for a beautiful woman. The pantuns are laced with erotica, though unwritten social rules dictate when and where crudities may be used. There is deep sophistication in many of these pantuns, for even Shakespeare could hardly have bettered "How honeyed are the words that pour from lips which coax but plan deceit," or "Your love sits lightly on your lips, within your heart it does not dwell." There is humor, too, much of it a gentle mocking comment:

> Wander, wander down the glen,
> Stopping at the neighbors' fences,
> Pretending to look for a hen,
> When his eyes are on the wenches.

The pantuns have been created over the centuries by many people, who drew their inspiration from the loves and hates and tragedies and ambitions of individuals and families in palace and kampong. If there is any one author, it is the Malay race itself, and so true was this collective author's observation of life that other races, especially the Chinese, have recognized the skill of the poet, the satirist, the humorist, and have adopted the pantun and built on it their own imagery and into it their own ideas.

But this copying from the Malays is not confined to pantuns. Generations ago many local-born Chinese women adopted the kebaya from the Malays, who in turn had taken a form of it from the early Portuguese. The kebaya is a long, loose, coatlike but collarless gown with long sleeves, often made of lace or flowered material, held together with gold pins or brooches, and worn with a sarong. These Malayanized Chinese women were known as Nonas, and you still see them about today, though the dress is regarded as old-fashioned now and the wearers are known as Babu Chinese. Older generations of Malay women wear the kebaya, but the modern girl generally favors a blouse, often of fine semitransparent material, and wraps an ankle-length sarong printed with gay flower or bird designs round her small waist. She hasn't the superb grace of the Indian woman in her most perfect costume, the sari, or the doll-like beauty and sophistication of the Chinese in her high-collared, leg-split Shanghai gown, or cheongsam, as it is known today, but she has more sex appeal than both of them combined. Her face is oval and soft, her eyes brown, her mouth big and friendly, her breasts small, and her hips perfectly rounded. She has an undulant, gliding walk and from the rear is a dream of steatopygous perfection. She loves jewelry, especially clashing bangles, and good sandals, preferably gold or red, and the lace scarf, or selendang, she sometimes wears over her black oiled hair is her final admission that she was once in purdah.

Sex, religion, talk, and betting on gamecocks would cover some of the main preoccupations of the Malays, so that they are not really much different from Americans or Frenchmen or Australians. They laugh, as the Chinese do, at novelist

Barbara Cartland's advice to British men that they should learn
from the Chinese, who consider six to seven hours normal
time for the thousand and one delights of love-making. A
Malay, I heard, had even composed a special pantun satirizing
this ambitious claim, including that word "normal," at the
same time pointing out that the Chinese, compared with the
Malay, was still an inferior lover. If the Malay claim is deserved,
and they have a sturdy reputation, then perhaps the reason
is the durian.

The Malay has a choice of delicious fruits—the claret mango-
steen, with its cool white sweet-sour flesh encased in magenta
pulp, the dusty-green hairy rambutan, with its sweet jellylike
flesh, the mango, persimmon, chiku, jackfruit, and many more
—but he still regards the durian as irreplaceable as both delicacy
and aphrodisiac. This curious fruit, which looks like a deflated
football covered with spikes, is filled with pips wrapped in thick,
creamy, stinking pulp. The smell of a durian is easily imagina-
ble, and its taste is just like its smell, only much worse. The
revolting flavor lingers for hours, and one durian will wreck
a refrigerator.

But a Malay with a durian tree owns treasure, and when the
fruit are ripening he and his family will guard them day and
night. Court actions have been fought over the ownership of
durian trees, and owners have been charged with wounding
in defense of their fruit. This passion for the durian is explained
by an old Malay saying: "When the durians are in, the sarongs
are up."

As a lover the Malay is an enthusiast. As a social man he is
kindly and tolerant. As a believer he is devout, but insult or reflect on his belief, and he can be fanatical. The higher-class
Malay will break many of the rules of Islam, but the common
man is a very strict Muslim. He won't even swallow his spit
during the long days of the fasting month of Puasa, and in
Malaya that is a penance.

It is the ambition of Muslims everywhere to make the hadj,
the pilgrimage to Holy Mecca. It is an ambition many fail to

achieve. But the Malays approach the hadj with such dedicated purpose that it is said that more of them, on a population basis, return from Mecca wearing the white stitched cap of the hadji than most other Islamic people. This may be an exaggeration, but the pilgrim ships leave regularly for the Red Sea with hardly standing space aboard, and some of the old men in sarong, baju, and songkok and the old women in dated kebaya have saved for a lifetime to make that coveted journey. It needs faith to spend weeks on open decks, particularly if you are old, waiting for that moment when, as they approach the Arabian coast, they can put on the cotton ihran and face Mecca and make that age-old call: "Coming, My God, Coming."

7

Singapore's loneliest man today is Stamford Raffles, the city's founder. Backed by ancient bombards, from which the paint is flaking, he broods on his pedestal under the clock tower of Victoria Hall in Civic Centre, staring across the traffic to the water front and his first landfall on Singapore Island.

The greatest compliment ever paid Raffles was generations ago when his statue was unveiled, for on that day, as the life-size dark-bronze figure was exposed, a deep murmur of pleased surprise came from the local population, followed by shouts in Malay, "Look, he's black, just like us."

"My Singapore," he called it, and spoke without arrogance, for Raffles was an appealing, intelligent, farsighted young man who took the trouble to learn the language and customs of the Malays, the people he ruled, and to practice their courtesies. The pity is that many who followed him did not also follow his example.

Today on a Chinese-governed and -dominated island he would be unable to understand what had happened to his city and would feel an alien in the no man's land between the end of the colonial era in Southeast Asia and an uncertain future. To him the frayed and flapping shirt tails of colonialism would be incomprehensible.

"Featherbedded colonialism," as I heard it described by an Englishman, was never designed to encourage independence of thought or action among the ruled, so that when Britain's slow evacuation from Asia began after World War II—an evacuation which is almost complete—it inevitably left a vacuum in Singapore—a political vacuum which had to be filled. Because of this I was not surprised to find that the struggle for power was still unresolved, or that new and significant political words, which were never heard in the Singapore I knew, had entered the dictionary of Raffles' city.

Words like *"merdeka"*—independence, freedom at last from the white man. "Yellow culture"—the term for what some Asians feel are the most undesirable, decadent features of the cultures of the West. "Malayanization"—replacement of Europeans in official and other jobs by local people. "Malayan consciousness"—development of a common identity by all races and religions. And ever more immediate, "Greater Malaysia"—the coming new state of Southeast Asia, of which Singapore will be an important and potentially dangerous part.

On first impressions, Singapore is orderly, efficient, stable, but, as a Malay proverb asks, "Do you think there are no crocodiles because the water is calm?" In the Singapore of the past, organized politics did not exist and clandestine political activity was far underground. Political opinions, except those of the rulers, were as elusive as fish in a pond. But today Singapore is more obsessed with politics than any place I have ever seen, with the possible exception of India before independence.

"There is so much distortion, lying, and personal abuse in politics here that it is hard to know what to believe," one man told me. "The spoken and published truth is often half or quarter truth and the real truth is often a rumor. You will change your mind about what is going on four times in the first week."

Which is a little harsh, but not entirely inaccurate. This is a small self-centered island world of prancing egos, a political society preoccupied with words, but not always too precise about their meanings, so that words are like a dangerous game played by children with the skill of a cardsharp. There is a breathless compulsion to talk, to explain, to deny, to denounce. Politicians will use a thousand words to say yes and two thousand to say no. There is no selectivity and no reticence. Controversy is unknown and argument hardly exists. Singapore politics is like watching two sluggers in a ring. Nobody has yet learned to box. This is a society so politically parochial that even the noises from other parts of Southeast Asia don't seem to penetrate. In Singapore you feel like a passenger on a ship at sea—the rest of the world is beyond the horizon and may never be reached.

Yet Singapore is in many ways politically unique. It is without corruption and for that reason alone is an example to the governing regimes of many countries. It has always been a popular game among Europeans to tell stories about the congenital dishonety of the Asian, but although many under-paid Chinese and Indians and Malays have had every reason to be dishonest, the Asian is no more corrupt than the Anglo-Saxon or the Latin. The Chinese cook-boy who squeezes the housekeeping money is reckoned a thief, but the white trader who beats a competitor with a dirty deal is a good businessman. Singapore's freedom from corruption gives its politics a singularly new perspective. It is rare indeed to hear from all sides the same story—that members of the Government of Singapore can't be got at, can't be bought, and that this incorruptibility goes right through the civil service.

Another intriguing thing about Singapore is the extraordinary honesty of some political statements and actions—honesty so bedrock that it appears to the stranger as incredible naïveté—until you realize that many of the politicians have known each other all their lives in this island community, have probably been to school together, have played football together, have grown up together. These men, among them personal friends who are political enemies, know each other intimately.

It is this long-established relationship which helps explain to the outlander some of their political acts and statements, but only some, in this city of disturbing undertones.

Raffles' Singapore, so peaceful on the surface, bubbles and swirls underneath. It is a danger spot, as I shall try to show through the events of the past few years and the personalities who are part of that history. But, firstly, a brief background picture is necessary.

The Japanese occupation of Singapore, which lasted from 1942 to 1945, was a grim and bloody business. But a new generation, to whom the Pacific war is as remote as your father's youth, finds nothing ironic in a night sign which proclaims "Mitsubishi" above streets once machine-gunned by that company's Zeros.

After the Japanese surrender, Singapore remained under British military control until civil administration was restored, on an unfortunate date, Fool's Day, 1946, when Singapore became the Crown Colony of the Island of Singapore.

Before World War II Singapore was part of the Straits Settlements—Singapore, Penang, Province Wellesley, a strip of territory opposite Penang Island, and Malacca—and British Malaya consisted of nine Malay states under different degrees of British influence and control. These states, all under their own sultans or their equivalent, were the Federated States of Perak, Selangor, Negri Sembilan, and Pahang, and the Unfederated States of Johore, Kedah, Perlis, Kelantan, and Trengganu.

In 1946 the British Government produced its plan for a Malayan Union under which the nine Malay States, Malacca, and Penang would come within a strong central government at Kuala Lumpur. Singapore was not invited to this geographical and political marriage because the British wanted to keep their military and economic control of the Island for as long as possible.

The Malay sultans and political leaders were glad to have Singapore excluded. They had enough trouble without being swamped electorally by Chinese Singapore. But they still opposed the Malayan Union because it would have extended the vote to all inhabitants of the Malayan mainland—and Chinese, Indians, and others would have then outnumbered the native Malays.

Under Malay pressure, the British Government canceled its Malayan Union plan, substituted for it the Federation of Malaya in February, 1948, and modified the citizenship laws at the expense of the big Chinese population in Malaya. Three months later the Malayan Communist party, almost entirely Chinese, went into the jungle and, helped by some of their own community and by Chinese in Singapore, fought what is evasively called the "Emergency" but what was in fact a full-scale guerrilla Communist civil war.

Because of this Communist war, unemployment and underemployment, Chinese nationalism and Malay antagonism, the underground Communist party and its many front organizations were extremely powerful in Singapore from 1948 to 1956. The party was helped by the strong support of Chinese-educated high-school students and ex-students, most of them not Communists, who rioted and supported Communist-organized strikes because of their lack of opportunities for jobs or to improve their educational status in a city where for generations the British had foolishly ignored Chinese education.

It was in 1955, nine years after Singapore became a Crown Colony, that the first limited but important elections were held, even though voting was restricted to the three hundred thousand people who were British subjects by birth or naturalization, a ruling which again deliberately excluded many of the Chinese.

The mildly socialist Labor Front won ten seats in the Legislative Assembly out of twenty-five, and its leader, David Marshall, a Singapore-born barrister of Persian-Jewish ancestry, formed a coalition government and became Singapore's first Chief Minister. The People's Action party, led by another barrister, the English-educated Lee Kuan Yew, and a radical, violently anti-British, anti-colonial party, won only three seats. The People's Action party included many known Communists and Communist supporters.

The Labor Front Government, when it took power in April, 1955, blamed the People's Action party for the Communist-led Chinese student riots, and demanded immediate self-government. David Marshall went to London in December, 1955, to begin negotiations with the British Government, but six months later, when independence had still not been won, he resigned. Talks with the British were resumed by the new Chief Minister, Chinese Lim Yew Hock, and in April, 1957, agreement was reached for the eventual creation of a State of Singapore with internal autonomy.

Before and during Lim Yew Hock's talks with the British Government, the People's Action party changed not its direction but its appearance. Its more moderate leftist leaders under Lee Kuan Yew were mainly English-educated Chinese. Its extreme left-wing leaders were mainly Chinese-educated Chinese. The moderates realized that they would not win political power and keep it, without British interference, unless they had a more appealing and less Chinese program. And so the P.A.P. became "Democratic, non-Communist, and Malayan." They were also helped in their new drive for power by two things: The arrest and detention of forty-one P.A.P. members and trade-union officials, including eight P.A.P. leaders, for subversive activities. And a revised electoral law which gave most Singapore adults the vote and doubled the total electorate to around six hundred thousand.

At the election on May 30, 1959, the P.A.P. won forty-three seats in the single-chamber fifty-one-member Parliament, but before the first mass government Singapore had ever known would take control, the successful P.A.P. demanded that its eight leaders, who had been in Changi jail for several years for subversion, should be released.

They were released by the British, and Lee Kuan Yew came to power as the first Prime Minister of a self-governing but not independent city-state, because the British controlled defense and foreign affairs and the seven-man Security Council, dominated by the British and a representative of the Federation of Malaya, controlled internal security—a control which will remain until the new Federation of Greater Malaysia becomes a fact.

But among those eight men who were released from Changi jail was a young Chinese, Lim Chin Siong, who was to become Lee Kuan Yew's most bitter rival for power, for when the extreme Left found they could not control the P.A.P. from within, they broke away, split the unions, and in August, 1961, formed the Barisan Socialis, or Socialist Front, party. It is Lim Chin Siong and the outlawed Communist party behind him who dominates the Barisans, and Lim whose aim it is to smash Lee Kuan Yew and the P.A.P. and one day take over Singapore.

8

Geese were drilling in the drive when the car turned off
Tanah Merah Besar and came to the house called "Tumasek,"
which means "Sea Town" and is one of the ancient names of
Singapore. The geese moved toward the gates until they saw
me under the trees which met above the drive. Then they
halted, heads questioning, tails flicking with suspicion, and as
I came closer they conferred, closed ranks, wheeled left, and,
still in formation, marched off among the dead leaves.

Now their place was taken by six dogs, who surrounded me
like a guerrilla band, frisked me for weapons, tested me for in-
tent, growled, tested again to make sure, and escorted me up
the rest of the drive to the lawn under shade trees where my
host, wearing brown batek shorts and an unbuttoned matching
shirt and smoking a bamboo-stemmed pipe, hoisted himself
from a long canvas chair to greet me.

I had first seen David Marshall, Singapore's first Chief Minister and one of the most controversial, liked, and disliked personalities in all Singapore-Malaya, at Kingsford-Smith Airport,
Sydney, a fortnight before. I had flown in the same plane and
had later called on him at his law office, where his room, which
overlooks the sampans in the Singapore River, is decorated

with banners "Presented to David Marshall," contemporary paintings, Chinese brushwork, and the full-length skin of a tiger he had shot in Malaya.

He had invited me to lunch on Sunday, and so I kept the day free to drive through coconut plantations to Tumasek, his two-story green-and-white home, with its sloping roof over a big open veranda room, on the low cliffs at Changi at the Island's eastern end. The house is fifty feet above a muddy green sea where the many kelongs, the brown thatch huts built on piles driven into the sea bed, and surrounded by staked fishing enclosures, seem to drift with wind and tide.

David Marshall is big with black, greying unparted hair which divides into the rippling snakes of the Medusa when he runs his fingers through it. His skin is deep tan, his forehead high, and aging lines slash his forehead and his cheeks, but his most characteristic feature is his eyes. They are brown-black, large and protruding, and they seem to be immersed in liquid, so that at times and in some lights it is like looking at them through water. They are extraordinarily receptive, sensitive eyes in a handsome proud face, and they tell you something about this man. They can be gay, hurt, angry, all in a few minutes. They are emotional eyes across which the little clouds of feeling drift and rush and scatter. When he is serious his face tightens and hardens and his eyes seem to protrude more and become cold and almost fanatical. But at other times they go away and brood and then his skin slackens until deep into his face comes an introspective sadness that is close to pain. He can smile, as gently and freely as a child, and his laughter rides straight from his big belly, but inevitably the pensive, bruised, questing expression returns. A lone and lonely man. A hurt man.

David Marshall is like one of those Pacific islands which anthropologists call "outriders." Tikopea, for example, between Fiji and Samoa, a Polynesian island in the middle of a Melanesian culture. It should not be there, but it is, and the anthropologists want to know why in order to help solve the riddle of Pacific migrations. He was born in Singapore and is part of it but not of it. He is an alien in his own home. He doesn't belong to any of the racial or cultural streams on this Island. His intellectual background is the West—English—his physical and emotional background is Asia. His instincts are local and regional, his tastes are international. He is an outrider who should not be there, but is.

Marshall first took me to his study to see his portraits, caricatures, and a large bronze sculptured head, and his many political cartoons, including an original by that famous New Zealander David Low showing Britannia, Marshall, Bandaranaike of Ceylon, and others above the caption, "I wonder why children never want Grandma to depart through the front door but always long to kick her down the back stairs."

From a glass cabinet he produced a Davy Crockett fur hat and an exquisite white jade bowl so fine that it was almost transparent.

"The hat was a personal present from Senator Kefauver when he was in Singapore."

David put it on and looked more like a villainous Cherokee than Davy or Daniel Boone.

"The bowl was a present in Peking from Chou En-lai. When he gave it to me he explained that old pieces were not allowed out of China these days—even apologized because it was not an antique. But experts here tell me it's a perfect Ch'ing piece at least a hundred and fifty years old. I'm sure Chou En-lai knew its age."

He returned the jade bowl to the case, carefully placed the fur hat beside it, and invited me to see his sea horses.

In a large glass bowl on a stand on the veranda two adult sea horses performed their stilted dance of dignified melancholy.

"They interest me, and I've been trying to rear them. Not these, the babies, those black threads there. I was told to feed the babies on small fish." He laughed. "The smallest fish I could buy were an inch long—whales beside these infants. All the babies died. I wasn't surprised. Then I heard I could get sea-horse eggs. They cost me a fortune. I was also told they would hatch in twenty-four hours. The advice was pretty right. They hatched in eighteen, and now I feed them on powdered fish food. See that one move."

That one was a thread, about two millimeters long, and black. It moved, sluggishly. I wondered if its diet was agreeing with it.

We went back to the garden, where a Malay kebun was slashing fresh coconuts with a parang and pouring the juice into a jug of ice cubes and adding the soft snowy flesh. When the jug was full, we pounded and stirred and tested its virginal flavor and added a little improving gin against the sodden heat of the day. We sat under the trees, glasses on the grass, overlooking a calm sea misted by the coming monsoon. An old Dutch cannon defended Tumasek, and near the cannon a large wooden hammer, about six feet long and symbol of his Workers' party, was propped against a low brick wall which prevented the garden from joining the driftwood on the beach below.

David Marshall's ancestry is generally described as Iraq-Jewish, but this is not entirely accurate. His grandfather was Persian-Jewish and the name was originally spelled "Mashall," and meant "The Torch," after an ancestor with red hair, before his father added the present "r."

Grandfather Marshall, to use the modern spelling, was an exchange broker in Teheran who made a comfortable living meeting the trading caravans from High Asia and buying and selling silver and gold. At least he bought and sold until the Shah introduced paper currency and called in all gold. The merchants and brokers, including Marshall, refused to co-operate. They manipulated the currency. They hoarded. They obstructed the new decree in every way they could. They had been dealing, and dealing profitably, in gold for centuries. They were not going to change. But the Shah had other ideas.

One night a Captain of the Shah's Guard and five soldiers called on Grandfather Marshall. The officer was polite but

firm. He gave him eight hours in which to leave the capital—
and the country. When Marshall protested, he was told that
six other brokers were outside in the street, in sacks, that the
only thing which had saved his life, and saved it only temporarily, was an honored personal service he had once given
to the Shah. Mr. Marshall would die, the Captain said, unless
he left within the time limit.

The special service to the Shah was several years before,
when the ruler's Queen had not been able to feed the infant
Crown Prince and Marshall's wife had been called in to suckle
the baby. The Shah repaid this service with a beautiful emerald,
which is still owned by a member of Marshall's family. Grandmother's milk saved her husband's life because, although he
continued to protest that he could not be ready in eight hours,
and was again warned that he would die if he failed, he
packed everything valuable he could carry, loaded it into two
carriages, and left the capital for Iraq.

David Marshall's parents, who were both born in Baghdad,
first went to Singapore in 1900, where his father started as an
importer of dates, later branched into Indian goods, including
materials, and later still became a real-estate broker. David was
born in 1908, one of five sons—a doctor in Singapore, a businessman and a salesman in Australia, a poet, who killed himself
in Australia, and a sister, as delightful as her name, Rose. But
just before World War I David's mother took him and one of
his brothers to see Grandfather in Baghdad, then Turkish
territory, where they were interned under house arrest for the
next three years. It is curious that Marshall saw most of both
World Wars from "inside," since he was also a prisoner of war
under the Japanese in World War II.

Marshall was nine when he returned to Singapore in 1917.
He had never been to school. He could not read or write. He
started at a convent school in the primary class, but the other
boys sang "Jody Jew, brush my shoe" and he had his first fight
and his first awareness of the anti-Semitism which has worried
him all his life. He moved to St. Joseph's School and survived

two years, until one Day of Atonement his father said, "You stay at home today, David," and David stayed and was expelled. Years later, on the centenary of that school, he sent a hundred dollars with these words, "I have forgiven you." From the Father in charge he received these words back, "Send us another hundred and we will be satisfied." There were other schools—St. Andrew's, Raffles Institution. There was also acute malaria and ill health and, while working sixteen hours a day, hoping that his reward would be a Queen's Scholarship to study in England, for he had early proved a clever scholar, he developed tuberculosis. In the slump after World War I Marshall's father had lost most of his money, but he managed to send David to Switzerland, where he learned French, and to Switzerland a second time after he had returned to Singapore "cured" and again developed the disease.

He was twenty-two before he got his first job, as a salesman. He sold cars, gold, and silverware, corks for medicine bottles, even a "denicotinizer" for cigarettes, and in his spare time he taught French for a few dollars a week. The best permanent job he ever held was with Messageries Maritime. He took it, at half the salary the poorest European was then paid in Singapore, and took it even though he was told, "You can never rise any further in this company. You're an Asiatic."

The deep rich voice, with the unmistakable mixed accent of the Singapore-educated, the accent which used to be known as Eurasian, stopped as we watched one of the puppies ambush Mrs. Marshall's Siamese cat, sunning herself beside the sea wall, and begin to chew her ear. David shouted, but the pup ignored him. The cat struggled and squalled. David got up, cuffed them apart, and returned to the chair and lit his pipe.

He was nearly twenty-seven when, with five hundred pounds he had saved in five years, he decided to go to England to study law. He chose law because medicine, which had always interested him, cost three times as much as the law course and took twice as long. He never made a better choice.

He lived in a cubicle in a London rooming house for a

guinea a week. His landlady, with that genius of English land-
ladies to ignore the simple lessons of Empire, referred to him
as "My Indian student." He was permanently cold, even in
summer. He was also extremely lonely, for "Indian" students
with little money made few friends in those days. To earn a
little more, besides teaching French, he applied to join the
London Police Force, but was rejected because he was half an
inch under six feet.

By working fifteen hours a day every day, by making a pact
with himself never to leave the library without reading something, even if he could not study, he finished his law course
with honors, then read for a year in chambers before being
admitted to the Bar of the Middle Temple and returning to
Singapore in 1937.

In London he was treated as an Asian, and not well treated
at times. In Singapore he again faced racial discrimination,
but mainly because he was a Jew, or at least had Jewish blood.
He was offered jobs with white law firms, but at less than the
pay of a chief clerk. A Chinese lawyer gave him a start and
this advice: "David, don't spend your life kicking against the
racial pricks. It will get you nothing but unhappiness." But
Marshall has been kicking ever since.

Early in his legal career he decided that the quickest way to
attract clients, and to make his name and a reasonable income
for the first time in his life, for he was already nearing thirty,
was in criminal law, and on this he concentrated. Just before
World War II he was opposed in court by one of the senior
members of the Singapore Bar. During an argument the barrister insulted him. Marshall snapped, "If you are rude to me
again, I shall be bloody rude." This clash led to a meeting
later, when the barrister apologized and asked him to join his
firm, but added: "You can have the highest salary of an Asian
in this firm. I will pay you seven hundred and fifty dollars a
month. But you will never go higher." Marshall accepted. He
could not reject the money he needed so urgently.

Around this time, with war coming, he decided to offer for

Army service. He felt that he wanted to "do something, even symbolic." He applied to join the strictly European Singapore Volunteers and wrote "Asian" on the entry form opposite "race." It was a defiant gesture, in a white-controlled colonial society. It expressed his hatred of German Nazi anti-Semitism, and also of the economic and social discrimination practiced against him as an Asian and a Jew in Singapore. His application was returned. He was told to apply to the Eurasian section. He refused. Finally he was accepted as a private in the Volunteers, but when he was paid the Asian rate of pay, which was about half the European rate, he protested that he would "see the General." He was confined to barracks, and again threatened to visit the General. He was given the European rate of pay. But although a member of the Volunteers, he was never really one of them. He was, in his own words, "intensely disliked," and some men who served with him still argue that even that description is a major understatement.

David Marshall's life story had to halt there because Sunday is open day at Tumasek, and the guests, with almost as many children and dogs, were international—an Indian woman doing postgraduate research in Malayan history, a Chinese professor, an American businessman, an English woman journalist, a Eurasian lawyer, and many more.

For two hours David Marshall was shouting greetings, pouring drinks, arguing politics, stopping dog fights, swimming with the children. An Indian guest called him a man with a big heart, and I found this to be true. He has warmth, as well as a first-class brain, which explains why so many people return again and again to Tumasek to be stimulated and amused and perhaps above all to be in contact with a generous, extravagantly energetic man to whom living is a challengingly crazy game beset with windmills and muddled with wineskins. There is something almost medieval about Marshall, the wandering irascible crusader lost from his time who has strayed into another world that is emotionally comprehensible but only partly makes sense. To expect Marshall to be logical is to hope for the impossible. He is logical only when logic serves a direct purpose, but he can never sustain it. His emotions inevitably take over, for he uses them as a weapon against others, as a whip against himself.

I watched him as he climbed the steps from the beach with a child on his shoulder and three wet dogs trying to get between his legs and up the steps. His hair was wild and he was laughing. His grey chest hair was weed. His eyes were humor and fire. He was like something that had just freed itself from the sea.

I went across to put some fresh coconut in my gin and to sit with the journalist, who was thinking of living in Australia. We were still talking when I felt a tug at my glass. A horse was standing over me drinking my gin. I couldn't rise from my low chair, and every time I moved my glass he followed and tried to get his nose into it. I don't mind horses, but this was the first time I had been almost under one. Then I heard a shout, and Marshall, changed once more into a new short suit of batek, ran across and slapped the horse away.

This was my introduction to Whisky, grandson of the famous race horse Hyperion, and yet another family pet. He could not be ridden because of a crippling fungus disease in his hoofs and so spent an idyllic life eating lavishly and enjoying the freedom of Tumasek. But Whisky was not a horse you could dominate easily. He moved away a few yards, explored a guest's handbag, picked up David's tobacco pouch and dropped it, and wandered off to pull up some of Jean Marshall's seedlings. Then he crossed the lawn, walked onto the open veranda, and stopped only when he was half inside the main living room. Even this was too much for Marshall.

"Get him some sugar," he yelled.

The Chinese Amah brought lump sugar and tried to coax Whisky out of the room. He refused at first, then agreed to back a few yards, but only if he got all the sugar.

"For God's sake, someone bring me a bottle of beer—and his tin," Marshall appealed. "It's the only thing that will bring him out. This horse has no morals."

Whisky was interested as soon as the Amah brought the bottle, and he was already backing off the veranda as Marshall poured the beer into a shallow tin.

Whisky drank the lot, shook his head, stamped back to the veranda, and dunked his frothy snout in the sea-horse bowl.

"Hassan," Marshall yelled, slapping the horse.

The driver came, and Whisky, chided with soft Malay words, allowed himself to be led away while the dying or intoxicated sea horses and the experimental babies were sieved from the beer-tainted water and transferred to another tank. I realized why my host's success at rearing sea horses had so far been limited.

With Whisky tied in his stall at the back of the house it was now possible to have lunch—a magnificent nasi goreng made with Malayan venison and served with iced rose. But first visitors to Tumasek were not allowed to start before a Marshall ritual had been completed.

David led three of us into the living room and from a wall alcove took four antique jade cups and a stone bottle like an old-fashioned Bols. The bottle was labeled "Mou Tai, Kwei-chow, China."

"When I was in Peking, Chou En-lai introduced me to this drink, and even gave me a bottle before I left. He said it was his favorite. The original bottle was finished long ago, so I now import Mou Tai from China through Hong Kong."

He filled the jade bowls, handed them round, and raised his own.

"There is only one rule at Tumasek. You must drink the lot."

We sipped, although it was a spirit you toss, as the Russians do, if you want to survive. An elderly lady spluttered and went pale. Her eyes appealed.

"The lot," Marshall warned.

I've drunk White Lightning made in the stills of the Great Smokies of North Carolina. I know well the crude rice spirit which cost us ten rupees a small bottle in Burma during the war—a spirit that would burn with a villainous green flame. But even they were gentle compared with the searing Mou Tai.

It tasted like degenerate methylated, and it cut across your throat like a blowtorch. I emptied the cup and, foolish exhibitionist, asked for more, and after that second cup my understanding of Chou En-lai and Communist China increased enormously.

The other guests, all of whom at some time had suffered this ordeal by Mou Tai, tried not to watch. Some looked sympathetic. Some were amused. Some could still taste Mou Tai and hoped that David would not suggest that they try it again. But the bottle was put away and the lovely cups washed.

It was middle afternoon when lunch faltered and stopped, and within minutes the sun was covered as a squall beat along the Changi coast. The faded blue Rhio Islands of Indonesia disappeared first, then the drifting kelongs. The first gusts bounced against the palms, and trailing them came the rain and a fresh smell of salt as the sea erupted under the downpour. The sky was full of slanting silver and leaves as the dogs stood in the cool rain and flapped their ears. The temperature dropped degrees. The gusts played with the garden and moved on and the rain followed them. The leaves dripped on an afternoon as fresh as a clean shirt.

I returned to Tumasek a fortnight later to find David Marshall pacing his garden, pipe in mouth, hair still wet from the sea. Birds were calling from the heat-limp trees. Whisky was browsing in the drive. The geese were asleep.

"How are the sea horses?"

He grinned. "Sick—very sick."

He has a mocking smile which makes him more English than Jewish. When he smiles he is Western. When the smile recedes Asia returns and with it you feel other thought processes take over.

We sat in the warm shade, the dogs at our feet. I reminded him of the graceful Afghan hound he had hugged before boarding the plane that morning in Sydney.

"That was Sonny's, my brother's, dog. Beautiful creature. The hound has a habit of wandering into other houses and flats at Elizabeth Bay and going to sleep. One afternoon a woman phoned Sonny and said, 'Your dog is on my bed.' Sonny replied, 'When you have finished with him, Madam, please send him home.' "

Our laughter woke the dogs. They looked at us in surprise.

In World War II Marshall spent three years as a prisoner of war, most of them in northern Japan, where, like so many others, he was starved, beaten at times, though he generally asked for it, and where he survived because he was determined from the first moment of captivity to return to Singapore.

He borrowed money to start in the law again and in a few years had built up a big practice in criminal law. He won major cases; then a brilliant defense in a murder trial established him as the most outstanding criminal lawyer in Singapore and Malaya, a position which no other lawyer has seriously challenged. It is often said that in his profession he has few equals when facing a jury, and perhaps this is because he breaks the rules and allows himself to become emotionally involved, because he worries so much about the person he is defending and his own conduct of the case.

"When I'm handling a murder case I'm not conscious at times of actually speaking in court. I become keyed up to a fantastic pitch as I seek for a way out for the accused. In one of my best-known cases, I was ill and full of penicillin. My doctor warned me that I must rest. But I couldn't. A life was in the balance. I had to go on. I got that man off, but I finished that trial beyond exhaustion. I may not have shown it, but I was hardly conscious at the close.

"When I fight in court I struggle against an imminent awareness of the death sentence. To hear a man condemned, even though I may not have been connected with the case, is something that has always deeply troubled me. When a man is told coldly and dispassionately that he will die, I can't sleep.

"I feel much the same about people generally and about justice. I feel that I am different from other people because I feel friendship toward all human beings. I am an internationalist. I am a man of no country, therefore I feel for all. I am a product of my Jewishness and my Asianness, yet I have imbibed, I am glad to say, through the British and through my English education, their concept of justice.

"I feel seriously about this. I get so excited about justice that I must battle against injustice and unfairness in any form. It gets me into a lot of trouble. I have not always been innocent in my own life—few men are—but British colonial rule gave me the spiritual concepts for which I have always been deeply grateful. British civil and criminal justice, allied to a sense of balance and fairness, is the greatest contribution by any race to man's progress. Even when the British exploited, there has always been a basic humanity behind that exploitation.

"People here will tell you that I am anti-British—even bitterly anti-British. I have criticized the British and fought them, but I have never been anti-British in the true meaning of that term. I appreciate their finest qualities far too much to feel antipathy toward them. They irritate and exasperate me. They drive me up the wall with their narrowness and smugness. They make me mad. But anti-British—never. The world would have been a poorer place—the world which produced a monster like Hitler—without them."

In 1950, when Marshall was forty-two and making a large income, he went through a period of indecision. He decided that he was "tied in a sack" of his own creation and that the life he was leading was not the life of an intelligent man. His conclusion was that an intelligent man should be able to lead "not one life but two."

Although he loved the drama, the conflict, of his profession, he had never completely lost his early urge to be a doctor. He believed that if he became a doctor, a psychiatrist, he would be able to help people, and especially young Asians, to adjust themselves to the revolutionary changes in their part of the world.

And so he entered the University of Sydney and went to Australia. He had ten thousand pounds, enough to see him through a medical course. But from the moment he arrived in Sydney he got "cold feet." He was afraid of something he couldn't define. He never even started his medical course before abandoning the whole idea and returning by the next plane to Singapore.

He tries to rationalize the violence of these decisions by claiming that the "atmosphere" was wrong, that nothing "inspired" him, that the only conversation he heard was of "horses and beer." But medicine, psychiatry, was a romantic idea he had never clearly analyzed until he faced a major decision of his life in Sydney. Yet he chose wisely, for Marshall would have made an unreliable doctor, just as he later became an erratic political leader who lacked real leadership and political instinct. But it is as a politician, not as a lawyer, that Marshall will be remembered, for his contribution to Singapore was far more significant than many people will yet concede.

David Marshall had long been interested in politics, and especially politics which would bring independence from British rule. But he was still almost politically illiterate when he went to England in 1954 to study British politics and the background of trade-unionism. And when he returned, to compare what he had learned with what he saw, he decided "from sheer anger" to enter local politics and to help fight for independence.

"I looked hard at the island where I was born and was furious at the stupidity I saw. I'm still not sure whether racial discrimination warps the governors, but I know how much it saps and devitalizes the governed, both morally and spiritually. When I looked around me I knew that a colonial subject at best was a poor human being. I knew because I was one of them. I looked at education, if you could call it that, and saw that all it was designed to do was to feed the commercial machine. It gave a man a poor living, and it gave him nothing else— neither respect nor hope.

"My basic feeling toward independence was to help remove the ceiling about our heads—the ceiling which weighed down on us and prevented us from seeing the sky. Lee Kuan Yew said, 'There is only one solution. Throw the British into the sea.' I opposed that attitude because it is a form of racialism—something I have been fighting all my life as a Jew and an Asian, and something I will continue to fight. Racialism is brutal, unintelligent, and often perpetuates just another extreme form of racialism. It is time we all began to mature a little as human beings living in one world. Let us begin to use our intelligence."

Marshall, as leader of the Labor Front, fought Singapore's first real election in 1955. During the campaign he spoke every lunch hour under what he calls the "Old Apple Tree," near the Singapore River and not far from where Stamford Raffles landed. He enthralled big crowds with his almost Churchillian oratory, showed then and later that he could sway a mob. Many Chinese who could not understand English, but who appreciated his dramatic gestures and the stirring noises he made, stayed to applaud this new form of political entertainment by a man who looks like a cartoonist's actor, whose manner is studied and grand, whose gestures are Shakespearean, and who could if he wished make a name on the stage or in films, for Marshall is an actor who becomes absorbed in a part. It is one of the reasons why he is so extremely attractive to women.

"I was astounded when I finished the election as the Island's Chief Minister. I thought when I began that campaign that I would be merely one of the names on the Opposition benches. I felt like that woman at the riding school who told the attendant that she had never ridden before. 'Don't let that worry you, Madam. I've got just the horse for you. He has never been ridden before either.' "

But David Marshall's fourteen months as Singapore's first Chief Minister were among the most frustrating and bitter of his life. They were also probably his most enjoyable, because he is not a man who sees himself in small letters. Chief Minister was all in capitals and in lights.

He began as head of state on an island in a vacuum. It had no free political traditions, sparse education, little concept of

democracy—an island where the British still held paramount
control and where the Governor under the constitution was
still the head of the Government. When Marshall was refused
four assistant ministers, he persuaded the Legislative Assembly
to vote for immediate self-government. He forced the British
to limit the power of the Governor. He went to London to
fight for independence, and failed, but in that failure he began
a process which could not be stopped.

From the start he argued, quarreled, and fought. The British
in Singapore behaved extremely badly to him, though not
without provocation. He was rude and unrelenting. Little tact
was used on either side. It was a time when subtlety would
probably have achieved much more than arrogance. But it was
also a time when the furnace of nationalism was being stoked
by many hands.

When he began as Chief Minister, he did not have an office,
and was even told by the British that he did not need one, or a
staff.

"From the beginning they showed what deep contempt
they had for us," he says.

Copying Gandhi, he threatened to work as Chief Minister
in the open at a table under the Old Apple Tree, and the
British, with long experience of non-violence in India, understood. He was given a cubbyhole under a stairway and one
messenger.

At one of the first big functions he attended he was placed
eighth.

"If I am Chief Minister I am not going to be graded as
Petty Officer of the Fleet," he protested, and walked out. He
was placed in number-two position, but overheard these words
from a high British official, "I am always willing to give way
to vanity."

He was kept standing for fifty minutes while the Governor,
adding insult by smoking his pipe while Marshall's beloved
bamboo had to stay in his pocket, for the Governor was the
Queen's representative, lectured him like a boy about behavior

and colonial government. Marshall retaliated by threatening to attend the Legislative Assembly wearing an open-neck bush shirt. The Governor's counter-threat was to refuse to hand over the Queen's speech in Parliament. Marshall wore his bush shirt. The press said it was an insult to Her Majesty.

All this was petty and rather like the third form at St. Dominic's. Yet it achieved much. For the first time in the history of Singapore, one man, an Asian Jew, leading an opportunist political rabble, which is what the Labor Front largely proved itself, stood up to the British, demanded a ruling on the status of his Chief Ministership, forced a Governor to lose face, called for self-government, began the Malayanization of the civil service, reached out for independence.

"Any decent Englishman in my position would have done the same," Marshall insists.

Marshall, who does not speak Chinese, could not have remained Chief Minister for long in a Chinese city where leadership is racial. He could not have remained because politically he is naïve and unstable, and although he can sway men, he is temperamentally incapable of leading them.

In Peking, Chou En-lai called him a "bourgeois idealist"— and he didn't realize that he was being insulted. In Singapore, some call him a Red, some even a traitor, some a political Ratbag. I would define him as an erratic, rather muddled, old-fashioned English liberal, too irritably emotional to be always responsible, too impatiently intelligent to fit any social or political pattern, too intolerantly individualistic to be a leader, too brilliantly legalistic to understand the earthiness of politics, too sentimentally diverted to have political instinct, too Western to fully understand Asians, too Asian to be fully understood by Westerners, and too much of a warm sensitive human being to think of cutting an opponent's throat.

But what he achieved and failed to achieve in 1955-1956 was immensely important to Singapore and its political development. In his sentimental, angry, amusing, histrionic way he was something the Island had hardly known before—an educator in a preacher sense in politics, yet an educator ill equipped for an exacting job in a multi-racial city. He hammered at independence, helped rewrite the constitution, and prepared the way for change. He proved, although he was probably not fully aware of it at the time, that the colonial regime was over.

Even today, since his return after several years' absence to politics, waving the hammer symbol of his almost non-existent Workers' party, and shouting *"merdeka"*—independence—from the front seat of his canary-yellow vintage Jaguar, he still seems to act as a catalyst in Singapore. As a political personality he is not important today, yet people still listen to him, still read his words, still argue about his ideas and about him, still criticize him. He is not British, Chinese, Indian, or Malay. He doesn't belong. Yet somehow this alien in his own birthplace is a necessary irritant in the political life of Singapore.

I once heard him called, by a well-informed, highly intelligent Englishman in Singapore, the "Father of Independence." Many will dispute this, but when the history of this period is written, and if any impartial historians exist to write it, I think they will agree that David Marshall deserves this title.

9

Lee Kuan Yew, Prime Minister of Singapore, came on stage at Radio Singapore's auditorium carrying a brief case and a large thermos flask. He poured tea, sipped, shaded his eyes from the television arcs, and said, "Please, could we save the light until we're ready to start."

The arcs flicked off, the bile-green walls of the auditorium receded. I reached for a cigarette, but Australian correspondent John Shaw touched my arm. "He doesn't like it at press conferences."

Some photographs of Lee Kuan Yew narrow his face and give him a sinister look, but at close range I could find nothing diabolic about this much-debated Chief of State, who faced us fresh-bathed and spotless in the "uniform" of his ruling People's Action party—white open-neck shirt, white trousers, black shoes.

Lee Kuan Yew is solid and almost moon-faced, with a forehead which races back to a high line of thick oily black hair. His eyebrows, which seem to have been polished, ask questions above his alert close-set eyes. You notice a curious bird's-feet pattern, a pock-marking of the skin, which accentuates his high cheekbones, and his fairness, for a southern Chinese—

more than fairness, an unusual reddish glow. It's said that as a youngster he was known in his family as "Little White Boy," and strongly resented it—an attitude which may help explain something of the character and attitude of the adult Prime Minister, and possibly future Foreign Minister of Greater Malaysia.

Lee has a strong resolute aggressive face which probably has not altered much since he was a baby. It is softened a little by his quick changes of expression, by a muted humor—although he is not a deeply humorous man—behind his eyes, which pick up and drop objects as quickly as a playing child. His voice, too, is strong and rich, but short-circuited visually and disconcertingly by sparks from a gold filling in a front lower tooth. Like David Marshall, he has the slurred accent of the local English-educated, but many individual words are middle-class English and whole sentences reflect unbroken his English university background. "Malaya" emerges as Sir Lawrence Olivier might pronounce it, and when Lee says "You chaps," he is very English public school.

He speaks with refreshing fluency and mastery of words and syntax, and uses logic and irony, allied to an exceptional memory, as devastating weapons. But when he answers a question he demands to be listened to, so that you soon tire of being talked at, talked down to, and wish that he would learn to vary his approach, to gain the sympathy, not just the ears, of his listeners.

He is an eminently logical, common-sense man, but he lacks subtlety and warmth. He talks but gives little in return except the absorbing spectacle of an agile mind functioning as smoothly as a finely adjusted machine. He has poise and command, but no grace, no charm, none of the casual irrelevancies, the stray gestures, the story told against himself, the endearing frailties, which reflect the warmth and sophistication of the mature personality. If you ran your fingers along Lee Kuan Yew, you would pick up splinters.

Practically everyone in Singapore-Malaya agrees that he is

clever, astute, efficient, a fantastic worker, extremely ambitious, and incorruptible. Many claim—and these are two of the most common criticisms—that he is arrogant and an intellectual snob. Some say that he is politically unscrupulous, that when he plays political chess he does not mind whom he takes off the board. And again, many people will agree that he is unpopular as a leader and as a man.

It is true that he gives the impression of being arrogant, but he is not arrogant within the dictionary meaning of that word. He is a serious, reserved man, even a shy man, who is impatient with chatterers, intolerant with the petty-minded and the lazy, wary and suspicious of people generally. It is not surprising that he has few friends, but that is hardly a criticism. He tries to cover his almost pathological reserve, this deep sense of unsureness, by abrupt and even crude behavior, by scoring off people with humor which hurts, by displays of his own mental agility. He is a little like the small man who makes a lot of noise to divert your attention from his sixty-two inches.

I was impressed by his handling of his long press conference, how for two hours he dealt with a wide range of political and social subjects, and how his answers showed his deep understanding of many problems. I mentioned this when I met him later, and meant it as a compliment for a craftsmanlike performance. His reply was one word: "Flatterer," he sneered.

You see what I mean.

Lee is so superior mentally to most of his political fellows that he is a danger to himself because he is far too conscious of this power. In this sense perhaps he is a snob.

Lee is clever, even outstandingly brilliant at times, but his ability is limited by his too-legalistic mind, his lack of human sympathy, his narrow background and interests, and his parochialism. One comment summed him up this way: "Lee has a local reputation for being an intellectual, but only local. He can't discuss with skill political philosophy or literature, and his general reading is slow. He has only one hobbyhorse, the local scene, and is out of his depth once he is away from it."

Lee's main problem is that he does not understand people. He need not like them. And because he is an adolescent at human relationships, at times a tactless egotist, at others bad-tempered or aloof, he needs guidance, yet is not the kind of man who would accept it. His relationship with the press, which should be close, is distant and bad, though it has improved as his political power in Parliament has declined. Reporters don't like him because he behaves to them like a seventeenth-century aristocrat. He would be a greater man if it were possible to drain some of the cold reason from his bloodstream.

As I heard one man say: "When Lee Kuan Yew tries to be friendly I feel acutely embarrassed."

And another: "The man who stands on his head is clever indeed. But the man who stands on his legs is sure of not falling down."

There is something inhuman about Lee Kuan Yew, the family man who never reads a novel, never listens to music, never goes to a cinema, never dances, never works less than fifteen hours a day, never. . . . It is almost a relief to record that he is a glutton, that he loves beer and drinks too much of it, that he once drank only orange juice for weeks, then, as he put on weight, chided the man who had recommended juice as a weight reducer, that he hates being beaten at golf—as he hates being criticized for anything he does or says—but like most golfers he will grin with childish glee if he makes one good drive in eighteen.

Lee Kuan Yew, whose name when crudely translated means "Bright" or "Brilliant," is a third-generation local-born Chinese with a middle-class background. He is still only forty years old. His grandfather made money as a trader. His father worked for the Shell Company and is now, while a Shell pensioner, a salesman for a jewelry firm in Singapore. His mother teaches cooking, at five dollars a lesson; you provide the ingredients. His wife is a Cambridge-educated lawyer, more brilliant than he is, who runs the family law firm while her husband runs

Singapore—and a Prime Minister who could earn from one good law case what he now receives in a month as Singapore's Chief of State. Lee Kuan Yew gives to Singapore much more than he receives.

As a schoolboy he showed exceptional ability. He liked argument, debate. His memory was uncanny. He was aggressive, and if he could not lead or dominate a group he joined the opposition. He was nineteen when the Japanese occupation of Singapore interrupted his studies, but the war years, when he worked as a contractor, played an important part in his development. He saw British rule humbled by defeat. He met many people, heard many arguments on political ideas, noted that the guerrillas who fought the Japanese in the jungle were mainly Chinese and Communists. For the first time he looked closely at the island where he was born, the area where his family had lived for generations.

His father had one ambition for his son. He wanted him to have an English education—he saw it was the only way to advancement—and to become "the equal of any Englishman—a model of perfection." He even borrowed on his superannuation with the Shell Company to send Kuan Yew to Cambridge University. There is a warning here to all parents who have an image of their children's future status and who will do anything to turn that image into their own reality, for father and Cambridge combined succeeded in creating an adult who was not only anti-British but also a model of socialist perfection.

Lee Kuan Yew, with money he had saved and his father's help, went to Cambridge in 1946, where he studied law and was an outstanding undergraduate. Cambridge was also the genesis of his political career. He was first interested in Communism, but later became a student and supporter of the British Labour party. He admired British democracy as he saw it in England, but the more he admired it, the more critical he became of the British colonial system—all colonial systems. As a British subject he felt it was anachronistic for a highly developed democracy to exist in England and yet a British ter-

ritory like Singapore to be still under what was a virtual autoc-
racy. He returned to Singapore in 1950 a nationalist determined to oppose the English because they represented the
colonial system he had decided to attack, and convinced that
in social democracy he had found a political philosophy less
tyrannical, less brutal, and less spiritually arid than Communism
as a way to liberation from colonial control.

He was admitted to the Singapore Bar in 1951—at a time
when the Communist civil war in Malaya was three years old
and when Singapore was being used as a Communist base for
that war—and almost immediately headed into politics, first
through his work as legal adviser to some of the trade unions,
which quickly won him a reputation as a skilled lawyer and as
a coming man politically.

They say in Singapore: In a murder case send for David
Marshall. If he fails, which is unlikely, then call in Lee Kuan
Yew to handle the dry legal arguments of the appeal.

In November, 1954, Lee formed with eight others the
socialist People's Action party, with strong trade-union support, including Communist support, and in the elections the
next year—when David Marshall became Chief Minister—Lee
won his seat in the Legislative Assembly as one of the three
successful People's Action party candidates out of four who
contested the election.

During that campaign Lee Kuan Yew said, "I would vote for
Communism if I had to choose only between Communism and
colonialism." It was a statement which expressed his belief that
of the two isms, colonialism had to be eliminated first before
Communism could be combated by proving it less attractive
than social democracy. He did not mean that he was in favor of
Communism. He sympathizes with some of its aims, but he
opposes it because he does not think it fits the Malayan ethos
and because of its revolutionary methods and its brutal subjection of the majority and the individual to undisputed minority
dictation.

The 1955 elections began Lee's climb to power. It also began his unending struggle with the illegal Communist party, whose key members, or some of them, were among the leaders of his People's Action party. Lee, as leader of the left moderates in the P.A.P., was able to consolidate his control and concentrate on the organization of his party as "democratic, non-Communist, and Malayan" through the arrest for subversion of the main Communist and fellow-traveler leaders in his party and their detention in Changi jail, and through police action which partly crippled, for several years, the Communist party's underground organization on Singapore Island. Lee, freed from the left extremists, was able to move on to become Prime Minister of Singapore by hammering at colonialism, by appealing for the mass support of the poor and underprivileged— the Chinese-speaking Chinese whose reasons for supporting Communism had been strengthened by chauvinism, by the new China of Mao Tse-tung.

On May 30, 1959, Lee's nationalist, socialist, anti-colonial People's Action party was voted to power with an overwhelming majority, and on June 3 Singapore became a self-governing though not completely independent state.

Despite British control of internal security, Lee and his party refused to form a government until the eight P.A.P. members detained in Changi jail for subversion were released. At the same time Lee upheld the law under which they were arrested and later broadened the interpretation of subversion to cover activities on behalf of any power, Communist or Western. The eight detainees were released on June 4, and the P.A.P. Cabinet, which averaged only thirty-seven years of age and contained eight university graduates out of nine members, appeared in their white uniforms before a hundred thousand supporters, who waved the jagged-lightning-symbol banners of the party and shouted "*merdeka.*"

Lee's action in demanding the release of the detainees, and therefore opening the way for them to sabotage him in the future, may seem, if not naïvely foolish, then at least curiously equivocal. But it was a move dictated by political tactics, and for important reasons. Lee and the P.A.P. leadership were mainly English-speaking Chinese, but thousands of their supporters, among the six hundred thousand who voted in this election, were Chinese-speaking Chinese, some Communists, many strongly chauvinistic. For Lee to have allowed the eight detainees to be kept inside would have alienated many of these P.A.P. supporters and would have branded Lee and the P.A.P. leadership as anti-Chinese-speaking Chinese almost in league with the British.

From the moment Lee took power, and even before, he began a struggle with the Communists on their own ground. He had to compete with Communism without antagonizing those supporters most attracted to it and driving them into the Red tents. This was a difficult and unenviable task, for Lee himself, no popular ideal of a demagogue, was not the natural leader of the Chinese-speaking Chinese. He was Chinese, true, but English-educated, English-speaking, and he had to learn Mandarin and Malay so that he could speak to his supporters, most of whom were Chinese. He was also a successful lawyer with a large income and a comfortable house—a total English setting, normal by Western standards, but already suspect to many a left-wing voter among the Chinese-speaking stream in Singapore.

Lee and the P.A.P. had early realized, with one eye always on the Federation of Malaya and its Malay Government suspicious of the big Chinese populations in both the Federation and Singapore, that any overemphasis of Chinese nationalism would inevitably set the Chinese further apart from other races and lead to a Chinese ghetto in both territories. Lee saw that the only solution was to convince his P.A.P. supporters that the future of the Chinese, both in Singapore and the Federation, depended on their willingness to think and behave not as Chinese but as "Malayans," to learn Malay as a national language, to develop a "Malayan consciousness," along with all other races in Singapore. Simply, this meant to replace British culture, which had proved divisive, with a new common loyalty to Malaya as a whole and to merge with the Federation. Yet even this policy was dangerous because of the risk that the chauvinistic Chinese-speaking Chinese would regard it as a long-range threat to their own ancient and powerful culture and would brand Lee and the P.A.P. as anti-Chinese.

Perhaps the most salient feature of Lee Kuan Yew's rise to the Prime Ministership was that with self-government and the creation of the city-state of Singapore on June 3, 1959, colonialism in Singapore virtually ceased to exist. Only its remnants remained and they, too, would soon disappear. From that moment, although the now almost meaningless word "colonialism" is still used carelessly and still used deliberately by propagandists, the nationalism-colonialism issue really ended on June 3 and was replaced by a much more potentially violent struggle—nationalism versus Communism—although this did not come into the open until later.

For at least six months after Lee Kuan Yew's Government took power—a Government which many people inside and outside Singapore regarded as wildly extreme—anyone who was not a member of the P.A.P. was denounced, by speakers who talked like British Labour politicians of the 1920's, as "colonialist" or as "English-speaking stooge of colonialism," and some Ministers behaved, in this period of violent reaction, with the unintelligence and arrogance of power-drunk leaders of an authoritarian regime.

The pay of civil servants—the local English-speaking group in the community—was cut to help balance the budget and their union leader was threatened with dismissal for political "criticism" of the Government. After the Government extended its powers to detain without trial, the Chinese owners of a strike-bound factory were warned that jail awaited employers who tried to "frustrate the Government's policy of industrial peace." The Principal of the University of Malaya in Singapore was attacked for "insubordination" when he objected to being told by a Minister, who had no control over the University, to cut academic salaries, and there were other attacks against schoolteachers and University staff.

But one of the most revealing things about the new regime was its attitude to the press. Lee Kuan Yew had earlier threatened to "fix" newspapers. "Any newspaper which tries to sour up relations between Malaya and Singapore after May will go in for subversion. We will put in any editor, sub-editor, or reporter who goes along this line and keep him in." Later he explained that this applied only to editors and reporters of foreign-owned newspapers.

The main newspaper, the conservative English-language *Straits Times*, protested, moved its head office to Kuala Lumpur, capital of the Federation of Malaya, and asked the International Press Institute to investigate freedom of the press in Singapore. An investigation was made; then this newspaper's resistance suddenly collapsed. The *Straits Times* continued to publish, from Kuala Lumpur, but the rival Chinese-owned Singapore *Tiger Standard* closed. Since then it would be an exaggeration to say that there is a free press in Singapore. There is no real criticism of the Government, no healthy comment or analysis of ministerial deeds and misdeeds. Prime Minister Lee Kuan Yew, without taking any direct action, has certainly fixed the newspapers. He never liked criticism, even as a small boy. Now he is free of it. As a believer in social democracy his conscience must twinge at times.

But in other ways Lee Kuan Yew and his Government set political examples almost unparalleled in Asia and even the world. They followed a regime that was lazy and corrupt, so that their new activity gave the impression of being efficient—and in most ways it was.

Ministers started work at eight o'clock and opened their offices to the public. They paid a third of their salaries into party funds. They took no graft, abolished political squeeze, and created one of the few completely honest regimes anywhere. They went on no tourist jaunts at public expense. They worked long hours and worked hard. And although the new bureaucracy they started, as the Malayanization of the civil service extended and the old British administrators continued to move out of government and semi-government departments, was inevitably more cumbersome and less efficient because of its inexperience and lower educational standards, it worked far better than many people had predicted. For the first time, for all the mistakes and arrogance of individuals in the regime, Singapore was alive, pulsing, planning for the future. For the first time, the majority of the people of Singapore, with little traditional concept of the rights of the individual or the freedom and restraints of democracy, felt that the Government was their Government. That the previous Government, of Lim Yew Hock, however inept, and before that the Government of David Marshall were responsible for forcing self-government and the creation of the state of Singapore, was conveniently forgotten in the general adoration of the P.A.P., which also ignored Lim's and Marshall's important contribution. That the Government of Lee Kuan Yew was heavy-handed didn't matter. It was the Government they had created and from which so much change flowed. And to a voter brought up under a colonial regime, that mattered.

The first six months of settling in, and of excesses and achievement, reached its peak on December 3, 1959, when the Government celebrated National Loyalty Week. The new flag of the city-state was unfurled—red and white with a crescent and five stars in one corner, the red representing universal brotherhood and equality, the white purity and virtue, and the stars representing democracy, peace, progress, justice, and equality.

The animal supporters of the new state's crest became a Singapore lion and a Malayan tiger. The new national anthem —and a fine of one hundred and twenty dollars if you don't stand up for it—was "Majulah Singapura" (Let Singapore Flourish), with words and music by a Singapore Malay, Che Zubir Said. And, as a final innovation, Inche Yusof bin Ishak, a Malay journalist and People's Action party supporter, became the Yang di-Pertuan Negara, or Head of State, one day after the last Governor, Sir William Goode, and transitional Head of State, had left Singapore.

By 1960 the decorations had been put away, the plates washed, the empty bottles sold. The long party was over.

Lee Kuan Yew and his Ministers had always talked and acted as if Singapore were a country. They knew it was no more than a big crowded city on a small island, but that was not the impression they gave or tried to give. Now, as reality returned, they began to see their island in more reasonable perspective, to shout fewer provocative slogans, to talk a little less of politics and more, much more, of the economic problems which their tiny city-state off the coast of Asia had to face.

Singapore, which has no raw materials and practically no industries, lives well on its entrepôt trade, its port installations, and the British Navy, Army, and Air Force bases, which employ forty thousand civilians and spend nearly forty million pounds a year or one hundred million if all service pay and allowances are included. Although a quarter of all Singaporeans exist in poverty and two thirds are badly housed, on the average they eat better, earn more, and work less than anyone else in Southeast Asia, and most other parts of Asia. The national income a head—about fifteen hundred Malayan dollars—is nearly ten times higher than in India. But Singapore's trade is slowly declining, her unemployment of forty thousand is rising, and her population is rapidly increasing. It is also such a young population that one third of the people keep the other two thirds.

Lee Kuan Yew's Government achieved little in its first year of office, although it talked loudly about industrialization as a solution to the Island's problems. It was only when Lee and his colleagues listened more seriously to their Finance Minister, Dr. Goh Keng Swee, that the Government began to face facts and designed a master development plan to expand agriculture and fisheries and to build up industries.

"What is regrettable," Dr. Goh once said, "is that the parents of Singapore in the past sixteen years have been so prolific in their capacity as parents that they have created a problem of terrifying dimensions."

This is true. Too many people with not enough work on a small island and nowhere to go is Singapore's main social-economic problem, and too many people is the reason why Singapore cannot exist without the Federation of Malaya, without Malaysia, behind it. People, survival itself, are why socialists like Lee Kuan Yew and his Cabinet have been forced to encourage the anathema of capitalism to build up industries and retard Singapore's downward drift.

They had to, as Dr. Goh early insisted. "Singapore is no place for normal socialist economic planning—it has no natural resources or industries that would do better in public than in private hands. You cannot take a great and complicated market and run it with civil servants. A socialist in Singapore has to plan for a just society without upsetting the delicate machinery of trade."

They were wise words, from Lee Kuan Yew's most able administrator—the poor Chinese boy from Malacca who won English-education scholarships which took him to the London School of Economics and who later, after social research in Singapore, returned to London to gain his doctorate. Like other People's Action party leaders who once made good incomes from the law, teaching, journalism, medicine, Dr. Goh, or Dr. Goh-ahead as the newspapers call him, had nothing to gain financially from politics.

But Lee Kuan Yew, who believes Singapore's future is tied to Malaya and Malaysia, that the Malay peasants, not the Chinese, are the key to socialism in Malaya, that all Asia will eventually be involved in the revolution which will make it either socialist or Communist, had more than a declining economy to solve.

Lee once defined political repression as a habit which grows, like making love. But often in the past few years he must have

felt the urge to use his powers to brake the gathering strength
of his political enemies. That he has not used those powers is
a sign of his political astuteness and also, in a way, of his rather
naïve conviction in the twentieth century that the political
party with integrity must inevitably prevail. It is a belief which
ignores the lessons of history—and particularly the political history of eastern Europe since World War II.

When Lee Kuan Yew formed his Government in 1959, his
party's leading political moderates became his Cabinet Ministers, and minor posts went to members of the extreme left in
the P.A.P. They had supported the party. They had to be
paid. It was expedient. For a year or so these extremists stayed
in the background, organizing quietly against Lee. Then they
began to move into the open. They demanded greater freedom
to preach Communism. They gained control of the major
trade unions—and largely because Lee had tried to tie the
unions to the P.A.P. and lost control of them.

Inevitably, the apparently strong but always shaky united
front between the Lee socialist and the Communists and
chauvinists collapsed. Sixteen P.A.P. members in the Legislative
Assembly, led by the extremists, split and in August, 1961,
formed a new political party, the Barisan Socialis, or Socialist
Front, with its all-too-familiar symbol, a five-pointed red star
penetrating the upper arc of a blue circle on a white ground—
the white symbolizing purity, the blue the unity of the people,
and the stars the socialist objectives of democracy, freedom,
equality, peace, and prosperity.

The split left Lee Kuan Yew only just in power but still able
to govern because conservative non-P.A.P. members in Parliament would support him in any real crisis to defeat the Barisan
Socialis.

The public policy of the Barisans was much the same as the
P.A.P., but the party's real control was Communist, its appeal
was to the chauvinistic Chinese-speaking Chinese stream, and
its eventual objective was an independent Singapore, a little
island China, a Nanyang China, governed by the Communist

party—the very opposite of Lee's argument and objective that the people of Singapore would be better off as integrated Malayans in a combined Singapore political and economic unit, Singapore-Malaya, and eventually Greater Malaysia.

The Barisan Socialis is an amalgam of Communists, travelers, genuine socialists, Chinese chauvinist, personal Lee Kuan Yew haters, and political nonentities, but the guts and brains of the party are six trade-union organizers who have been called the "Young Turks" or "Beerhall Revolutionaries." Lee calls them the "Lunatic Left." They in turn refer to the Prime Minister as the "Emperor Lee."

The six, whose average age is only twenty-nine, are Lim Chin Siong, Fong Swee Suan, Sandra Woodhull, Jamit Singh, Dominic Puthucheary, and S. T. Bani, and those are all names worth remembering. But at the top of the six is Lim Chin Siong—a name to watch in Southeast Asia. He is an old friend of Lee Kuan Yew and his most bitter enemy. He is also one of the youngest and shrewdest extreme-left Chinese politicians rising in Southeast Asia.

10

The small room above Victoria Street resembled a cell in a monastery dedicated to poverty. Old cane chairs stood at attention on the concrete floor. Bare walls were part of the petrified greyness. Only a glimpse of the ragged tiles of Chinatown, streaming below the window like a stained and choppy sea, saved the room from total isolation.

This "lounge" at Barisan Socialis headquarters must have reminded some of the men of the "Lunatic Left" of their time in Changi jail before Lee Kuan Yew insisted on their release after the People's Action party victory at the 1959 elections. And particularly one man, Lim Chin Siong, one of the most discussed political personalities in Singapore, whom I talked to for hours while he drank orangeade and answered my questions in English that was slow and often hard to follow, though an interpreter was needed for only stray words.

People in Singapore will tell you that Lim Chin Siong is a member of the Central Committee of the illegal Malayan Communist party, chief front man in Singapore for the party, the most politically dangerous man on the Island, not a Communist but a socialist, a paranoic, and many other things. The Prime Minister, who knows him extremely well, has called him the most important open-front leader the Malayan Communist party has built up, but when I asked Lim if this was true, he said he was first a nationalist, then a socialist, and denied that he was a Communist—a denial he has repeated many times. He once said, "I am not a Communist or a Communist front-man or, for that matter, anybody's front-man."

Denials like this are pretty meaningless in a city-state where the Communist party is illegal and where a public announcement of party affiliation or even sympathy would open the gates of Changi jail within half an hour. The only way to assess Lim Chin Siong is to ignore statements about him and by him and to look at his history and political record.

The overwhelming conclusion is that he is a dedicated Marxist-Leninist and a devoted supporter of the Malayan Communist party. He may not be a ticket-carrying member of the party, but there is not a line, a suggestion, an implication in his political history that he has ever been anything but a loyal and undeviating worker for the Communist cause.

As a good Communist, who believes that the end justifies the means, that any switch is expedient if it aids the cause, his denials that he is a Communist are irrelevant. He has been inside once; he is not likely to put himself in again. Nor would being inside be of any value unless he were jailed by his political opponents and could then use the propaganda of local martyrdom. Lim is much more valuable to his party working openly, within the law, and continuing to say whenever he is asked, "I am not a Communist or a Communist front-man."

Lim Chin Siong is one of the most extraordinary infant prodigies this tropical city has spawned. It is jolting to sit with him and realize that he was twelve when the Pacific war ended, still in his teens when he was already active in politics, a member of the Legislative Assembly at twenty-two, and today, still under thirty, is a dynamic personality behind the Communist-controlled Barisan Socialis movement and one of the most politically powerful men in Singapore.

Powerful, but not the most dangerous. He is still only the open-front worker and mouthpiece of the underground group in Singapore-Malaya, the group which numbers no more than a hundred or two and does the thinking and organizing of the Malayan Communist party, whose lines of communication go direct to Peking.

Lim Chin Siong, who looks no more than twenty, is boyishly handsome and, like Lee Kuan Yew, is pale for a southern Chinese. He is small and slight, with the slender wrists of a girl and thick hair parted on the left side. He looks like a young student. His large film-star eyes are disarmingly innocent and frank when you first meet him, and he has a mocking elfin expression which the girls of Singapore find particularly appealing.

I knew he was interested in a girl and used this information to pull his leg just to watch his reactions. I told him I'd heard he was soon to marry.

"Who told you that?" he said quickly.

"It's a strong rumor about town."

"Who told you?"

"I've heard it in half a dozen places."

He stared at me half smiling, puzzled. Then he relaxed.

"It is not true. . . . Poor girl . . . poor girl."

It was my turn.

"Why?"

"Nobody will marry me. The Prime Minister will put me inside." He made a face. "The poor girl would suffer."

He seldom misses a chance to sneer at Lee Kuan Yew.

There is nothing infantile about baby-face Lim. He is astute, quick-witted, and almost indestructible. Even when he is being his most attentive and charming—and warmingly attentive he can be—he watches you all the time, and there is a guarded stillness about him which rings little bells of warning.

Observing him in return, and later while he talked to others in the workrooms below the lounge, there was little doubt who was in command of the Barisan Socialis, although the nominal head of the party is Dr. Lee Siew Chop, a thin, long-faced nonentity who calls himself a socialist and says he does not believe the Barisan Socialis is Communist-controlled.

Lim Chin Siong is tough and determined, with perhaps his greatest advantage—although it limits his experience—his youth in a city of youth. He can speak to young people in the idiom of their time, and he can stir them, as he has proved many times from the public platform. Mob-rousing words from an innocent baby-face appeal to chauvinistic youth in rebellion against the past.

Lim Chin Siong was born in Singapore in 1933. His father, who was a clerk in a rubber factory, was also local-born, but his grandfather was a Hokkien immigrant from South China. Lim is the senior son in a family of twelve. One brother is a political prisoner who was not released in 1959. One is in charge of the library at Singapore's Chinese Nanyang University. The others are still at school or just leaving.

At Lim's Chinese primary school at Bukit Timah, a suburb of Singapore, he was nearly always at the top of his class, but he was also lazy and easily diverted. At his Chinese high school, where languages were his best subject, he spent most of his time reading Chinese and Russian novels in Chinese translation and avoiding as much routine work as possible. He particularly liked Dostoevsky and Turgenev, and from them and other novelists developed the beginnings of his interest in politics.

Lim was nineteen when, in his final year at the high school—his studies had been delayed by the war—he took part in the boycott of an examination and was expelled.

"I was not the leader. I was one of many. It all seems silly now. But I did not mind. It started me in politics. I joined the Bus Union."

Lim has never had a job, has never worked at anything except politics. He is a professional union organizer and politician. At least he was until he began to move higher in the ranks of Singapore's extreme leftists.

At twenty-two he was prominent in the Chinese High School Parent-Teacher Association—a group which was not as innocent as it sounds—secretary of the Singapore Factory and Shop Workers' Union, which was Communist-controlled, a member of the Legislative Assembly, and as a Parliamentarian was one of David Marshall's independence mission to London which failed.

Lim admitted that he was involved in the serious school riots of the mid-1950's, but would not agree that he helped organize them, as many well-informed people claim. He never admits being the initiator, which is probably technically true, since he acts on instructions from the hidden party hierarchy, instructions that have come to him in the past by courier from the Malaya mainland.

For his part in the school riots he was arrested and spent more than two years in Changi jail, where, in the six months before he was released, he read a translation of Boris Pasternak's *Dr. Zhivago* many times to help improve his English and for what he called a good critical study of the Soviet system.

When I asked him whether he had read deeply on Communist history and philosophy, he gave me an amused little-boy smile and said: "I know little about Marxist-Leninism. My reading has been very limited. I have never had the opportunity. When I became interested in politics, socialism was vague to me. But I was aware of the need to produce a free society because I felt humiliated where I had been brought up. I felt it was my duty to do something to produce a happier life for the people of Singapore. It is easy to be called a Communist in Singapore if you come from a Chinese school."

I asked him what prison had meant to him, whether he had learned anything from those years inside.

He sipped his orangeade and wrinkled his nose. "I like beer or brandy better, but I'm not a drunkard. I don't have the big stomach of Mr. Lee." Then he put down his glass and twisted his fingers together, a habit he has when he is thinking. "I looked at the past and I felt I was far too young in politics. I still feel this. I did not know enough. That was my first lesson. I felt it was wrong to be locked up. I felt it was a form of violence against me. I did not like it. I came out of Changi hating violence—against me or anyone else. I still feel violence is wrong. I feel that nothing should be achieved except by peaceful means. I am opposed to violence. That was my second lesson."

When Lim and the other detainees were released in 1959, he was made, as a leading member of the People's Action party, political secretary to the Ministry of Finance, but was given no access to confidential information and no power in the P.A.P. This did not matter, for while working for the P.A.P. Government and while still a member of the P.A.P., Lim and his friends set out to complete their domination of the trade-unions and to smash the P.A.P.

The trade-union story in Singapore-Malaya covers nearly forty years of work by men like Lim Chin Siong. Singapore has little tradition of trade-unionism, but the tradition it has is intimately linked with Chinese Communism. The Nanyang Communist party was formed in Singapore in 1927. Some of its members had come from China to escape the purges of Chiang Kai-shek, some from the Netherlands Indies (now Indonesia) to escape the Dutch. The Indonesian members, most of them Javanese, strongly urged the party to start work immediately among the Malays, since they saw that the future of the revolution would depend largely on the indoctrination and support of the Malay peasantry, whose Islamic anti-Communism undoubtedly helped preserve Malaya for the British. The Chinese-dominated Nanyang Communist party, who could not see beyond their own people and aims, refused to listen to the Javanese, who, if they had been successful with the Malays, might have won Malaya for Communism many years ago. Rebuffed, the Javanese party members left Singapore and moved on to Moscow, and they did not return to Indonesia until well after World War II. It is some of these men who lead the powerful Indonesian Communist party to-day.

In the 1930's the Nanyang Communist party controlled some of the worker organizations, and organized strikes, but progress was slow. It was the Japanese occupation of 1942, when white Tuan Besars became coolies in twenty-four hours, which acted like a time machine and advanced Communist work years in months. When the Japanese arrived the Communist party was the only political party in the area. The Communists who went into the jungle fought them and fought well, but at the same time, with their eyes and ambitions on the future, they concentrated on the training of their cadres in the jungle for the real struggle for power after the war.

One of the grim stories of this war period concerns Loi-tek, a Communist leader who had been sent from Shanghai to take command of the party in Singapore and Malaya. This man not only accumulated nearly one million Malayan dollars in graft, he was also a Japanese spy. He had been caught by the Japanese and tortured and had gone over to their side. In December, 1942, he told the Japanese that seventy-two leaders of his own Communist party would meet at the Batu Caves near Kuala Lumpur in Malaya. The Japanese sent five thousand troops, and only eighteen of Loi-tek's friends escaped. Loi-tek deliberately arrived late for the meeting so that he would not be suspected by party members and, although arrested, was later released by his masters the Japanese. After the war the Communist party caught up with him in Hong Kong. He died with a knife in his back.

Trade-unionism began in 1946 when the British allowed registration. The Malayan Communist party had already been organizing the unions from August, 1945, when the Island was still under military control, and the best known of the new unions, the General Labor Union, was already Communist-controlled, although at that time the great mass of its members were not Communists.

This phase lasted until 1948, when the Communist civil

war began in Malaya. Then the Indians took over union leadership, especially in Malaya, where they have kept it ever since, but by 1951 the Chinese Communists had become more active, most notably in the Singapore Factory and Shop Workers' Union which was the General Labor Union under another name and still Communist-led.

This was the period when Lim Chin Siong was starting his political career—when he was moving up to become secretary of the Singapore Factory and Shop Workers' Union in 1955, to help organize the school riots and strikes which led to his arrest and detention, and to the disbanding of the unions. But when the unions were allowed to re-form in 1957, the Factory and Shop Workers' Union appeared once again, with the Communists still in charge. This time it was called the Singapore General Employees' Union.

Back in 1950 the Indians had formed the Singapore Trade Union Congress, and the Indians still controlled it in 1959. But when Singapore became a city-state and Lee Kuan Yew and his P.A.P. won power, the Government took control of the Trade Union Congress—and hastened its destruction—for once Lee had released the detainees, they were free to restart their work in the P.A.P. and the unions—work which other Communist party members and supporters had continued during their detention.

Lim Chin Siong, as leader of his ex-detainee group, the "Union Six," as they are sometimes called, took charge of the white-anting of the unions. His chief lieutenant was his personal friend Fong Swee Suan, whom Lee Kuan Yew had appointed in 1959 not to a political job, where he could do no real harm, but to a key position as political secretary to the Ministry of Labor, even though Fong, who had promised to behave himself, had for years been as loyal as Lim to Communism.

It did not take Lim, Fong, and the others long to do their work, aided by highly disciplined groups within the unions. In July, 1961, Lim moved—and it was an impressive month for Communism. Right-wing unions, largely Indian, became the National Trade Union Council. Left-wing unions, largely Chinese, became the Singapore Association of Trade Unions. The significance of this split was that Lim Chin Siong and his followers gathered into one group all the major manual-worker unions in Singapore—harbor, river, and dock workers, the bus companies, the Naval Base workers—and all led and directed by hard-core Communists who kept discipline among the rank and file by threats, by bashings, and by intimidation which led straight back to the families of the workers in Communist China itself.

This control of all the strategic unions of Singapore gave Lim the industrial power to stop Singapore and paralyze its life almost any time he wished.

In addition to his union victory, Lim Chin Siong organized a major breakaway from Lee Kuan Yew's P.A.P. and formed the Barisan Socialis. He also made sure that the Communist vote would be strong enough to give David Marshall, Singapore's first Chief Minister, who had returned to politics, victory against a Government candidate in an important Parliamentary by-election.

July, 1961, was a memorable month for Lim Chin Siong, the young man who at Barisan Socialis headquarters that day denied he was a Communist or Communist front-man, insisted that he was still far too young for politics, denied that he liked power or had any ambition for leadership, grinned when I suggested to him that one of his greatest assets was a well-developed imagination capable of turning black into white at will.

Sandra Segaren ("Sydney") Woodhull, one of the Union Six, who had supplied a word here and there when Lim struggled for the right one, provides a miniature of his colleague. Woodhull, a good-looking man of education and charm—he is only thirty, with an Arts degree from the University of Malaya—is a Ceylonese whose great-grandfather discarded his own name and took the name of a Presbyterian missionary in Ceylon.

Woodhull, who was a member of the P.A.P. from its beginnings and personally close to Lee Kuan Yew, is called by some a Communist and by others a socialist. Although his record is heavily weighted toward Communism, he lacks the fanaticism of a Lim or a Fong and seems to be far too sensitive a man, too divided in his loyalties, to ever be a good party member. He is the dedicated socialist, I feel, to whom much of Communism appeals, except its tyranny.

I didn't expect an answer when I questioned him about this, and was surprised when he said:

"I do not think I am made to be a martyr. I am not built for the Cross."

He was looking directly at Lim Chin Siong at the time.

"And what of him?"

"Lim is an interesting person. He is modest and very self-possessed, as you have seen for yourself. He refuses to let things get loose."

"Loose?"

"I mean that he always keeps himself, his emotions, his thoughts well under control. He never breaks out."

"Can you ever get at a controlled man like that? Is it possible to influence him?"

"Yes, he's amenable to argument. You can talk to him and he will listen and learn. He's nobody's fool."

"What do you feel is his chief asset—as a man and a politician?"

"His greatest strength is his acute sensitivity to popular feeling. He knows instinctively—just like an animal. If something is going wrong he can sense it."

"And his weaknesses?"

"His greatest is his lack of English, because this cuts him off in many ways, but he is learning and learning quickly."

"I suppose this limits the range of his reading. Would you say that he has read much on politics—Marxist-Leninism?"

"Quite a lot. He is very well read politically."

I couldn't help smiling to myself, because Lim had denied this.

"Has he any other major weaknesses—faults, if you like?"

Woodhull pondered this one.

"His immaturity—his youth. But he is intelligent, quick. He will go far politically."

"To go back to your earlier statement. You say you are no martyr for a cause. Is he?"

"I can't answer that. I don't know."

"I've heard people say that Lim is something of a Yogi. They don't mean that he practices Yoga. They mean more a Yogi in a political sense. I haven't put that well, but perhaps you get what I mean?"

Woodhull nodded. "He could be, but I haven't detected it yet. He could even be a combination of the Yogi and the Commissar."

I went down the concrete stairs knowing that it is men like Lim Chin Siong, dedicated, tireless, ruthless, who are winning the battle for Communism in Asia.

Prime Minister Lee Kuan Yew gave a picture of the activities of Lim Chin Siong and his friends in a series of broadcasts in English, Mandarin, and Malay which covered many phases of the struggle for power between the Lee socialists and the Lim Communists. For Singaporeans the talks covered much old ground, but to an outside observer they were a fascinating and revealing document of Communist penetration.

Because the Prime Minister's talks covered many thousands of words, this is a summary of a section of them, and it starts in the early 1950's, when Lee Kuan Yew was acting as a lawyer for some of the unions and when his political career was beginning.

"One morning in January, 1951, I woke up and read that Mr. John Eber had been arrested, that Mr. Lim Kean Chye had disappeared and escaped arrest. Shortly afterward a reward was offered for his arrest. Politics in Malaya was a deadly serious business. They were not clowns or jokers. They had decided to go with the Communists. . . .

"I got in touch with the people who were detained in the same batch as Mr. John Eber. They were an English-educated group of the Anti-British League, a Communist organization. The A.B.L. relation to the Malayan Communist party is like a volunteer force compared to a professional army. I was instructed to act for one of their members. I came to know and like him. In 1953 he was released from detention. We became friends. He told me that he was a Communist. I will call him Laniaz. He is still a most important Communist cadre member, spreading propaganda on behalf of the Communist cause. Through him I came to know Devan Nair, who was the most determined Anti-British League member I have ever known. Later I discovered that Devan Nair was in fact on the way to being a full-fledged Communist party member. . . .

"Devan Nair knew I was not a Communist. He knew that I knew he was a Communist. In 1956 he landed in jail with Lim Chin Siong and Company. After spending a great part of his life with the Malayan Communist party he came to his own conclusion that their leadership was inadequate to meet the needs of the revolution in Malaya. . . . Devan Nair is now on our side, but Mr. S. T. Bani (one of the Union Six), who had for years worked together with me in the unions competing against the Communists, decided to throw in his lot with the Communists. He had been won over to their side. So the battle went on for the hearts and minds, first of the political elite of the population, and ultimately of the whole population. . . .

"Laniaz joined us, a core of English-educated, to fight colonialism. We were all non-Communists other than Laniaz. . . . Then one day in 1954 we came into contact with the Chinese-educated world. The Chinese middle-school students were in revolt against national service and they were beaten down. Riots took place. Charges were preferred in court. Through devious ways they came into contact with us. Laniaz bridged the gap to the Chinese-educated world—a world teeming with vitality, dynamism, and revolution, a world in which the Communists had been working for over the last thirty years with considerable success. We the English-educated revolutionaries went on trying to tap this oil field of political resources and soon found our pipelines crossing those of the Communist party. We were latecomers. We were considered by the Communists as poaching in their exclusive territory. In this world we came to know Lim Chin Siong and Fong Swee Suan. They joined us in the People's Action party. In 1955 we contested the elections. Our initiation into the intricacies and ramifications of the Communist underground organization in the trade-unions and cultural associations had begun.

"It is a strange business working in this world. When you meet a union leader you quickly have to decide which side he is on and whether he is a Communist. You can find out by the language he uses and his behavior whether or not he is in the inner circle which makes the decisions. These are things from which you determine whether he is an outsider or an insider in the Communist underworld. I came to know dozens of them. They are not crooks or opportunists. They are men with great resolve, dedicated to the Communist revolution and to the establishment of the Communist state, believing that it is the best thing in the world for mankind. Many of them were prepared to pay the price for the Communist cause in terms of personal freedom and sacrifice. Often my colleagues and I disagreed with them, and intense fights took place, all concealed from the outside world because they were Communists working in one united anti-colonial front with us against the common enemy, and it would not do to betray them. Eventually many of them landed in jail, in the purges of 1956 and 1957. I used to see them there, arguing their appeals, reading their captured documents and the Special Branch précis of the cases against them. I had the singular advantage of not only knowing them well by having worked at close quarters with them in the united front against the British, but I also saw the official version in reports on them. Many were banished to China. Some were my personal friends.

"They knew that I knew they were Communists, for between us there was no pretense. They believed that I should join them. They believed that ultimately I would be forced to admit that what they call the bourgeois democratic system could not produce a just and equal society, and that I would admit that they were right. I used to spend hours arguing with some of them, trying to prove that whatever else happened in China or Russia, we were living in Malaya and, irrespective of Communism or democratic socialism, if we wanted to build a more just and equal society in Malaya, we would have to make certain fundamental decisions, such as being Malayans, uniting the Chinese and Indians and others with the Malays, building up national unity and national loyalty, and rallying all the races together through a national language.

"In 1953 I became legal adviser to the Naval Base Labor Union, fought their case and won the confidence of the committee and the men. They were looking for a union secretary. I introduced to them Sandra Woodhull, a person I had known in the University of Malaya Socialist Club. I knew that he was anti-British and anti-colonial. I also knew he was reading Marxism and that he was initiating himself into the mysteries of world revolution. But he was not a Communist or member of the Anti-British League, although they were grooming him for recruitment. He was then prepared to work for a cause. On my recommendation he became secretary to the union. He worked hard and by 1955 he had organized, with the help of a handful of dedicated Communist ground workers in the union, ten thousand workers in the Naval Base. He had organized them into a coherent force, not because the workers believed in socialism or Communism, but because they knew him to be a trustworthy and industrious man who worked with me for them. The strength of the Communist party lies not in their mass as such, but in the band of trained and disciplined cadres who lead the mass into Communist causes, often without the masses knowing they are Communists. . . .

"Let me tell you the inside story of the P.A.P. and the people who made up the leadership. In 1954, when it was formed, we the non-Communists were in complete control of the party. The only persons who could press the Communist point of view were Fong Swee Suan, Chan Chiaw Tor, and Devan Nair, three out of twelve members of the Central Executive Committee. After the election of the new Central Committee in 1956, pro-Communist strength in the party had increased to four out of twelve. They were Lim Chin Siong, Devan Nair, and two others. . . . The Communists, through James Puthucheary, were also pressing hard for a constitution which would allow the branches complete control in the party. Such a constitution would mean that the Communists would be able to capture the party. In 1956 they were all detained in a purge. . . .

"When they were detained . . . I used to visit the leaders, who were kept separate from the others in what they called a 'camp' outside the prison. These six leaders were Lim Chin Siong, Fong Swee Suan, James Puthucheary, Sandra Wood-hull, Chan Chiaw Tor, and Devan Nair. They were detained for two and a half years. Lim Chin Siong was the most important open-front leader the Malayan Communist party had built up. By 1955 he knew that I knew this. He is a friendly and quiet person. He is prepared to devote his life to working for the creation of a Communist Malaya. But once you resist and fight the Communist cause, then you can expect all that personal friendship to mean nothing in the ruthless and relentless struggle for supremacy.

"Lim Chin Siong was once Devan Nair's closest open-front comrade. Devan Nair was his constant guide. But when Devan Nair decided that the Malayan Communist party was wrong in continuing the armed struggle after independence in the Federation and not coming to terms with Malayan nationalism, Lim began to fight Devan Nair relentlessly and ruthlessly, by fair or unfair methods, by smears and intimidation, to destroy every influence that Devan Nair had with the workers and in the unions. His personal friendship with Devan Nair meant nothing.

"In June, 1959, we won the elections. We got the detainees released from prison—Lim Chin Siong and seven others who were closely connected with P.A.P. leadership. When they were released they published a signed statement in which they endorsed wholeheartedly and without reservation the non-Communist aims and objectives of the P.A.P. For all of them, except Lim Chin Siong, it was at that time a genuine change of heart. Devan Nair, Fong Swee Suan, Sandra Woodhull, James Puthucheary, and Chan Chiaw Tor all told me that we must not go back to the mistakes of 1955-1956 and allow the Malayan Communist party to make use of the P.A.P. And they solemnly declared to me that if the Malayan Communist party fought the P.A.P. because of this, they would fight with the P.A.P. against the M.C.P.

"We accepted this declaration as sincere and appointed them political secretaries. Lim Chin Siong also signed this statement. But I had my doubts as to Lim's sincerity. We hoped that he genuinely and sincerely believed with us that the right road for us was merger with the Federation and the creation of a democratic non-Communist and socialist Malaya. But just in case they were not honest and sincere, we took care to see that there were safeguards and guarantees to ensure that they could not do the country great harm. They were given no access to secret matters. And Lim Chin Siong was specially put in the Ministry of Finance, where he could do no harm. They were not, like Fong Swee Suan, given their citizenship papers. None of them was made a P.A.P. cadre member.

"After the first year we became more and more convinced that Lim Chin Siong was only playing a game and was only interested in building up Communist strength in the unions and slowly undermining the influence and prestige of the Government with the workers. He was not sincere in his signed declaration. And over the last two years he has been

able to persuade many, like Fong Swee Suan and Sandra
Woodhull, to go back to the Communist side. . . .

"There may be people who say that all this talk of the
Communist underground is a fairy tale. I shall have to tell
you something which is known to very few people. In March,
1958, someone whom I knew to be connected with the Communist organization approached me and arranged for me to
see a man who he said would like to discuss some matters. I
met him in Singapore one afternoon on the road between
Victoria Memorial Hall and the Legislative Assembly and took
him to a room in the Assembly. He was a Chinese-educated
young man several years younger than myself, an able and
determined person. He told me that he was a representative
of the Communist party in Singapore. I told him that I did
not know who he was and I had no way of knowing the truth
of his claim. He explained that his purpose in seeing me was
to establish co-operation between the Communists and the
non-Communists in the P.A.P.

"I shall call him the 'Plen,' short for plenipotentiary. We
spoke in Chinese. Sometimes I used English words to clarify
my meaning and I found that he understood English. I asked
him for proof that he was a genuine representative of the
Malayan Communist party. He smiled and said that I had to
take his word for it. I then asked him whether he had authority
over the open-front Communist cadres in the unions and
the political parties, and I gave as an example Chang Yuen
Tong. Chang was then a City Councilor and Executive Committee member of the Workers' party. I knew he was one of the
pro-Communist trade-union workers. I told the Plen that I
thought the Communists were trying to make use of David
Marshall's Workers' party to fight the P.A.P. I said that as
evidence of his credentials that he was a real representative of
the Communist command in Singapore and his good faith in
not wishing to attack the P.A.P. by using the Workers' party,
he should give word for the resignation of Chang Yuen Tong
from the Workers' party and the City Council and let the

Workers' party and David Marshall go on their own. He said, 'All right. Give us some time. We shall see that it is done.'

"Several weeks later, in April, 1958, while I was in London, I read in the newspapers that Chang Yuen Tong had resigned from the Workers' party and from the City Council. The Malayan Communist party had given orders. The Plen had proved his credentials. Subsequently, in the City Council by-election at Kallang, David Marshall, without Communist support, found himself with just over one hundred votes at the end of a campaign in which he was most times talking to empty fields. The Communists had withdrawn support, and the Workers' party collapsed. . . .

"Before the general elections in 1959 I met the Plen on four occasions, all in Singapore, each time at a different rendezvous. He was trying to gauge the P.A.P. intentions and purpose. He wanted again and again to find out if we were prepared to let the Communists work together with us in a united anti-colonial front in the P.A.P. I told him that I did not see much virtue in this, because from time to time we would have repetitions of the troubles of 1956 and 1957. Each time the Malayan Communist party decided to take a different line, we the P.A.P. would be involved. I told him that it would be far better from the P.A.P. point of view that the Communists left us alone. They had their other open-front organizations. They could work on parallel lines if they chose to, but if they decided to change policy they could please themselves and it would not damage the P.A.P. He tried to allay my doubts. He said that Lim Chin Siong and the others I had dealt with might have given me an unfortunate impression in 1956 and 1957. But this time I was dealing with the top, the men who decided and gave the orders, and they would keep their word. He said Lim could not decide policy. I did not commit myself to anything in reply. Never in any one of our meetings did I say or do anything which would commit the P.A.P. We left things at that. The general election came in May, 1959. But I was to meet him again in May, 1961. . . .

"In one of my election speeches I said that the real fight would begin after the elections, when the ultimate contestants would be the P.A.P. and the Malayan Communist party. This would be the fight to establish the democratic system in the hearts and minds of the people. I said: 'In this fight the ultimate contestants will be the P.A.P. and the M.C.P.— the P.A.P. for a democratic non-Communist socialist Malaya, and the M.C.P. for a Soviet Republic of Malaya. It is a battle which cannot be won by just bayonets and bullets. It is a battle of ideals and ideas. And the side that recruits more ability and talent will be the side that wins.' . . .

"From about March, 1960, when Lim Chin Siong had got back his intimate friend Fong Swee Suan to the Communist side, both began running down the P.A.P. Government to the workers. Openly these two were with us in the Government as political secretaries. But privately they told union secretaries and rank-and-file workers what a reactionary lot of fellows we were and how all our actions and policies, which were benefiting the workers, were all the result of their pressure. These sly propaganda lines all came back to us and hastened the antagonism that grew between the pro-Communist party and us, the non-Communists.

"Some time after I assumed office, in September and October, 1959, I went around the various Ministries, including the Special Branch. There on October 6 at about 4:00 P.M. I was shown a bundle of files of people on the 'arrest at sight' list. I came across a file which had a photograph I recognized. It was the Plen. I mentally noted who he was. But I did not tell and have not told the Special Branch what I know of him. The Special Branch would have to, and probably will one day, find out for themselves in their own way.

"The Plen made contact with me again through a courier in March, 1961. He asked me to indicate a secret nom de plume that I would use. He had always used the name 'Lee Yuck Han' as his. He used my surname as his nom de plume and characters Yuck Han in Chinese for John. I then gave him my nom de plume, a name using his surname, which, for the sake of anonymity, I shall say is 'Chen,' and Pin Ann, Chinese characters meaning peace and tranquillity.

"After we lost Hong Lim [an important by-election], I openly and publicly told Lim Chin Siong and his friends where we stood, where we were going, and that if they were not coming with us, they could go their own way. A few days after that, on May 11, I met the Plen again in Singapore. He thanked me for having been very kind to one of his relatives, whom I had occasion to help. In this way he indicated that he knew by the fact I had used his surname in my nom de plume that I knew who he was. We had a four-hour session in which discussion ranged over many subjects, such as more democratic rights, more cultural freedom, more free importation of books, and more free immigration permits, all of which meant, in short, more opportunities for Communist activities.

"He asked me whether I was likely to get merger soon [with Malaya] from Tunku Abdul Rahman. I told him there was no immediate likelihood of it, but that I was hoping for common market arrangements with the Federation of Malaya. He pressed me to agree to the abolition of the Internal Security Council as the immediate target for the 1963 constitutional talks [with the British Government] while deferring the question of independence for Singapore alone or through merger with the Federation. . . . I did not commit myself. . . .

"Three weeks later Lim Chin Siong got five other friends to join him in a statement to demand the abolition of the Internal Security Council in the 1963 constitutional talks with the British. I knew that, like Chang Yuen Tong, he had received his instructions from his organization, the Communist underground."

11

The red-and-white barred flag of Lee Kuan Yew's city-state and the red star of Lim Chin Siong's Barisan Socialis both symbolize, among other things, "purity."

This is no coincidence, for an obsessive puritanism has been imposed on Singapore and is also noticeable as a new social force in many parts of Asia, where many things Western are under attack.

David Marshall, a student of society if not of politics, insists that among the young people of Singapore, particularly the Chinese, there is a "new concept of living reminiscent of Cromwell's puritans," and he is not the only one among the many people I discussed this with in Singapore who looked back to the English Commonwealth to find an explanation of this phenomenon.

"Wowser," an Australian word which means drab-souled philistinism, aptly describes the new puritanism which has transformed this city. Singapore used to be a reasonably adult place, but today it is haunted by an austere spirit and talk of corrupting influences and sin in capitals, and although it is the fastest-breeding city in the world, sex is a word that is Western, decadent, and avoided as much as possible. The "Paris of

Asia," as some optimist once described Singapore, has become as dull and respectable as an Australian Sunday.

This new puritanism is due to a combination of forces. It is a violent reaction to British rule, to generations of colonialism, and it reflects the thinking of the anti-white political left. It is largely Chinese-inspired and comes indirectly from the social austerity of Communist China. Its strongest behind-the-scenes advocates are a formidable bloc of anti-Western Chinese women, daughters of the Asian revolution, behind the men of the governing People's Action party.

By deliberately concentrating on some of the shoddier products of the West—products which many Westerners themselves reject—the new puritans proclaim: "Look what a corrupt lot they are. Our purity must be contaminated no longer."

One of the first acts of the Lee Kuan Yew Government was to attack "Yellow Culture." The term, Asians told me, was invented in Peking. It is clever, subtle propaganda, since it uses a word with a derogatory meaning in the West—"yellow press," "yellow streak"—to attack things Western.

In Singapore, Yellow Culture was, and still is, used to define and denounce anything Western which the P.A.P. and the Government disliked or could use as propaganda in its anti-colonial struggle, and the Government's Minister for Culture, a soft-voiced handsome Indian ex-journalist, has turned it into a weapon of censorship and social conformity.

The much-traveled Mr. Rajaratnam, who has been widely "contaminated" by Western culture—he once worked in London's Fleet Street—and has survived remarkably undamaged, probably has his own private opinions about Yellow Culture, but although a worldly man, he denounces it with the same enthusiasm as his less sophisticated colleagues, who need little convincing that jazz and rock 'n' roll are inventions of the devil with a white face. That some of the popular and harmless fashions of the young West were just as popular with young Asia was regarded as an affront by some of the pure-minded administrators of Singapore. And so Mr. Rajaratnam, by banning jazz, rock, jukeboxes, magazines, films, books, entertainments, shared the responsibility of acting like an adolescent with the less liberal and enlightened members of his party.

A policy was introduced to "eliminate sex-obsessed culture and all activities which are detrimental to a new and healthy society and culture," words Hitler could have used as he publicly burned books in Berlin which pure Aryan Germans should not read. That sex-obsessed publications are still available under many a counter and are still bought by determined Asians who have been keenly interested in sex for millennia, merely shows that the Chinese and Indians and Malays who sell them are businessmen first and puritans last.

Even the film *Solomon and Sheba* was banned because it was allegedly offensive to Muslims, who regard Solomon as a prophet and not a bit like Mr. Brynner embracing Miss Lollobrigida, as the posters showed.

Under Yellow Culture came a concentrated attack on prostitution, through the closing of hotels, brothels, bars, and massage establishments, though how the most universal profession could have been labeled Yellow is hard to understand. The P.A.P. Government conveniently ignored that some girls will be girls in Sydney, Singapore, or San Francisco and that in a city where unemployment is heavy and many people employed work only part time, prostitution is the sole reason why many families, and especially Chinese families, eat.

The police have more than two thousand girls on their books, but the real number is many times that, and as fast as hotels or boardinghouses or massage shops are closed, others open. There are more prostitutes in Singapore today, even allowing for the increase in population, than ever before, many of them, like the Communist party, underground, and the reason is economic—too many people struggling for too few jobs, too many rice bowls that are permanently three parts empty.

During the campaign against the girls, a member of the P.A.P., which tried to rehabilitate prostitutes, found a job for an attractive member of the profession, but some weeks later he heard that the girl was working after hours at a house in one of the European areas. The P.A.P. man was shocked. He couldn't believe that his personal drive for purity had failed. He rushed out to the house and described the girl to the Madam.

"Yes, one of my best girls. In number two, up the stairs."

The P.A.P. man climbed and knocked. The door opened. For a moment he could not decide whether to embrace her or hit her. Then he took her in his arms and wailed, "My Maisie, why have you done a thing like this—to ME."

While it is understandable in a young population to prohibit the pathological pulp of the West, you can't isolate a community and keep it in childhood indefinitely. And there is always the danger that censorship will breed on censorship. The Yellow Culture attack has produced many absurdities which reflect, more than anything else, the little minds and big political motives of the attackers. The entertainer, for example, who was refused permission to perform because she had large breasts—fully covered. Half the women of the world would be Yellow on this basis. The appeal to women to stop spending money on clothes and jewelry, the excuse being that spending on personal adornment was wasteful, inherited from the West, and by implication a Yellow habit. The filthiest filthy postcards I have ever seen were not French or Egyptian but Chinese, and you can still buy them in Singapore.

In a society where the leaders appeal for racial harmony—a society which will soon be part of the wider Greater Malaysia, whose existence will depend on the co-operation of all races—the attack on Yellow Culture is largely racial and political, and also ninety per cent spurious, but all disguised in moralistic cellophane phrases and as transparent.

But, as Dr. Goebbels proved, if you stress a propaganda point long enough, some people will believe you. I was shown essays by senior students, most of them Chinese, which showed how Yellow Culture had been absorbed and how the words were used with parrot-like smugness.

"Yellow films make me want to go out and seduce a woman," one essay said. "If I see a prostitute soliciting a man I know I should tell the police," said another. "Yellow culture is bad. Our culture is good," said a third.

Turn out enough students of this caliber and Mr. Rajaratnam will produce a society thinking like infants and acting like storm troopers.

Fortunately, as Singapore's classic Yellow Culture case proved, there were enough students sufficiently unimpressed with Yellow Culture propaganda, sufficiently selective and sufficiently concerned with free discussion to spank members of the Government.

It all began when Professor D. J. Enright, Johore Professor of English at the University of Malaya at Singapore, a long-haired English poet of note and a man of widely liberal views, gave a lecture on the poetry of Robert Graves—and created a small cultural typhoon. What he said is worth reading—anywhere:

"I must at once apologise for bringing you here tonight merely to listen to a talk, and moreover to listen to a talk merely about poetry. About a commodity in large supply and short demand whose social value is problematical at the best. And I am not even going to talk about poetry at its best. I abase myself for failing to slant my inaugural lecture to local needs and interests. I realise that I cannot expect to be offered a commission in the Cultural Brigade on the strength of it.

"But it seems impossible to avoid altogether the pressing question. How is a culture built up? So let us, by way of propitiation, make a short and modest proposal. A culture is built up by people listening to music and composing it; reading books and writing them; looking at pictures and painting them; observing life and living it. Now, using the word 'culture' in its widest sense (and its sense grows wider day by day), we must admit that the cultures of the old world were extremely cultural—in the sense of being very distinctive, very idiosyncratic, very different from one another. Today the most

distinctive national cultures are those which involve cannibal-
ism, head-shrinking and other forms of human sacrifice. Alas, it
sometimes seems that the most striking national elements are
also that nation's most deplorable mannerisms. I had compiled
a list of examples, but on second thought I won't read it out.
Enough to say that these days 'national culture' is chiefly
something for the tourists from abroad: the real life of the
country goes on somewhere else. The world is growing smaller,
and therefore more homogeneous, and the cultures of individual countries are bound to draw closer together than they
used to be. . . .

"In the new countries—Singapore, Malaya, Ghana and so
forth—you will often be told in an envious tone that England
is blessed with a firm and long-established culture. Yet when
we look at England, culturally, as it is at this moment, are we
so impressed by its solidity and assurance? We are not. Which
is not to demand any jeremiads about poor sick England,
or poor old broken-down Europe. Things aren't what they
were, of course: they never were. My point is that there is a
danger in being so conscious about culture; culture is not an
orchid, true culture does not have 'the look of flowers that
are looked at.' It more nearly resembles the asphodel, that
Elysian flower, beloved of literary souls, but as Robert Graves
describes it: 'a hardy, tall, tough, unscented and commercially
valueless plant.'

"I am not setting up shop as a prophet. I only wished to
suggest that at this point in time it would be as ridiculous to
institute a sarong-culture, complete with pantun competitions
and so forth, as to bring back the Maypole and the Morris
dancers in England just because the present monarch happens
to be called Elizabeth. The important thing for Singapore
and Malaya is to remain culturally open. Who can decide in
advance which seeds will fall on barren ground and which
will grow? Arising from this is a further consideration: Please
don't think that I am advocating legalised pornography if I
suggest that there is a trace of 'yellow' in most works of culture (as in most of us). Art doesn't begin in a test-tube, it

doesn't take its origin in good sentiments and clean-shaven
upstanding young thoughts. It begins . . .

> '. . . . where all ladders start,
> in the foul rag-and-bone shop of the heart.'

Art is not good manners and proper behaviour: to obtain art
you cannot use the same methods of discipline and control
by which you encourage these social amenities. To obtain art,
to build up a culture, you must leave people free to make
their own mistakes, to suffer and discover, to come to terms
with the foul rag-and-bone shop of their own hearts and whatever else, less foul, more fair, their own hearts may contain or
be capable of.

"It is an old-fashioned view, but I persist in thinking that
the greater part of a people's culture lies in the art which those
people produce and consume. I say 'old-fashioned,' because
these days we are forever being told that actually 'culture' is
a much wider conception altogether, which comprises things
altogether more important, such as whether people eat with
their right hand or their left, whether they carry their babies
on their backs, their hips, their fronts or their heads, and so
forth. If we allow my old-fashioned view, then we should re-
mark that a woman who has been sterilised will not produce
a baby. An artist who has been successfully psycho-analysed
will not produce any more art. A society which has been
thoroughly swept clean and garnished, brought to a high degree of spiritual hygiene, will not produce any art. Remove
all the 'dirt' from a human being, and you will be left with
an invertebrate. The boundary between 'cleaning up' and
'brain-washing' is very uncertain. For that reason, and although I am not addicted to juke-boxes, I deplore their banning from Singapore. Singapore, we hope and believe, is a real
place inhabited by real people. We hope that they will continue to be real people, more active and independent than
before, less narrow in their interests. We do not wish to see life
here decline into an interminable Sunday-school meeting.

"Shakespeare spoke of 'Art made tongue-tied by Authority.'

Authority, when it is kindly, achieves that end by fighting our battles for us, by providing us not only with social welfare—no one can decently object to that—but also with spiritual welfare. That is, by imposing subjects upon the artists and bestowing prescribed, as it were rediffused, art upon the audience. This has its advantages, of course. A successful totalitarian state affords the most civilised society you can have: it is civilised because, temporarily at any rate, its citizens are essentially dead. Authority must leave us to fight our battles for ourselves, especially our personal battles (and that is what culture is: personal). Authority must leave us to fight even that deadly battle over whether or not to enter a place of entertainment wherein lurks a juke-box, and whether or not to slip a coin into the machine.

"This serves to bring me to the announced subject of my talk: a poet who, though he is not of the world's greatest, has always insisted on fighting his own battles. Perhaps, after all, my theme is not utterly irrelevant to here and now. . . ."

Professor Enright had just finished lunch the next day when . . . But he has described objectively what happened after his "preliminary comments on the nature of 'culture' " were sensationally reported in the *Straits Times*:

"That same afternoon the Professor was summoned to the Ministry of Labor and Law on a question concerning his 'professional visit pass.' He there met the Minister for Culture and the Acting Minister for Labor and Law, who informed him that if he again interfered in 'local political issues' he would at once be deported.

"A Government press release, in the form of a long letter to the Professor, had already been sent out to newspapers and to Radio Singapore. Among other things the letter described the recipient as a 'beatnik professor' and a 'mendicant professor.'

"The Students' Union of the English-speaking University of Malaya called an emergency meeting on the following day and passed (by five hundred and twenty-two votes to five) a resolution condemning the Government's attempt to 'strangle free discussion in the University and to cow an individual into silence for expressing views which do not coincide with official ones.'

"The Government [People's Action Party] were clearly unprepared for such firmness on the part of a group whom they had hitherto considered politically decadent. Thereafter the 'affair' degenerated into a complex of intrigues, extra-and-inter-mural, public and private, cheering and depressing, comic and sinister. The nastiest development was a move by certain interested parties to persuade the Malay minority that its customs and way of life had been insulted.

"A formula of reconciliation between the Professor and the Government was eventually arrived at; but the general issue of academic freedom remains in the air—no formula has yet been found for that.

"In retrospect the 'affair' can be attributed to a mixture of ministerial pique, the hypersensitiveness of an ex-colonial state, the nervousness of a left-wing Government harried by its ultra-left wing and other elements, inter-racial tensions (as ever, deplored by politicians and exploited by them), disingenuous newspaper reporting, a confusion of the various senses of the word 'culture,' and the Professor's tactlessness in advancing abstract commonplaces in terms all too concrete and topical."

As the official critics of Yellow Culture seem to frown on most things except pure thoughts, I was not surprised to find that the once-big entertainment centers of Singapore had degenerated into dull acres of food stalls, advertisements, and whirlem cars. In a city notoriously lacking in "cultural" amenities, though a National Theatre has recently been built, the Worlds—the Great, the New, and the Happy—used to be centers where thousands could find harmless outlets for their collective boredom. Today people still visit them, but there is a new aimlessness about these thinning patrons, as though a visit is now a disinterested habit they can't break. The

Worlds today are shabby places suffering the general puritanical malaise, but they are still worth a visit if you are an addict of Cantonese opera or have never seen Malay dancing.

Peter, my cultured taxi-driver friend who spoke English, Malay, Mandarin, and several Chinese dialects, and who had suffered the advantage of being a sailor, drove me to the New World and talked about girls, his favorite subject, as he weaved through the heavy night traffic.

"Bad girls, many sick, are in Jalan Besar, but best high-class girls live near Sea View Hotel. They go there because it quiet and away from police. Very expensive. Twenty dollars. But good."

I asked about Lavender Street, which used to be full of houses.

Peter shook his head. "All gone. Lavender Street all engineering shops now. Man can't do much with a lathe, can he?"

He grinned and missed a cyclist by half an inch.

"Bloody Indian," he shouted.

"Peter," I scolded.

"Bloody Indian, yes, but not because Indian. Because Indian worst bloody bicycle rider in world."

We returned inevitably to the girls.

"My grandfather say best girls in Singapore Japanese, worst girls Europeans. Malay Street when he lived all European. Terrible women. They got drunk and fought in the street. They shocked the Asians, even the Chinese. Later Europeans not allowed work in Singapore any more and Japanese girls came. Japanese quiet and clean. In last forty years most girls Chinese. Many to buy food."

Peter dropped me at the New World, and within minutes of getting inside the big amusement park I had received quotes from three Chinese and a hideous Malay who obviously had not heard of Yellow Culture. The World was half empty, but beyond food stalls steaming with rice and fish and noodles, a merry-go-round circling at a loss, and an open café where Chinese families were sipping tea, I found what I was looking for.

The door curtain at the Cantonese opera was unattended, so
I walked in and sat down. Much later I was asked for my
dollar. Dragons, fearsomely neon, climb columns on either
side of the broad stage. The suspended microphone wears a
frilly skirt of pink garlands. The Prince is in blue robes with
long white sleeves. His costume glitters with sequin embroidery. The Princess is in pale gold and carries a large black fan.
Both wear the traditional make-up, though the old rice-
powder mask has been replaced by a heavy carmine which
accentuates the eyes, the red mouths. The Princess is talking.
Her voice is like a scalpel.

The audience sits under garlands of paper flowers, watching
with that supreme indifference of Chinese audiences until
something happens on stage which amuses or calls for applause.
Then the sudden bark of *"How"* is music to the hard-worked
actor. The theater is full of children and babies of all shapes
and sizes. They wander up and down the long sloping aisle.
They stand and gape at the orchestra. They sit on the floor
among the crackling peanut shells and spittle. Near me an old
lady has a pot of tea, two small bowls, and a plate of rice and
vegetables—the lot on a tray clamped to the back of the seat
in front of her. Large portraits of the visiting stars from Hong
Kong adorn the peeling green walls. Cymbals and drums
clash and thunder, sticks rattle on wood, the Princess hits an
impossible note and holds it against the deafening competition.
The scene shifter, in black pants and a filthy singlet, comes
on stage, against a scarlet-and-gold moongate backcloth, tosses
a cushion on the floor, lights a cigarette, and scratches himself.

The opera tells of a jealous King in love with a Princess who
is already betrothed to a Prince. The King forces the Prince
to swear to love the girl to eternity and proclaims the Princess
his sister. But this of course is only a dirty ruse to get the
beautiful girl into his clutches—as the next three hours prove
if you have the patience to stay.

As the curtain comes down on the act to show three enormous glittering characters on a turquoise cloth, I ask the Chinese sitting beside me for a translation.

"I speak Chinese, but I can't read it," he says. "I was born here and know only a few characters. Many local-born Chinese are slowly forgetting their language."

I moved on at last to the Malay dance hall to watch not the traditional Ronggeng but Baruh Joget—modern dance—performed by dancing girls to American, English, Malay, and Indonesian music, none of it Yellow. Malay taxi dancers were unknown in the Singapore of the past. They would not have been allowed by their parents or their religion, for a Malay girl had only one place, the home. But here were Malay girls dancing for money. This was indeed a revolutionary change.

The girls were attractive, slim and small-waisted, with perfectly rounded bottoms. Many wore the Malay blouse and tight sarong, but others chose a modified Malay form of European dress. Their dark faces and piled hair were flowers above blouses of rose, black, white, wine.

Baruh Joget, to the halting rhythm of a Malay band, is a dance of advance and retreat in which the facing couples never touch. It is a slow dance of swaying hips, moving arms, fluttering hands, which play an expressive part, and shuffling, tapping feet. It is a dance of no physical contact, not even the hands, but it concentrates more sex into five minutes than a Western dance gets into sixty.

The audience, all Malays in their late teens and early twenties, sat around the dance floor drinking beer or orange and selecting the girl they hoped to dance with next, for the competition was strong. They wore white shirts and dark trousers and some the songkok, or velvet cap. Their teeth looked painted in their dark faces as they watched the girls and hurried to the floor as each dance started.

"Three dances for a dollar," an older Malay near me explained. "Some girls make three hundred dollars a month. Many are married. They dance here to help husbands out of work or to get more money for their homes and clothes.

"No, the old people don't like this Baruh Joget. They still say a daughter's place is at home learning to cook and sew.

But I am forty and old and I like to see it. It is modern and I like the modern. The old is still good but it does not appeal to the young. We live in a new age, and the past is the past. I will not argue, as many of the old do, with time."

Any moment now I expect to hear that Cantonese opera has been declared decadent and Baruh Joget proclaimed Yellow Culture.

Kuala Lumpur II

12

The day train to K.L. crawls across the mile-long Causeway which links Singapore Island with the mainland, stops for a moment at Johore Bahru, the most southerly town in mainland Asia, then begins its slow climb into the Federation of Malaya.

Nothing seems to have changed since the last time I came this way. The same dun-painted carriages twist and straighten through the same jungle hills. The little stations, gay with flowers in pots and clipped hibiscus hedges, are still suburban neat. The palms shake their heads above kampongs hiding from the train. And on either side, through the air-conditioning windows, is the endless silver mathematics of rubber trees misted by the steam of early morning.

Even the warning to restrain yourself at stations still proclaims its international message in English, Chinese, Tamil, and Malay, and the Malay script reminds me as ever of expertly written Pitman's shorthand improved by an interior decorator.

The train crawls on through the Sultan states—up and through the indigo hills of Johore, across Negri Sembilan, toward Selangor. South only a few miles is ancient Malacca, facing the steamy straits of the same name which separate Malaya from Indonesian Sumatra. At Malacca modern history began in these parts to the cannon tympany of the Portuguese four centuries ago. At Malacca, St. Francis Xavier, the Apostle of the Indies, was once buried in the church on the hill, before his body was moved to Goa, and a Chinese Princess of the blood still sleeps in her womb grave on the soft green slopes of Bukit China.

Northward the jungle mountains lift into the other Sultan states of the Federation—Pahang and Perak, Kelantan and Trengganu, Kedah and Perlis—lift and reach north to names like Alor Star, which once featured in England-Australia air-record attempts in the pioneering days of aviation, to Kota Bahru and its Beach of Passionate Love, where the Japanese invaders first landed to begin their conquest of Malaya and Singapore twenty years ago, to the tangled valleys along the southern border of the ancient Kingdom of Thailand.

The pleasant English Army wife I share a gin-and-tonic with at noon hasn't changed much either. Her accent is middle class, she copies her clothes from Vogue, she has spent half her life making transitory homes for her husband in many parts of the world. Now she looks forward to going "Home" to a cottage near London, and she talks about color schemes, the cost of living on a soldier's pay, terrorists, and tells a long story about a tiger-loving rubber-planter friend who refuses to let anyone carry a gun on his estate, where a tigress and her four growing cubs have complete freedom to keep down the pigs.

At Seremban, halfway across Negri Sembilan, my ticket provides a free newspaper with the compliments of the Malayan Railways, and on the front page one story alone is enough to convince me, if I need convincing, that I am back in the long thrusting peninsula of the charming Malays, for no race on earth has greater appeal or appreciation of magic or closer connections with the hantus, the spirits of the jungle, or greater need of the pawang, that learned gentleman who has the power to make the hantus behave themselves.

I read that Aladad Khan bin Taizullah Khan, a cowherd of

forty-two, had prayed for help when fifteen of his grey water buffaloes died. His prayers had been answered by a dream in which a holy man had directed him to a spot five feet from the railway line near the town of Klang and ordered him to dig a small hole and "wait for the magic waters to flow."

Aladad Khan followed instructions and the water flowed. He sprinkled the magic water on the rumps of his ailing buffaloes and they were cured of the mysterious disease that was killing them. The news got about faster than a hantu can travel—and a good hantu can ride the clouds like a jet—and within hours the pilgrimage had begun to the holy well.

One old lady with a nasty backache poured three cups of water over herself, walked without pain for the first time in months, and cried, "It is amazing. I feel wonderful." An asthmatic bathed in the water and stopped wheezing. Aladad Khan's own son after washing was "complete cleansed" of his ulcers. Hundreds of people filled bottles to take back to relatives too ill or crippled to visit the magic spring.

And then some official busybody, some scientific bureaucrat, who was quite free of aches and twinges and allergies, had to spoil everything by having the water analyzed and proving that it was contaminated and should not be drunk under any circumstances unless boiled.

When told that his magic spring was packed with bacteria, Aladad Khan bin Taizullah Khan shrugged and made a sensible but resigned statement: "If the water is boiled it will lose its healing properties. But if the authorities want to take action, there is nothing I can do."

I was glad that he had the last word. At least Aladad Khan knew that all his sick buffaloes had recovered. And if the old lady's back stopped aching, even for half an hour, her visit to the spring had not been a complete failure.

The attendant brings tea, and the same piece of raisin cake I had rejected a generation before, and on page two I find another reminder, this time from Kuala Kangsar, that the rest of the world is far away.

"The Sultan and the Raja Perempuan of Perak and other members of royal families were wet through when water hoses were turned on them, as part of a traditional ceremony observed in the palace grounds here yesterday evening.

"The ceremony was the 'Mandi Sampat' [ceremonial bathing] performed in connection with the wedding of the Sultan's granddaughter, Tengku Mariam Khalidad binte Tengku Ibrahim Shah, and Tengku Zabir bin Tengku Nasir, chairman of the Tanjong Malim Town Council.

"Earlier in the afternoon the young couple drove through the town at the head of a procession of thirty decorated cars. On their return to the palace, the newlyweds mounted a five-tiered dais. A fire engine then arrived and the Raja Muda of Perak drenched all the guests with a hose. The ceremony marked the end of the four-day celebrations of the royal wedding."

But the story I like best is at the bottom of a page—a story of man's dark beliefs and his greatest quality, his compassion.

For thousands of years the world's biggest turtles, the great Leather Backs, which are eight feet long, weigh more than a ton, and live for several hundred years, have returned each year from temperate oceans to the same dozen-mile stretch of Malayan east coast beach near Dungun in Trengganu to lay their eggs.

But in recent years local Malays and Chinese have been digging up the distorted rubbery white eggs and selling them as an alleged aphrodisiac—destroying so many hundreds of thousands of the annual laying that scientists estimated that there are probably no more than a thousand pairs of giant turtles left in the world and that if the destruction continued this rare species would soon be extinct.

But destruction of the eggs is only part of the story, for the old belief, inherited from who knows where, has led to pilgrimages to Dungun to dance on the turtles to bring good luck. Official notices, "Do not dance on the turtles," have not prevented this rite and, although the mother turtles don't seem to mind as they drag their ton weight up the beach or grunt and sob as they lay two to three hundred eggs in the dry sand, scientists think that continued dancing may eventually frighten the females away from their traditional breeding beach.

To save the Leather Backs, thousands of eggs are now collected each year and put into hatcheries, and the babies later released. Last year Professor J. R. Henrickson of the University of Malaya collected about ten thousand eggs, and seven weeks later gently put two thousand babies, each weighing about one ounce, into the South China Sea to begin a life cycle which will bring some of the mothers-to-be among them back to the ancient breeding place of their ancestors and the sign that appeals, "Do not dance on the turtles."

I put the paper aside and finished my tea. The train moves on, wearily now. It is seven hours since we left Singapore and the sun is dipping toward the Nicobars, out in the Bay of Bengal, which I last saw from the bridge of a British cruiser in almost-forgotten World War II.

The land of the Malays still seems unchanged as we cross Selangor—but not for long. Slowly the hills fold back and uncover squares of red tiles, high tubes of glass, blocks of concrete shuddering in the glare and piercing the tamed jungle roof. The village I knew has almost overnight become a city.

When I first saw K.L.—for Kuala Lumpur, capital of the Federation of Malaya, is never called anything else—it was a toy town created by an Islamic child, a miniature film set, fresh hammered and painted, ready for an Aladdin spectacular. It was then little more than a large hill-encircled village gathered along a thin pipe of river khaki with mud, still smelling of jungle only just pushed away from its front and back doors, and dominated by four things: its great green Mosque beside the river; the onion domes and endless colonnades of its "Moorish Byzantine" government buildings; the "Elizabethan Suburbia" of its European club, commonly named the

"Spotted Dog" because a formidable late-Victorian female once hitched her pet Dalmatians to her waiting carriage outside; and its Railway Station.

K.L.'s Railway Station deserves to be listed among the modern wonders of the world. It has been derided as "Victorian Moorish," and it was either designed by an architect with delusions of grandeur or was an administrative mistake, because it is large enough to serve New York or Tokyo.

It is a museum collection of domes, towers, arches, columns, pillars, pinnacles, and little twisting exterior staircases. It looks like a Maharajah's palace or a crazy mosque or an overdecorated fort or the tomb of some dark horde leader out of High Asia. It is the Taj Mahal redesigned by a commercial artist, the Tower of London given a face lift by a Moslem master builder from Baghdad. It is anything you like to name—and its purpose is to serve each day a few slow trains which meander into its vast vaulted inside and never seem to come out.

The Station, the Mosque, and the rest are still landmarks of K.L., but they are overshadowed today by flat buildings and business blocks, by vertical acres of steel and glass, for the sterile matchboxes planned to catch and store the thin sunlight of northern Europe and North America have been transplanted to Asia, where the sun is not a friend but an enemy, and one to be defeated by shutters and shade as any simple kampong Malay has known from birth.

K.L. is not an ancient city. It is not even old. It began in 1857, year of the Indian Mutiny and the Black Hole of Calcutta, when eighty-seven Chinese tin miners rowed up the Klang River to its junction with the Gombak and named the spot where they landed, and found tin, Kuala Lumpur, or Muddy River Mouth. Most of them soon died from malaria, but others followed to spread and find more tin, to pay royalties to nearby sultans, to open shops and brothels and opium dens, and to establish the genesis of today's capital in a jungle where man was much more dangerous than tiger or elephant or krait.

Years before nineteenth-century settlers were fighting their last battles against the American Indian, K.L. was a wild jungle settlement where Chinese and Malay combined or fought and where throats were cut for a few cents. In the seventies the British, who had been fighting among themselves for a thousand years, decided that the Malay States were far too valuable commercially and strategically to be left alone. And so Queen Victoria stopped most of the throat slitting, much to the disappointment of the Malay sultans and the pugnacious Chinese, who regarded wiping out an enemy as something between a profession and a hobby. With order more or less restored, the invaluable rubber tree arrived about sixty years ago, and following it came the Indians, mostly Tamils from South India, to work on the expanding rubber estates, to open shops, to build roads and temples, to clean the streets, and to do most of the other dirty work of the growing towns.

Until a few years ago K.L. was a small and attractive sleepy tree-filled hollow, and even the Communist civil war, which began in 1948 only fifty miles from her Moorish minarets and colonnades and lasted for twelve years, did little to disturb her virginal provincialism. Then, in 1957, when the British gave the Federation of Malaya independence, K.L. suddenly grew up.

Today it is a city, and a multi-racial city on the way to half a million people, which has never known adolescence. It is crude, brash, noisy, crowded, and still in many ways provincial. It is a new jungle rising and spreading and destroying. It is that ugly creation of modern man—an unplanned city. Skyscrapers shadow thatch. Crumbling shop-houses where Chinese families lived and worked for generations touch elbows with new hotels. Riverside kampongs survive, but not for long, washed in the flickering amber and orange of night signs. K.L. jars with picks, hammers, riveted steel, shop radios in four languages, impatient car horns, massed bicycle bells. It smells of wet concrete, new paint, bitumen, petrol fumes, all mixed up with tamarind water, bean curd, curry, steaming rice, roast duck, flowers, and incense.

You can eat French food, stinging Malay curry, sharksfin soup, all within a hop-step-jump. You can buy California grapefruit, Australian apples, grapes from Spain, jars of dried beetles to ease your sore throat, powdered deer antlers to help your potency, torches from Japan. You can have your hair cut in a first-class saloon or be shaved under a tree not ten yards from the traffic jams in Jalan Mountbatten. You can join the shouting argument of a food market or know the peace of the Great Mosque, where the pillars are inlaid with bronze panels, the rafters are duck-egg blue, and the swallows flick through the arched windows facing the khaki river.

You can buy a boy child for a thousand dollars or a girl child for a hundred, or dine in cool luxury at the Lake Club facing floodlit velvet-lined alcoves filled with fresh orchids. You can see Chinese girls riding motor scooters and Biblical bullock carts passing silent on rubber tires. You can find hand-beaten Kelantan silver, thin as eggshell, or walk in spacious gardens of English or Chinese mansions with pillared entrance halls and forty rooms.

It is above all a city of unforgettable glimpses, of far-off smiling hills, of clouds trailing their skirts on frail peaks, of near-black jungle, of mighty trees like beautiful antique furniture.

K.L. is a friendly tolerant city without the sour puritanism of Singapore and without the official Yellow Culture cult, which is Chinese and which the Malays feel reflects Chinese arrogance and Chinese politics. In K.L., too, you can't help noticing that the Chinese, who are not in the majority, are much more polite than in Singapore.

I set out one day to find two things—things that would represent to me the past, unchanged and unchanging, in this Asian city, and things that would symbolize the changing present. What was I looking for? I didn't know. But I was certain

I would recognize these symbols of yesterday and today and that they would tell me more about change than curtain walls of steel and glass.

I first saw the blue-and-white kite climbing above the trees and stopped to watch. It had nothing to do with my search, but Malay men and boys have been flying kites for centuries—the originals made from sewn leaves—and Malay craftsmen are among the most expert kite makers in the world. And, anyway, I like kites.

A father, stripped to his tucked-up sarong, was teaching his small son, for he pulled the kite down as I watched and showed him how to grip the center part of the frame with his right hand, while the boy held the string, and how to launch the kite upward facing the wind. The kite was a Wau Bulan, a Moon Kite, but smaller than the beautiful Bird and Fish and Frog kites you see in Kelantan, which have a wing span of up to six feet and are gay with color, tassels, and other decoration. This Wau Bulan was shaped like an African shield with a red sickle-moon tail suspended below it and a busar, or bow, and bowstring, attached to the head of the kite. The bowstring vibrates when the kite is flying and makes a soft humming sound which some claim will lull you to sleep. In some parts of Malaya competitions are held, with prizes for the kite which makes the most sound or the most pleasing sound, or for the kite which will fly with its string vertical. There are even fights, four or five hundred feet above the kampong, with string rubbed with powdered glass to cut an opponent's kite adrift and send it fluttering to the palms like a broken bird.

When the lesson was over, the father held up the kite, the boy lengthened the string, and prepared to run. Up went the Wau Bulan, above the trees, higher, its blue body and red tail brilliant against the pale sky. The boy squealed with delight. Father clapped his hands. But although I listened for its humming bowstring, all I heard was the wind in my ears.

I went on, my shirt already gripping me in the morning heat, to watch another once-familiar sight—Malay youths in a side street kicking a rattan ball and keeping it in the air for minutes without touching it with their hands or arms.

This was Sepak Raga, or Malay football, which has been played for about six hundred years and which the immigrant Chinese have adopted as one of their own games. It used to be contested by teams of nine, and the team which kept the ball in the air with the most kicks won. I think that was it, although it might have been the fewest kicks. But a modern and popular version, Sepak Raga Jaring, or Malay net-football, is now played by teams of three on opposite sides of a net on an area about the size of a badminton court. The winning team is the one which kicks or heads the rattan ball the most times over the net without it being returned.

A boy, when he saw me watching, threw me the ball, and they all laughed at my futile attempts to keep it in the air. Then one of them showed me how, with instep and ankle, and even with his heel from behind, he could keep it moving like a Yo-yo—until the others decided his skill was becoming monotonous. I left them scruffing on the ground for the rattan ball.

Later that morning I was strolling along the river bank, where majestic rain trees bow over Ampang Road, when I saw the man squatting on the grass playing to Chinese schoolboys. I stopped to listen and to watch his elegant fingers fondling the two long strings of his battered pear-shaped instrument, not unlike a mandolin and called, I think, a "khim." He was playing a Cantonese nursery rhyme, one I recognized, since a friend in China had once collected them, and I was amazed at the delicacy of his touch, the way he created so much music from two strings. At last he finished and got to his feet. He was tall for a Chinese and frail, and his face, like his fingers, was slender and sharpened. He was so thin, I found it hard to judge his age, but he was much older than he looked, for his eyes had that smeared look of years. He wore an old felt hat with a wide brim, a faded jacket unbuttoned to expose his bony chest, and half-mast pants. His feet were bare and his toes were long.

He pushed the shaft of his instrument toward me. From its end, which was inlaid with yellowing ivory, hung a metal disc and from it were suspended strips of wood inscribed with scarlet characters. He spun the disc and held out his hand. I found thirty cents. He spun again and I caught one of the whirling strips. He looked at the characters, smiled, and touched the strings. And as he began to play people stopped and crossed the street to listen, as they had throughout history to this ragged man's wandering tribe, the Minstrels of Asia.

"It is an old love song," a well-dressed Chinese said, first in Chinese, then in English. "What you would call traditional. He has great skill."

"What is the use of love," an old Malay said.

"Love is good."

"Love is only for the young."

The Chinese again translated and added: "No, no. Love is for all. It is the one thing all feel."

"Love is for the young," the Malay repeated.

The Minstrel played on while the river flowed to the sea. The love song did not end; it faded into the water and into the high rain trees when he left us at last without a backward glance and walked along the bank gently plucking one string with his little finger.

This was my first discovery. My second was under the arches of one of the government buildings where the letter writers sat in a row before their stool-like tables. These professionals are as old as character and script. They have been writing for the illiterate of Asia since writing began—letters for the lovelorn, the absent son, the distant soldier, the trader, the job seeker, the petitioner, letters written with brush and stylus and pen, letters dusted with powder and sand.

But the pads and the ink blocks and the rice paper had

disappeared, and in their place was something I never expected to see a traditional letter writer use in Asia—portable typewriters made in Switzerland.

To me this was a change more revolutionary than buildings of glass rising from the smoking rubble of shop-houses around K.L.'s old Market Square.

K.L. today is a twentieth-century frontier town designed not by malarious Chinese miners and feudal Malays but by real-estate agents, land developers, foreign companies, get-richer-quicker tycoons of all colors, and a Government determined to change an upcountry rubber-and-tin-trading village into one of the capitals of the world.

Millions of dollars have been spent on it and millions more are earmarked. K.L.'s International Airport, with its twelve-thousand-foot runways, will cost fifty million Malayan dollars. Its Parliament House, and already finished Parliament Road to the Lake Gardens area, will cost ten million and will include a sixteen-story building for Cabinet Ministers alone. The King's Istana Negara, or Royal Palace, plus its eighteen-hole golf course, five million. The new Mosque, to hold nine thousand people at prayer, five million, much of it from public subscriptions. The National Monument, by the designer of the Iwo Jima Memorial, nearly one million. The National Museum, another million. The Indoor Stadium Negara, to hold ten thousand people and now completed, a million and a half—and brother to the two-million, open Merdeka Stadium, which holds thirty thousand.

These are only a few of the major projects. Some people regard them as wild extravagance, waste of money in a country emerging from semi-feudalism, where so much still needs to be done. But it must be remembered that almost no major building has appeared in K.L. since the famous Railway Station was completed about sixty years ago, and show buildings are more than glass and steel; they are symbols of independence, of what was ignored under colonialism, of that all-important necessity in Asia—Face.

But much more impressive than the built and building showpieces in K.L. is Petaling Jaya, the city's outer-suburb satellite town, which is unique in Southeast Asia.

During the early years of the Communist civil war, its site was an old rubber-estate and tin-mining area which was used to resettle Chinese squatters and segregate them from the Communist guerrillas. Today you drive seven miles from K.L. on a four-lane, speed highway to a planned town of fifty thousand people who live in their own pleasant homes, have their own government offices, banks, town hall, market, and cinemas in a seventeen-acre commercial center, and their own industrial area of six hundred acres where more than one hundred modern factories, and another hundred building, manufacture products which range from soap and sulphuric acid to biscuits and furniture, and assemble air-conditioning plants, tractors, cars, trucks, and machinery.

To encourage factory development at Petaling Jaya, the Government grants "pioneer status" to many industries. A company which invests less than one hundred thousand Malayan dollars is tax free for two years, but the tax concession stretches to five years for a factory with more capital involved. Pioneer status has attracted both local and foreign firms— some of them from Singapore to the more politically stable environment of the Federation.

Petaling Jaya, racially, is K.L. in microcosm. All the people of K.L., of Malaya, are represented, and all their places of worship, too. Among the European-style buildings, some like English council flats, are Chinese and Indian temples, a Moslem mosque, and Protestant and Roman Catholic churches. You even discover the curving yellow tile roof of a Siamese temple, built by the Governments of Siam and Malaya at a cost of more than one hundred thousand dollars.

Petaling Jaya is unique not because there is anything distinctive about its temples, factories, or homes, or that it is a planned satellite town, but because less than a generation ago, even if it had been suggested as an idea, a vague possibility, for the dim future, Petaling Jaya would still have been regarded as fantasy.

Petaling Jaya is more significant than a new industrial town carved from a rubber estate and old tin-mine workings soon to be turned into decorative lakes. It is more portentous than new royal palaces and stadiums and driveways. Petaling Jaya, if you read its real meaning, is the beginning of the new Malaya, the new Malaysia, where people, free from colonial rule, are thinking, deciding, and doing for themselves.

13

The Federation of Malaya has been a politically stable independent country since Merdeka, or Independence Day, August 31, 1957. It is a prosperous and booming society for some; it provides little more than a semi-feudalistic existence for the many. Its social and industrial revolution is only just beginning. It is the fourteenth century desperately trying to catch up. So don't be too diverted by the tall buildings of K.L. or the spreading factories of Petaling Jaya. K.L. is not Malaya.

Malaya, which is much closer geographically to Peking than to Sydney, is a thin peninsula four hundred and fifty miles long by two hundred miles at its widest, between the Indian Ocean and the South China Sea. It is a small area about the size of England or Greece or North Carolina—so small that it would fit nearly twenty times into Australia's largest state, Western Australia, and five times into America's largest, Texas.

Four fifths of this country between the Thailand border in the north and Singapore Island in the south is under jungle, including all its central mountain backbone, which lifts to seven thousand feet, yet Malaya supports seven million people, only four million less than Australia, and its population is growing rapidly. Half its people are Malays, about thirty-eight per cent are Chinese, eleven per cent are Indian, and the rest are Eurasians, Europeans, and other races.

About ninety per cent of the Malays are poor peasants and fishermen living in kampongs, often without the simplest amenities, and above the peasant mass are the wealthy Sultan families and a thin aristocracy, a minute middle class, and a servant and small-clerk class.

The Chinese are the urban dwellers of Malaya. Many of them are poor—as poor as the great mass of the Malays. A few are extremely rich—the rubber-tin-trade-land millionaires. But at least twenty to thirty per cent of the Chinese are far better off than most of their own race in the Federation, and most of the Malays. It is these Chinese, with a few Malays, Indians, and Eurasians, who form the real middle class of Malaya.

This in itself is the source of the country's greatest problem. Singapore is a small city-state with an overwhelming Chinese majority. Malaya is a country with not one but two racial majorities—the Malays and the Chinese.

The Malays distrust or fear the Chinese because there are so many of them, because of their wealth and commercial power, and because of their potential political power. The Malays also distrust or fear them because across their southern border is Chinese Singapore. This is why, when Malaya became independent, Singapore was deliberately excluded from the Federation.

The Islamic Malays, who have already survived a Communist civil war designed to turn their country into a satellite of Peking, have every reason to be anti-Communist—not non-Communist like Singapore—so that it is not by chance that wherever Chinese groups are concentrated anywhere in Southeast Asia today, local races are at worst fearful, at best suspicious or uneasy.

The Federation of Malaya is a constitutional monarchy, but a monarchy in which the King is a Sultan elected by his fellow Sultans, or Conference of Rulers, for five years, and a Sultan-

King who can be deposed by these Rulers if he misbehaves himself or becomes unable to rule.

The present King, or Yang di-Pertuan Agong, as he is known in Malaya, is Sir Syed Putra ibni Al-Marhum Syed Hassan Jamalullail, Raja of Perlis, the most northerly and smallest state of the Federation, on the Thailand border. The Agong, as the King is generally called, has been Malaya's ruler since January 4, 1960, but he is a paper ruler, a King only in a constitutional sense, since the real control of the country is in the elected Government of the Prime Minister, Tunku Abdul Rahman.

The Agong, who is of mixed Arab-Malay ancestry, is large, fat, boyish-faced, and only forty-two. He normally wears Western clothes, but on state occasions appears in the splendid coats and sarongs of the royal Malays.

When he was installed as ruler, to the music of flutes and the drums of the Court Orchestra, he dressed in black with gold thread and wore the Tengkolok di-Raja, or Royal Headwear, decorated with its crescent and star of platinum and sixty-six diamonds. He was attended by his Regalia Bearers, in black-and-magenta coats, carrying the silver-and-gold Mace of the Universe, the silver Mace of Religion, the silver Orb, and the State Swords and Kris, and by the Bearers of the twenty Royal Yellow Umbrellas and the twenty Plumed Lances.

The Agong's wife, Raja Permaisuri Agong, wears on state occasions the Gendik, or Tiara, of platinum and diamonds which can be broken to form a locket and two bracelets, and the diamond-studded Kalong, or Necklace, which can be separated into earrings, brooches, and a choker.

The Royal Standard is yellow and carries the arms of the Federation—two tigers supporting a shield—the crest is an eleven-pointed star representing the eleven states of the Federation and the Islamic crescent, and the motto changes from the resounding Malay *Bersekutu Bertambah Muter* into Unity Is Strength—a translation which always gives me a let-down feeling. The Royal Standard is quite unlike the Federation's flag, which resembles the American Stars and Stripes and has eleven red and white bars and the yellow star and crescent on a blue ground.

The Agong, who is not noted for his intellectual interests, has two major passions, films and golf. In his own projection room at the Istana Negara, he sees every film which comes to Malaya, including some which the public does not see because of censorship. But when he is not watching films or tending his orchids, he plays golf—left-handed and with a handicap of eighteen. On the handicap board at the Selangor Golf Club the King takes his place simply as "H. M. Agong—18."

Golf in the Federation and in Singapore among heads of state, politicians, top government servants, and others is hardly a game. It has become both a symbol of status and a public joke. If you don't play golf, you're out, politically and socially. It opens the doors of the Istana Negara in K.L. or the Prime Minister's office in Singapore. It is not uncommon to find the Agong and the Prime Ministers of Malaya and Singapore putting on the same green, so that the golf course has become a second Cabinet room. There is something almost frenetic in the way these heads of state attack their golf. They bet hundreds of dollars a game. They bet on a slice, a pull, a putt, a drive. The Agong once won three hundred and sixty balls in a weekend, which was not a cheap outing, with balls at one dollar and sixty cents each.

Golf is so important that the senior diplomat who does not play or who plays indifferently might as well ask for a transfer. A low handicap is a great advantage in a country where everyone talks so freely that security in any form must be almost impossible to maintain. As one low-handicap diplomat observed, "How do you think we get our information?"

The outstanding personality of Malaya is not the golf-playing Agong, but my host on a mild K.L. evening only a few hours after arriving in the capital. His full title and name is Tunku Abdul Rahman Putra Al-haj ibni Al-marhum Sultan Abdul Hamid Halim Shah, but he is known to the world as Tunku Abdul Rahman, and in Malaya as just the Tunku—the Prince.

The Prime Minister of Malaya lives in the old Residency, a bungalow on Federal Hill above K.L. It is an undistinguished white building with wide tiled verandas, and its large rooms are tight with dull Victorian furniture, valuable pieces and junk. The house is a decorator's nightmare, but it has something so many decorators can never achieve—an atmosphere of lived-in warmth, the marks of playing children on worn sofas, the feeling that human beings don't just perch like suspicious birds, but live here. The house was once a British official residence, and some of its contents are from that time, but its muddle and order, its corners and hallways of understanding, its touches of taste and beauty, reflect with uncanny accuracy the character of its present occupant.

The bronze bust in the hall, under the glassy scrutiny of a stuffed tiger's head, wore glassless spectacles and a Malay songkok. The glasses, I'm sure, were the Tunku's joke. The cap was the Tunku's, as he had turned his own sculpted bust into a hat stand. In the reception room, where the walls seemed to sag inward under the weight of indifferent Western paintings, a glass case shimmered with the gold, silver, and brass scabbards and polished wood hilts of a wonderful collection of ceremonial and fighting Malay kris. On a side table, below a framed Chinese scroll, black on scarlet, was a row of books, including a biography of India's Prime Minister, Pandit Nehru, and a pictorial volume on Australia, plus a stuffed possum-like creature, running swiftly on an artificial branch, afflicted with permanent mange.

Glimpses of other rooms: full-length paintings of sultan ancestors, Royal Academy portraits as stiff as old wax. Gilt Victorian mirrors. Persian carpets and brocaded sofas. Sporting guns on walls. A doll tossed in a corner, one leg in the air.

The bright eyes of a little girl, probably the Tunku's adopted daughter, watching the coattails of yet another reception from a half-opened door.

In the big dining room were Ming and Ch'ing plates, five faultless pieces of blue trade porcelain, Chinese scrolls, plaques, including one of the Indian poet Rabindranath Tagore. There were silver bowls and cups in cabinets, a Japanese Samurai figure in sixteenth-century gold and crimson, a collection of exquisitely dressed dolls, some Chinese, some Malay, some Indonesian, all smiling stiffly behind glass like social ladies at a reception.

And in an alcove made by an ancient carved wood screen was a Chinese brush painting of a tiger, and a large mournful autographed photograph of the British Prime Minister, Mr. Macmillan. Studying this picture I could not help speculating whether the Tunku was responsible for its sly juxtaposition.

Tunku Abdul Rahman is one of those ugly-attractive men. He is short, with thin hair beginning to grey, a woman's mouth, a mustache that is little more than a smudge of greying stubble, and extremely alert humorous eyes behind thick horn spectacles.

He is darker than the average Malay, due to his mixed ancestry, and looks more Indian, more Hindu. As a child he was known by his family as "Little Dark Boy," and resented it, just as the Prime Minister of Singapore, Lee Kuan Yew, resented being called "Little White Boy." The Tunku is conscious of his darker pigment and doesn't like cartoons of himself where the artist has used a slight wash shading to indicate his darker skin. This sensitivity is difficult to understand in a many-race society where the only skin color which to me looks bleached, unpleasant, and completely alien is the European. Yet the fairer skin is prized among the Malays, who regard a fair girl as more beautiful. The darker Malay girls suffer by comparison. They are only *Hitam manas*—black but sweet.

The Tunku this night wore a dark blue suit, which is almost a night uniform in Malaya, a blue shirt, a Cambridge University tie, and black patent-leather shoes, and as he moved among his guests telling stories, listening with head characteristically twisted to one side, laughing through his curling cigarette smoke, he reminded me of one of those smaller socially adjusted breed of dogs who the moment they enter a room have the gentlemen bending to pat them and the ladies stroking their ears.

Les Hoffman, editor in chief of the *Straits Times*, presented me.

"Welcome to Malaya," the Tunku said, shaking hands. "We were just talking about the Malays and what an easy tolerant people they are." He held up his glass. "Here I am a good Muslim, and yet I'm drinking brandy and soda."

Even the very good Muslims present laughed, and seemed to mean it.

Some fires lose their heat up the chimney, but the Tunku's warmth touches everyone in his presence. You feel it and know that others feel it. It is an amalgam of simplicity, natural courtesy, a sly tongue, and deeply comprehending eyes, which look at the frailties of others and see their own reflected.

The Tunku's frankness intrigued me, for alcohol and Islam are normally not companions, at least in such a public place as a Muslim Prime Minister's reception room. But he is Western-educated, a Prince, and only the fanatical would forbid him his favorite brandy.

A friend of the Tunku, while dining at one of K.L's hotels, saw the Prime Minister at a far table and sent across a special bottle of wine with his compliments. Later he joined the Tunku, who thanked him and said, "I'm drinking coffee. I'm sure you would like some." The Tunku poured from the coffeepot and handed him a cup. The man swallowed a mouthful and nearly choked. The coffee was straight rum.

Again and again I heard from people who know the Tunku well, who have observed him for years, the same explanation of his success as a man and as a leader.

"He is not clever, but he is completely sincere."

He doesn't pretend. It's as simple as that. He never poses. He behaves with the simplicity of a very ordinary man whose charm has never been learned or studied. It is an asset built in from birth. His mother had this charm, and he has inherited it.

One of the best analyses of the Tunku came from one of his friends: "It's true what people say. He is not smart. There is nothing intellectual or clever about him. He doesn't know the meaning of the words. Beside a man like Lee Kuan Yew, he is educationally an infant, though Kuan Yew is often overrated for his brilliance. The Tunku has only what I would call a fair average brain, and his I.Q. would probably shock you. But he has other attributes. He is extremely shrewd—the shrewdness you find among peasant Malays. He is a good judge of character, is difficult to fool, and he has a political sixth sense which helps him a lot and keeps him out of trouble. This is quite intuitive. He seems to be able to smell the right thing to do, and when he makes a mistake—and he has made many—some kindly Malay hantu watching over him steps in and gets him out of the mess. When he first entered politics, he said and did some silly things. He once publicly burned newspapers which criticized him, which wasn't a good start for a politician. I've heard him make the most foolish and naïve political statements and then watched the words swing later to his own advantage. But don't forget that this is Asia, and the Tunku is deeply, intuitively Asian. When I use the words foolish and naïve I'm thinking with my Western brain. To Asians the Tunku's words often have a different meaning. This is when the Asian side of my brain understands."

But all agree upon one thing about the Tunku: his understanding of people, his sympathy for human weakness, his genuine liking for that most unlovable creature, the human being. As he once remarked: "If anyone says I have nothing up here [he tapped his head] I don't worry. But if anyone says I have nothing here [he tapped his heart] I am damned annoyed." A statement like that could be construed as propaganda, a politician's trick. In a way it is, for the Tunku is a politician. But it is also genuine.

Tunku Abdul Rahman prefers Malay food during the day and Chinese food after dark, but this night on Federal Hill he ate sate, and we all joined him round the long dining-room table.

For an old hand, sate is one of the delights of a return to Malaya. There used to be a sate man, a Chinese, who made so much money selling it to tourists near Raffles Hotel in Singapore that he was able to retire to his village in China and live well—until the Red Chinese took over. But the sate prepared by the Tunku's chef—or his wife, who does much of the Residency cooking—was the most delicious I have ever tasted.

Sate is grilled beef, mutton, or chicken served on a thin stick and eaten with a hot sauce. But it is the preparation of the meat and the sauce which determines whether the sate is good or a work of art. Sate à la Tunku was beef rubbed with saffron, white gintang, and sugar. The sauce was a mixture of oil, chili, saffron, powdered nuts, pulped onion, butter, a little water and milk, and, believe it or not, a pinch of starch as a thickener.

The sate arrived like smoking lances, and the smell of grilled meat and hot spices filled the room. The Malay art of eating the skewered meat, as the Tunku demonstrated to the uninitiated, was to dip into the sauce, place the skewer sideways in the mouth, grip, tug, and slide the meat off in one delicious sweep. The only problem is that occasionally a piece of meat sticks and you're left, struggling, like an impaled headhunter.

Sate is an insidious dish, for one lance invites another and another until your plate is heaped with wooden skewers. But after slices of coconut meat, which cools and cleans the palate, I sat at the end of the dining room, beside the glass case filled with dolls, and talked to the Tunku, or, more accurately, he talked and I slipped in a question here and there.

His accent is strongly Malay and at times he talks so quickly that he runs words together and is a little hard to follow. He talked of many things—the place of the Chinese in Malaya and Chinese education, British bases, Malay as a national language, the urgency for all races in Malaya, and in Singapore, to feel that they are Malayans. He talked, too, of the urgency of establishing Greater Malaysia.

During a rare pause I was able to ask him whether it was true that he was never guarded.

He looked genuinely surprised. "Guarded—never."

He lit yet another cigarette, and the heavy gold ring he wears flickered in the match light.

"I do not have a guard—here or when I move about. Why should I? There is no need for a man with a gun to protect me. I am an ordinary citizen—nothing more."

"In Singapore," I reminded him, "Lee Kuan Yew's home is guarded day and night and he has a gunman near him all the time."

The Tunku nodded. "I know—and even on the golf course."

I repeated the story I had heard that at Merdeka Stadium in K.L. a foreign visitor had said: "You mean to tell me you have nobody to protect you—no personal bodyguard," and the Tunku had spread his arms to embrace the packed Stadium and replied, "I've got thirty thousand."

"It is true," the Tunku said, simply.

Tunku Abdul Rahman, who is sixty, was the seventh son of His Highness Abdul Hamid Halim Shah, Sultan of Kedah, and a child of the Sultan's sixth of eight wives, who had forty-five children. The Tunku's mother was half Burmese, half Siamese, the daughter of Luang Nara, a chief of one of the Siamese Shan states, and a woman of great warmth and charity and the Sultan's favorite wife.

The Tunku was born at Alor Star, Kedah, in northwest Malaya, and was brought up in his father's palace at a time when servants dropped to their knees and averted their eyes before the members of the royal family. The young Prince was neither physically strong nor scholastically bright. He went to school in Bangkok, where an elder brother was a captain in the Siamese Army, then in Alor Star and Penang, and he just managed, after tutoring in England, to enter Cambridge University, where his chief interests were fast horses, fast cars, and fast women. He was an above-average undergraduate.

He still managed, against stiff competition from these distractions, to leave Cambridge with his bachelor's degree, but after a visit home to Kedah he was sent back to study law. Then began one of the most often interrupted and longest law courses in academic history, all intermingled with passionate love affairs, marriages, work in the civil service in Kedah, and the Japanese occupation of Malaya. The Tunku was around thirty when he began to study law. He was forty-five when he finally graduated as a barrister, being admitted to the Inner Temple in London in 1948.

While moving between Malaya and England as a mendicant student, he fell in love with an English girl but was not allowed to marry her because she was a Christian. Instead, he married a Siamese-Chinese girl, who died, leaving him with a son and a daughter. He then married the forbidden English girl, a marriage which ended in divorce, and finally married his present wife, To'Puan Sharifah Rodziah binti Syed Alwi, daughter of a Kedah civil servant of Malay-Arabic blood and granddaughter of a Malay judge.

This last marriage, in 1939, was childless, but the Tunku's love of children is so deep that he picks up strays, as some people collect lost cats, and either adopts them or looks after them. Mariam, his adopted daughter of ten, he found in a welfare home in Johore after he had been refused permission to adopt a deserted Chinese baby, rescued from the jungle, and believed to be the daughter of a Communist terrorist. He was refused permission because the parents might one day claim the child. Sulaiman, his adopted son of five, he and his wife found in another home in K.L.

During one of his trips in Malaya he met an orphan boy who showed intellectual ability far beyond his years.

"Put him on the plane," he told his secretary, "I'm taking him home."

There are others he cares for. There are always others. Nobody has even counted the number of children he has befriended. Perhaps the Tunku doesn't know himself, for at times he is forgetful and at others quite naïve. He could never learn his school lessons properly, but he has always possessed something much more valuable—compassion.

Many stories are told of his vagueness. At a big party in London he broke off a conversation with a Foreign Office official to greet another guest. He brought the man across and introduced him.

"This is an old friend of mine," he told the F.O. man. Then he turned to the guest and asked, "What's your name?"

The Tunku was once talking to the New Zealand Commissioner, a Maori of aristocratic blood, and referred to the "natives" of Borneo.

"I'm a native, too," the High Commissioner said.

The Tunku smiled, but clearly did not understand what the distinguished New Zealander meant.

One of the most dramatic episodes in the Tunku's life was at the start of the Pacific war, when the Japanese had landed in northern Malaya and were advancing on his home state of Kedah. The Tunku heard that the British were preparing to evacuate and intended to take his Sultan father to Penang and out of the country. The Tunku intercepted the convoy in which the Sultan was traveling and kidnapped him. He did this—and the reason is revealing—because he believed his father's right place was with his own people in a time of national emergency.

The Japanese occupation deeply influenced the Tunku, as it did all Malaya. The invading Japanese brought a new product with them, nationalism, and the Indonesian struggle later against the Dutch helped fan national ambitions. The Tunku emerged from the war years a more serious man, interested in politics, and strongly anti-Communist as the Chinese Communist guerrillas came out of the jungle at the Japanese surrender and threatened to take over his beloved Kedah, then part of the northern Malay States which the Japanese had handed to Siam during the war.

Early in the 1950's the Tunku became president of the Malay political party U.M.N.O., the United Malay National Organization, which had adopted as its slogan *"Merdeka."* This was not original, because the Indonesians had used this Sanskrit word meaning independence or freedom for nearly fifty years as a political rallying call against Dutch rule. Later the Malayan Chinese Association and the Malayan Indian Congress joined U.M.N.O. to become the Alliance party and Government when the Federation of Malaya became an independent country.

The early fifties were busy years for the Tunku. He led the Alliance and became Chief Minister of Malaya after the first federal elections in 1955. He began to preach the unity of all races in Malaya, a platform which horrified the more fanatical Malays. And he was co-respondent in a divorce suit which had minor social significance in Malaya, where under Islamic law a man is allowed four wives anyway.

He also played a leading part in the official attempt to end the Communist civil war—after it had been going for seven years—by the declaration of an amnesty to the Communist forces in the jungle and a meeting with the leader of the Malayan Communist party, Chin Peng, who was then worth thirty thousand pounds if captured alive. The Tunku, the Chief Minister of Singapore, David Marshall, and others met Chin Peng on December 27-28, 1955, in a barbed-wired schoolhouse at Baling in Kedah after the dapper and outstanding Communist leader, who had been Secretary-General of the Malayan Communist party since the age of twenty-six in 1947, had walked across the border from Siam and had been brought to Baling under escort for the two-day meeting.

The talks were fruitless. Chin Peng, after trying for seven years to turn Malaya into a Communist satellite, was prepared to lay down his arms only if the Malayan Communist party was allowed to continue to operate in Malaya—and everyone knew what that would mean with a dedicated man like Chin Peng still directing its activities. The civil war went on, for another five years.

But if Comrade Chin Peng did nothing else, he made certain that when the Federation received its independence on August 31, 1957, and the Tunku became the country's first Prime Minister, the official policy of his Government would be strongly anti-Communist and the Communist party would continue to be illegal.

Midnight August 30, 1957, when the British flag came down in K.L. and the new striped flag of the Federation was raised, was an emotional moment for Tunku Abdul Rahman. He was a small sickly boy when his father, the Sultan of Kedah, had signed a treaty with Britain which gave protection to his state from Siam, whose King had been overlord of Kedah since early in the nineteenth century. He was fifty-four when not only Kedah but all Malaya was given its independence by Britain. And Merdeka Day, August 31, 1957, was more than one hundred and seventy years since the trading port of Penang, on Malaya's west coast, had been ceded to Britain by his own Sultan great-great-great-grandfather. It was not surprising, as those flags changed places, that the crowds on Merdeka night shouted for "*Bapa Merdeka*"—Father of Freedom.

14

Down a slope from the Prime Minister's office, on a hill above the muddy Gombak, is a long low air-conditioned building, the glare from its white paint and glass softened with panels of grey and black.

In this building is the Operations Room, sometimes called the "Red Book Room." It is big enough for a banquet, ornate enough for a millionaire's office in a film extravaganza.

There are polished desks, soft chairs upholstered in scarlet and grey, wall panels which slide and unfold to disclose flagged maps, illustrated charts, multi-colored graphs to delight the rectangular eyes of a chartered accountant. There are projectors which roll silently forward, and screens and tape recorders and telephones and colored lights. And the Red Books, huge ledger-like tomes, are along one side, and black words on the far wall, *Pembangunan Luar Bandar*, mean Rural Development.

This room would appeal to Winston Churchill, because it is in many ways a replica of the actual war room from which the British Army and Administration fought its twelve years' war in Malaya against Comrade Chin Peng and his terrorists.

The Communist civil war is over. Chin Peng and the few

hundred remnants of his guerrilla army have retreated to jungle camps among the mountains of the Siam-Malaya border. Defeated, yes, but still a nucleus, intact, organized, and deadly, if the revolutionary opportunity comes again, as it easily could.

In K.L. a war room is no longer needed, but its idea has been put to peaceful use by the Tunku's Government through its Ministry of Rural Development.

The Operations Room today is the Government's link with the fourteenth century, between officials in K.L. and the Ra'ayat, the People, the mass peasantry of Malaya in their jungle-shadowed villages and kampongs.

The Red Books are the heart of the Operations Room. They contain master information on every district and every district's needs, and are invaluable for reference and as a source for the briefing and interrogation of officials by the Minister for Rural Development and his top administrators.

The Books record the five-year plans, one completed and one running, to open new land, settle the landless, introduce new crops, build roads, bridges, and water supplies, improve hygiene and health services, crash through mass illiteracy, and encourage that almost unknown commodity, democracy, or perhaps an Asian variant of it, in a society almost akin to Agincourt's.

I am always a little wary of Operations Rooms, particularly if they are show places like the one in K.L. Perhaps that is old newspaper training. I never feel certain that a chart which occupies most of a wall or a statistical map decorated with colored flags tells the real story of what is happening a couple of hundred miles away in some remote, dirty, sub-standard village. But that the Red Books exist and that they are the symbols of an intelligent attempt to help the peasantry is in itself significant and encouraging.

For Malaya, the work these Red Books represent and record is more important than the country's industrialization, much more important than those glass boxes and palaces and stadiums rising and built in K.L., since the future of Malaya, of Malaysia, will not be decided among the electric signs of the capital but under kampong thatch. If the Ra'ayat, the peasants, can get land, power, clean water, if their miserable incomes can be raised, there is hope. But if the Red Book plans are not successful, then Malaya will be in trouble from within, for the time has long gone when a peasantry asked no questions and did what it was told. There would have been no Communist China today if that country had not been a landless peasant society drained by absentee landlords, corrupt officials, and an inept government which did not deserve to survive.

Much more reassuring than the efficiently kept and attractively presented Red Books, and the elegance of the Operations Room, is the Minister in charge, who is also Deputy Prime Minister and Minister for Defense. This is Tun Abdul Razak bin Hussain, the Tunku's personal friend.

If the British had remained in Malaya, this man may have been allowed to reach a relatively minor post in the government service—perhaps a magistrate or something like that. Yet the Tun, as he is called, is a future Prime Minister, the logical successor to Tunku Adbul Rahman, and the man who before long will probably lead the new Federation of Greater Malaysia.

Tun Abdul Razak, a product of the new Malaya, is outstanding as an administrator and is an impressive answer to the old British-Chinese myth, which in turn was probably inherited from the Portuguese and the Dutch, that the Malays are a feckless people.

It used to be said, in the days not long ago, when the Malays had no say in the real government of their country or of its captured trade, that one Chinese would start his own business, two would compete bitterly for that trade, and three would form a secret society; that one Malay would go to sleep under a tree, two would sit down to gossip and if they saw a third pass would wonder why he was out in the sun and ask him to join them; that one Englishman would drink a whisky-and-soda, two would play tennis, and three would look for somebody to divide and rule.

Only an English or Chinese businessman could have invented that old story or its many variants, just as only a rare and perceptive observer—a famous British official of Malaya's past like Sir Hugh Clifford, or a highly creative writer like Henri Fauconnier—could have recognized the Malays as an energetic, determined, sensitive people with unlimited potential.

Tun Abdul Razak—the Tun is a modern revival of an ancient Malay title, and is a corruption of the word "Tuan," meaning "master"—is small and dapper, with regular features, honey-colored skin, well-brushed thinning hair, and friendly eyes.

At the Ministry for Rural Development he offered cigarettes with slender manicured hands and relaxed and laughed when I told him that every word I had heard about him was so much in his favor that he must have some gruesome weaknesses and habits I would like to hear about.

The Tun is only forty-one and is already more important in many respects than the Prime Minister. The Tunku is the front man, the traveling salesman, at times even the circus and the clown, but above all a man with deep understanding of the people he leads. But Tun Abdul Razak, although he lacks the Tunku's spreading warmth, is the brains, the organizer, the manager. He is a man of patience and skill, the planner who thinks a lot and talks little, the clever logical man with a kind of in-built control.

He was born near Pekan, on the coast of Pahang, Malaya's most central state, facing the South China Sea, where the waves come unbroken for more than a thousand miles from the Philippines. He is an aristocrat of Pahang, one of the four major hereditary chiefs of the state, and is the eleventh generation of his family to hold the title Orang Kaya Indra Shahvandar.

The Tun was nineteen when the Japanese invaded Malaya. He joined Wataniah, the Malay Resistance Movement, organized by the secret British Force 136 from India, and finished the war in the jungle a captain in command of a guerrilla company.

He had early shown brilliance as a student, and after the

Pacific war a scholarship enabled him to study law in England, at Lincoln's Inn. He passed his law examinations in only eighteen months and was called to the Bar in 1950. England and law were also the beginning of his friendship with Tunku Abdul Rahman, a close relationship based on mutual respect and liking despite twenty years' difference in age and widely divergent personalities and intellectual ability. They came together when the Tunku, at forty-five, was still studying for his finals and when Abdul Razak, at twenty-five, was just beginning law. The young man almost acted as a tutor to the Tunku. He helped him with his work, even read to him, and in their spare time they studied English politics, particularly Labour politics. They both strongly supported the British Labour party, although, ironically, the British Government which gave Malaya its independence was Conservative.

The Tun has played the part of the king-maker. He encouraged the Tunku, who had been a playboy in his time, to take a serious interest in politics. He originally recommended and supported him for president of the United Malays National Organization—an act which led the Tunku to the Prime Ministership.

Between these two men, as there was between Mahatma Gandhi and Jawaharlal Nehru, is almost a father-son relationship, which has lasted unbroken for fifteen years and has been of great benefit to Malaya. Now Tunku Abdul Rahman is sixty and has several times mentioned retirement to friends, so that it may not be long before the son succeeds and the king-maker becomes king.

Only a few years ago the Pantai Valley outside K.L. was jungle and old tortured rubber. Today its low hills have been sliced and leveled, its cool little stream, the Sungei Anak Ayer Batu—Ayer Batu in Malay means "ice"—has been halted to form a lake, and its hundreds of acres of jungle and rubber have become mown-grass billiard-table green.

Here in the Pantai, which almost symbolically means a beach

or a shore, a starting place, is one of the world's newest centers of learning—the low white buildings of the University of Malaya, with covered ways supported by pale-blue pillars and, wherever you look, subtle touches and splashes of saffron and red, gold and lime, blue and grey on concrete and shutters and posts.

From the top of the New Malay Language Institute next door, with its decorative Malay roof like an upturned boat flickering in the morning sun, the planned University is as fresh and sparkling as a new idea.

The University of Malaya is international in its best sense, for here more than a thousand students—Malay, Chinese, Indian, Ceylonese, Eurasian, and others—study with English, Australian, New Zealand, Dutch, American, Canadian, Chinese, Malay, and Egyptian professors and lecturers in faculties built or equipped at a cost of ten million dollars by Malaya, with major help from England, the United States, Australia, New Zealand, and Canada.

It was in one of these new buildings, after trailing a finger in the infant lake and wandering in the dappled sunlight of the faculty walks, that I found yet another example of the resurrection of the Malays—the good-for-nothing Malays.

"You must see Aziz," a friend in Singapore had said. "One of the best brains in the country."

The man who came round his desk to shake hands was medium height, with good shoulders and strong arms. His pointed beard, blacker than the inside of a cupboard, accentuated his fine regular features, the fairness of his skin, and black penetrating eyes which seemed to have a separate existence from his body. He was more than extremely handsome. He had some dramatic quality about him, though not in the least theatrical, so that merely by being in his presence you felt more alive. He was dressed in grey slacks, a white shirt without a tie, and old shoes. He made you think of Inca priests.

This was Ungku Abdul Aziz, Professor of Economics at the

University of Malaya, and the first professor in any subject in the history of his race.

The Professor is also a Malay Prince, because Ungku is not a name but a title. A Tunku, like the Prime Minister, is a Prince in the direct line from a Malay Sultan, but an Ungku is a minor Prince. Abdul Aziz is a Prince of the royal house of the State of Johore. The present Sultan's mother is his aunt.

"I have Turkish blood mixed with Malay. My wife [a journalist and one of the beauties of Malaya] has Arab and Malay. We have one daughter who speaks Mandarin."

He spoke in clipped almost English English flavored with only a faint accent of southern Asia.

"We're a thoroughly mixed-up lot in these parts. But that isn't surprising. Every race has been through here at some time to mix with the people of this total area. The Romans and the Greeks, for this was the Golden Chersonese, and long before that, early people from southern China, India, Thailand, Indochina, and in more recent times Arabs, Portuguese, Dutch, English, and others. The top families of Malaya have many blood mixtures. They could afford it, because a foreign wife, although she might have been fashionable, was generally expensive."

Ungku Abdul Aziz, who is bilingual in English and Malay, speaks fluent Japanese and above-average French. He would make an impressive diplomat, but has refused foreign appointments in his country's service because absence from his own soil for long is to him unendurable. He has concentrated instead on university life and teaching, and to fit him for this he has lived among rice farmers, among rubber tappers, and with Malay and Chinese fishermen. He knows how to plant paddy, how to tap and cure rubber, how to handle a boat and pull and mend nets.

"How can I possibly understand my own people unless I know them and their problems?" the Prince asked. "How can I sit in a university chair unless I understand the economics of a kampong or a fishing village? This is why I insist that my students use all their spare time living and working on plantations, in rice areas, in mines, in fishing ports, in factories. Those places are where my students do their real study toward their economic degrees. Knowledge and thinking is not in dull lectures. It is people, where they live, what they do."

We talked about Malaya and change, and about rural development. He agreed that the Red Books had started a new method of administration, a centralized system of departmental control, discussion, and explanation, but he still thought, while admitting the value of the work already completed, that the Red Books were a luxury.

"You can't measure if the real things are happening. And the real things today are not to move charts, but people's minds, not to draw graphs on walls, but to fill people's bellies. Ninety per cent of the Malays live in the rural areas. Seventy-five per cent of all Chinese live in the towns. There are no hospitals in the rural areas, no secondary schools, yet the great wealth of the Federation comes from the land. Roads, water supplies—physical things like that—are being built and are important, but the critical item for the peasants is their income—and peasant income is not rising. If incomes are not increased, peasant dissatisfaction will lead the people to the fanatical Islamic groups, whose thinking is dangerously narrow, or to the Communists."

And why were the peasants not getting a better return for their labor?

He stroked his beard with one finger as he gazed out the window.

"Partly historical, partly the Chinese. The productivity of our land is pathetically low, although this problem is being tackled with some success. We are many years behind in research because we have concentrated far too much on the growing of rubber. We inherited these weaknesses from the British. The other problem is that markets are monopolistic and are tied up by the urban Chinese. It is often said that the economy of Malaya is controlled by the Chinese, but that is far too simple. The real truth, although you don't hear this mentioned often, is that the Chinese are no more powerful economically than the major European business houses will allow them to be. A dozen British, European, import-export companies really dominate this economy, so that Chinese economic power is held largely by courtesy. But it is the Chinese middleman who buys and distributes what other people, particularly the Malays, produce."

He hit the desk. "What would happen if the rice grown by half a million Malays was sold, not through the Chinese, but by a Government marketing organization? The Chinese would be put out of business. What would happen to the country's two thousand-odd Chinese rubber dealers, who buy and sell to the export houses and handle about one third of our national income, if we set up a rubber-marketing board? The Chinese monopoly would disappear overnight."

As the Malay was the producing peasant and the Chinese the buying and distributing capitalist, had the low-income Malay to become a capitalist to survive?

The Prince laughed. "We're generations too late for that. There is no point in producing Malay capitalists. The Chinese rice and rubber barons, who are in on the ground floor and who control the markets, would merely use the Malays, as some of them are doing. Take my own case. If I, as an economist, wished to join a number of companies in Malaya it would not cost me a penny. The shares would be presented to me and my present income would be five to ten times higher than it is. But I would lose my independence to my Chinese or foreign owner. Many have taken this easy way out—some in high places. This is a bad system and I am against it. I am more interested in my university work than I am in a large income. I am more interested in speaking out than shutting my mouth.

"The only way is to give all a fairer share of what Malaya produces, and this could be done, not by trying to create

Malay capitalists, but by fostering co-operative or marketing boards and by introducing public auctions for some commodities. In this way you would make it possible for all races to compete equally and would eliminate the present racial friction between the have and the have-not groups, which is a direct result of Malay poverty, Chinese monopoly and wealth, and foreign control."

The kampong is, as the Prince and others know, the key, and the political key, to the future of Malaya—the Malay kampong, which the visitor to Malaya seldom sees, where the peasant can afford less than one third of a Malayan dollar a day for food, where malnourishment is serious, where infant mortality is high, and where disease, especially malaria, reduces the vitality of the people.

It is the kampong which needs aid, especially foreign aid, if the life of the peasantry is to be made more tolerable and the infant and still only vaguely understood democracy of Malaya is to grow. Colombo and other aid which never reaches the peasant has little place in a society where a five-per-cent increase in the present standard of living of the Ra'ayat would mean a revolutionary improvement in peasant life.

Professor Aziz has lived and worked among the farmers and fishermen of his country to become better equipped as a teacher, as an economist. But his time among them, including much of one year moving round fishing villages alone, was not spent in detached academic study, but in getting to know his own people intimately and making many close personal friendships.

"Professionally I'm an economist, a product of this small Malayan world and its university. Although I have traveled and lectured in many countries, I have no foreign degrees. Personally I'm obsessed with people and the things people create. I'm never bored so long as there is evidence of people around. To me a beautifully made fishing net or basket is just as important as a fine painting or a well-written book. I collect

Picasso prints, but only because there is something in that man's work which speaks to me. I read Lawrence Durrell or Chekov because they too are obsessed with people, with mood, with color. I like listening to Indian drums, which make for me the most beautiful music in the world—music which comes traditionally from the lowest classes in India, so that in a halting drum beat you hear a people speaking. I am a passionate lover of Negro jazz, not just because of its wonderful human virtuosity, but because it is the kind of music a man must try to like if he is to keep in touch with young people, as I must as a teacher, and to hope to understand them. Jazz speaks to youth because it is vibrant, pulsing, incredibly alive. Jazz is a means of discovering what the young think. I love it for itself and for what it teaches me. Jazz is not something to be banned, but to be encouraged. If you understand jazz you understand how young people feel. And how young people feel and think and react is vital to the future."

The driver who took me to Petaling Jaya was a thin, nervous Pakistani who spoke in Army English, learned during service in the war against Chin Peng, and who drove his dented Morris like a tank making a breakthrough.

He talked about his wife and two children, the one room they lived in, the cost of food, and how he earned an average of six Malayan dollars a day, out of the thirty to forty dollars he took in fares, by working from daylight to midnight six days a week.

When I paid him off at Plantation House, he jerked his head at the headquarters of the National Union of Plantation Workers.

"This good union. My friend tell me. Taxi men should have."

Minutes later, while drinking tea with the union secretary, I repeated what had been said by a man who was earning just enough to keep his family alive.

He nodded. "One of the unprotected many to whom union-ism is coming in this country and other parts of Asia like a revelation."

The man across the table was not a Malay or a Chinese, but a southern Indian, a stocky sharp-eyed immigrant, and one of the most astute and respected personalities in trade-union-ism in Southeast Asia.

P. P. Narayanan is not yet forty, but he is one of the men responsible for turning a worker rabble into the biggest and best-organized union in Malaya, and probably in Asia.

He was fourteen when he went to Malaya. He has known hunger and intimidation. He was an electricity student at K.L. Technical College when the Japanese occupied Malaya. He worked on rubber estates and then as an apprentice winchman on a tin dredge for one dollar a day. But even when he was hungry he continued to read, and in time to teach English and mathematics to private students for a few dollars a week.

His black fingers plowed the black waves of his hair as he told me this, his shoulders hunched, his bright eyes measuring and assessing.

"I worked and read to find a place under the sun. If a man, any man, is determined to go forward, nothing can stop him. It is the same with a good union, whose members make de-mocracy work. And ours we feel is almost a model union."

Nothing stopped P. P. Narayanan. He knew what life was like on some of the rubber estates. He knew that more than half the people who worked on them were mostly his own people, Indian, many of them existing in dirty leaking bar-racks, some without even the amenities of a domestic animal. He joined the trade-union movement, fought the planters, led strikes, and forged divided and badly organized groups of rub-ber workers into one union, the National Union of Plantation Workers.

In 1954, when the N.U.P.W. began, it had seventy thousand members. Today it has nearly two hundred thousand, or two thirds of the membership of the Malaya Trade Union Con-

gress, and a quarter of the country's work force. It is still growing. In 1954 a weeder, the lowest-paid worker on any estate,
earned sixty cents a day, compared with the more than three
dollars now, and his hours and conditions of work, his housing
and health, have shown corresponding improvements. Thanks
to men like P. P. Narayanan, the N.U.P.W. is concerned
not only with wages, hours, and conditions, but also with the
unionist and his family and every phase of their life.

"We feel that the old approach that a union exists only to
improve wages and conditions is out of date. The unionist
who thinks that way ignores the revolution around him. Just
as important is the welfare of a man's wife and children, the
state of his home, the hygiene and health of his family, the
education of his children, and even his own education. We see
no reason why plantation children, with the union's help,
should not become lawyers and doctors if they have the skill,
or why aged workers should not live in homes the union provides. A union is a community of free-thinking, free-deciding
people. It is a unit of genuine democracy. A good union is
probably the most democratic body in existence."

Thanks to men like P. P. Narayanan, the N.U.P.W.—and
the badly organized plantation groups which went to create
it less than a decade ago—has always been free of Communist
control because it is a good union, because it regards its members and their families and their problems as at least equally
important to industrial problems, because it recognizes that
Communist control will destroy not only the N.U.P.W., but
unionism, and because it uses special techniques which work.

"Before the Emergency [the civil war] all unions except our
own were heavily infiltrated. Many attempts were made to get
control. Many of us were intimidated and actually threatened
with violence or worse. We knew what was going on and we
kept them out. We knew that if we failed, that would be the
end of free trade-unionism in Malaya, that democratic union-
ism would be replaced by totalitarian unionism, which would
not be trade-unionism at all, but the servant of a dictator party.

We knew that if we failed, the Malayan Communist party and it alone would rule.

"How did we keep them out? How do we still keep them out, because the Communists are still active although the party is illegal? We made sure that anyone who wants to be elected to the executive level of a local union committee must work for at least two years on an estate. This way we can check on anyone Communist-inclined—and don't make any mistake, we check. To reach state-committee level a man must have been a member of the union for at least three years, and, if elected, holds office for only two years. Again we watch. To reach top executive level a man must have been a member for at least five years. The proof of our method is the union itself. We have kept the Communists out. And many other unions now follow our example."

A dozen years ago a union like the N.U.P.W. would have been regarded as fantasy, yet today the administrators and the records of this strong, well-organized force are housed in a central headquarters which cost more than two hundred thousand dollars—and every two dollars of this money came voluntarily from a union member. Many unions in the world can't claim such success or, more important, such confidence from its membership.

Back in my air-conditioned K.L. room I sat for a long time remembering some of the things P. P. Narayanan, once an immigrant boy, had said:

"If the leaders of tomorrow fail to hear the small voices of men and what small men are thinking, they will fail and their world will go down with them."

"A Gandhi or a Nehru are wise because they never frighten their people with their thinking. Thus they draw people to them and are able to talk to them and win their confidence. They give out their ideas in small doses like a good doctor telling comforting stories to a sick child. This is a virtue, and virtue has molded millions in Asia."

"I am part of everything I have seen and read. I am part of

the total experience of Man. I am not obsessed with the idea that I know all the answers. Thus I grow and learn humility."

"The new Malaya that is emerging is like the buses in K.L. Look at them and you will see that the driver may be a Malay, the conductor a Chinese, and the passengers from many races. But remember that there isn't just one bus, there are hundreds on the streets and roads of Malaya. Remember, too, that this blending of work and the mixing of races is going on all the time, without argument, without friction. In the buses of Malaya I see great hope for the future."

Across Jalan Mountbatten, in the heart of K.L., a white cloth streamer proclaimed that the "Young Artists" were holding an exhibition. This public announcement, in a city where many people can't even write their own names, interested me, but I did not realize its significance until I met Frank Sullivan, an Australian journalist who is Tunku Abdul Rahman's secretary and who has adopted Islam as his religion and Malaya as his country.

Frank Sullivan can be a testy fellow but, like the Tunku's, his heart is warm, and he has a sensitive eye for beauty and originality. He has also done more than any other individual in K.L. to encourage Malayan artists of all races and, through the presentation of many paintings from his own private collection, to help form the ever-growing and impressive collection of indigenous work in the Balai Seni Lukis Negara, the National Art Gallery.

Nobody is expressing the new Malaya more dramatically than its painters, and especially its young painters from Singapore to Penang, many of whom even at student level are producing work of great strength and originality. Through the catharsis of paint they seem to be abandoning their racial backgrounds and setting out to see and feel and interpret their country not as Chinese or Indians or Malays or Eurasians, but as Malayans—Malaysians.

For almost the first time they are creating from their own

world, the Southeast Asian world about them. Their work shows the influences of Indonesia, China, Thailand, of Christ, Malay legends, the Ramayana. In a land which lacks color, they are finding it in thatch, costume, pigment, the intermingling of races—and color which smolders and flames as though they had been starved of an essential ingredient in their diet.

I followed the sign across the street and went to the Young Painters' Exhibition. Nearly three hundred and fifty artists had submitted five hundred paintings, and these painters, the majority in their teens, ranged from fourteen years of age to twenty-two. Some of the work was derivatively Western and revealed the academic guidance of the school art teacher, but even the dullest canvas mirrored the Southeast Asian eyes and hands and minds which had conceived it. Here was a new approach, a new vitality.

Out of the multi-racial catalyst of independence, from students still at school, from experimental painters so poor that they have to save for months to buy paint, from the sons and daughters of professional people and coolies, could come painting neither Asian nor European, but an art form which the world has not seen before.

One of these days, if the work of these youngsters is any guide, we may see painting which comes from the emotional blending of many races—an art form that is excitingly Malaysian.

15

An old barefoot sailor in the small town where I grew up chilled us with his stories of Malay pirates slitting throats with gleaming kris. This was long before I knew anything about the Indies or that sea rovers from what is Indonesia visited North Australia, or Marega, as they called it, as far back as Elizabethan times, and probably earlier, to collect trepang and pearl shell, to build temporary settlements, to influence Australian aboriginal myths and corroborees, and to leave shards, wild rice, and tamarind trees to remind us today of their passing.

The sailor of my childhood was a remittance man who had been "deported" from England by his family to become a wanderer and to end his life selling prawns from house to house in a small Queensland sugar port. He was a man of some education, improved by an inquisitive mind and scattered reading of history, and he often sat on our back steps, after selling us a quart, and talked of his adventures while he wriggled his toes and smoked a pipe.

He had been in Macassar in the Celebes. He had lived in Kuala Lumpur, Singapore, and Batavia, which is now Djakarta. He even claimed to have been captured by Bugis pirates in the eighties of last century and to have saved himself by diving overboard when the pirate vessel had been sunk by a Dutch man-o'-war.

He loved telling stories of famous kris or, more correctly, keris, as he called the traditional Malay dagger. One he had seen in Macassar was reputed to poison anyone, except the owner, who touched it. Another, a famous kris of the Selangor Sultanate in Malaya—Brok Berayun, or Swinging Monkey, was said to have been brought to Malaya from the Celebes at the start of the eighteenth century by the Bugis family, from whom the present Sultan of Selangor is descended. This kris, which is carried at state ceremonies as part of the Selangor regalia, is said to have the blood of a hundred deaths on its wriggling blade.

I recalled some of these stories when I saw the collection in the home of Tunku Abdul Rahman. I recalled others as I stood beside a table laid with beautiful royal kris in the office of one of the last of the old Malaya hands, M. C. ffranck Sheppard, Malaya's Keeper of the Public Records, Director of its Museum, noted historian, and an English-Irishman who has become a Muslim and, even more unusual, has made the hadj to Holy Mecca.

The kris scabbards gleamed among old Malay ornaments and jewelry. Some were full sheaths of beaten metal, some wood bound elegantly with metal strip and wire. Some scabbards were carved or embossed with animal, bird, or abstract designs, others had tapped into them fine spidery script which spelled the names of the original aristocratic owner or proclaimed passages from the Koran. The curving wood hilts were carved into many shapes, some vaguely recognizable as birds or crocodiles or faces, but nearly all, whatever the design, curving to form a crude sort of beak.

I challenge almost anyone to unsheath a royal kris, grasping the hilt in the correct way, with the thumb down the flat of the blade, without a feeling, however slight, of excitement, perhaps even of awe. As a weapon its flat, waved, tapering blade, with both edges sharpened and reaching a needle point, is malevolent, as though its inventors, the Malays, had deliberately tried to produce a dagger different from all others, which was both efficient to use and intimidating in appearance. Even the theories of the origin of the kris seem to support this, for the common birdlike hilt is believed by some authorities to represent the Lord Vishnu's steed, the bird-god Garuda, and the cruel, waved, twelve-inch blade the Nagas or giant snakes which Garuda slew in the Valley of Khatmandu in the Himalayan State of Nepal.

But I did not call on Mr. Sheppard to discuss kris, which he is collecting for his new National Museum, now rising in K.L., before the finest examples of the work of Malay armorers are lost or destroyed. I came to ask him, among other things, about his conversion to Islam.

Haji Abdul Mubin Sheppard—for that is what his fellow Muslims call him—has been entitled since 1960, when he became the first European since World War II to make the hadj or pilgrimage to Mecca, to put Haji before his name. He is a tall, sensitive-faced man who, seeking tolerance in an intolerant world, found it exemplified most in the religion of the Prophet Mahomet.

"I came over a long period to believe in Islam because I felt that it was the best religion and the one which plays the greatest part in everyday life. It is not a religion of one day a week, as Christianity is to many people. It is an important part of life from hour to hour, from day to day.

"Perhaps most important was its tolerance. This, and its understanding of human behavior and motives, appealed tremendously to me. It is above all a personal religion. I have lived in this country for a long time, for more than thirty years, among the Malays, whom I like and admire. Their religion brought me so much closer to them that after much study and thought I wanted to share their beliefs. And so I became a Muslim and made the hadj."

He fingered an article he had written as he described the

journey to Mecca, among thousands of other pilgrims, many of them from Malaya, and how for the first time he, a European, was able to make it, and penetrate the most sacred areas of Islam, without any restrictions, without even the police protection always given to European converts in the past.

Before he landed from the pilgrim ship at Jedda, the Saudi Arabian port on the Red Sea, he first put on the *"kain ihram"* —one garment like a sarong of white cotton, and one like a Roman toga covering his back and chest but leaving the right shoulder bare. In the past a pilgrim either walked or rode a camel nearly fifty miles from Jedda to Mecca, sometimes in a temperature of one hundred and twenty degrees or even higher, but Sheppard went by bus along a modern highway through a wasteland of sand and treeless hills, making a traditional stop only once, at monuments thirty miles from the coast which marked the boundary of the "Forbidden Territory," which no non-Muslim may enter if he wants to stay alive.

He reached Mecca, birthplace of the Prophet, city of antiquity built on rock and sand and circled by barren hills, where the population of one hundred and fifty thousand was even then expanding to four hundred thousand with pilgrims in white from Malaya and Pakistan, Indonesia and Nigeria, Afghanistan and nearby Egypt.

The hot wind, the Samoun, flung fine dust in his eyes and dust under the carved doors of the stone houses of Mecca as he walked to the two-hundred-yard-long Great Mosque, the Masjid il-Haram, and saw for the first time, inside the walls and open to the sanded sky, the Ka'aba, the very heart of Islam. It is not Mecca, but this fifty-foot-high square of stone draped in black cloth which Muslims face when they pray five times a day in Singapore or Zanzibar or Istanbul. They do not pray to the stone itself, but face it as a symbol of the unity of Muslims everywhere. But only inside the Masjid il-Haram, and nowhere else in the world, do Muslims pray facing the Ka'aba from all points of the compass and therefore facing each other.

Sheppard's first act of faith was to circle the Ka'aba seven times, praying and calling the ancient cry of Islam, *"Allah Ho Akbar"* (God is Great). This ritual, known as the *"tawaf,"* was followed by the *"sa'i,"* walking seven times between two mounds a quarter of a mile apart. Then three hairs were cut from his head, and he was free to replace his toga-like *"ihram"* with ordinary clothes until the eighth afternoon of the Muslim month of Djul-hijjah, when he traveled the eleven miles from Mecca to 'Arafah and camped in a tent on the desert plain with hundreds of thousands of other pilgrims.

At 'Arafah he prayed for two days, then moved back to Mina, near Mecca, to stand before the three ancient stone pillars which must be visited three times before Mecca can be re-entered and the *"tawaf"* and *"sa'i"* rituals completed in the Masjid il-Haram to complete the hadj.

An unforgettable experience, Haji Abdul Mubin Sheppard added, describing finally how, during the pilgrimage to the plain of 'Arafah and back to Mina, Mecca was deserted of inhabitants and pilgrims, yet its homes and shops were empty, unprotected, and completely safe.

An interesting experiment for Christian London, Sydney, or Chicago.

Nymphs on pedestals under Italian chandeliers gazed coyly at their parts in gilt mirrors hung against stained paneling. The marble staircase was Victorian, the paintings fake French, the screens Chinese. The chairs were inlaid with mother-of-pearl.

The old house was daringly modern about the time of the Zulu War, when a Chinese millionaire with more money than taste built it, but now it is one of the decaying Great Houses of K.L. which has become an expensive restaurant in its advanced age.

The food was French and good, but the setting was wrong for my guest across the table, who had spent many years of his adult life, much of the time alone, among the jungle he loves, the wild animals he admires, the wild men who are his friends.

"Places like this . . . cities . . . people . . . give me claustrophobia," he said. "I feel strangled sometimes, even in a small place like K.L."

Jim Hislop is another old Malaya hand who has remained in the country after Malayanization caught up with him and forced him out of the job he loved with almost religious dedication and into an office in the capital.

But he is more than a former Chief Game Warden, to whom life in the jungle, with all its discomforts and dangers, was fulfillment. He is among the last of the breed who for centuries found satisfaction, and even some form of personal magic, in escape to remote places in search of new frontiers, and who found fortunes rarely and death often at an early age, but who felt, as journal remnants and faded letters tell, that life had meant more than the boredom of a village or the drudgery of a city.

Jim Hislop knows the real Malaya, the wild Malaya of blue-green jungle ranges, steep ridges, rocky outcrops, seven-thousand-foot peaks, of giant trees, mossy forests, trailing vines, rhododendron clumps, hidden flowers. He knows what it means to be alone and lost and how to find his way by recognizing individual trees, the shape and turn of leaves, by watching the script of nature, run of streams and their color, by following game trails along the ridges, by observing the behavior and marks of animals, the habits of wild men.

Since I was last in Malaya, I discovered from Jim Hislop, the anthropologists had changed the names of the primitive aborigines of the country. The tribes, many of which have been there since prehistoric times, could not care less about these changes, but they are confusing for the visiting layman.

A generation ago everyone seemed happy to refer to the Sakai, who dressed in the briefest of bikinis, killed their game with poisoned darts fired from blowpipes, and sensibly spent as much time as they could in the shade, and as far away as possible from civilized people. But Sakai today is, anthropologically, almost a dirty word, and the Semang, the Jakun, the

Orang Mantra, and others, who were once very real people, might almost have never existed.

Thirty years ago a British official, who had probably never seen a Sakai or a Semang, guessed thirty-two thousand as the total population of the Malayan aborigines, and advanced the theory that they were decreasing through assimilation with the Malays. Today, the slightly more accurate guess—and guess it is, because some tribes have still not been contacted—is about fifty thousand, broken up into a number of main groups and mixtures and all with brand-new names.

In the north and east of the Malay peninsula are Negrito peoples, short, chocolate, frizzy, who are like similar peoples in the Andaman Islands, the Philippines, New Guinea, and parts of Indonesia. The Senoi, who live among Malaya's central mountains, are probably Mongoloids and resemble primitives in Indonesia, Cambodia, Laos, and Vietnam. They are taller than the Negritos, with wavy hair, paler skins, and finer features. The Senoi are in two groups, the Temiar Senoi and the Semai Senoi. To the south of the Senoi are mixed tribes of Mongoloid blood.

The Negritos are nomadic hunters, though some are beginning to settle and grow food. The Senoi practice shifting cultivation, and related families live together in rectangular houses, known as longhouses, some fifty yards long and up to ten feet aboveground.

The main hunting weapons are still the blowpipe and iron-bladed spears. The blowpipe darts are tipped with a poison from the ipoh tree or creeper, which quickly paralyzes the heart. But when the flesh around a dart wound has been cut away, an animal or bird can be cooked and eaten with safety.

Most of the aboriginal peoples, except those who have lived near Malay settlements for years and have intermarried, are animists, living in the jungle peopled with good and evil spirits and practicing a way of life little different from that of their remote ancestors. The witch doctor still presides at jungle births. One aboriginal child in two dies before reaching the age of six. One aboriginal in ten has tuberculosis, and malnutrition is widespread.

Until the Communist war in Malaya, many of the aboriginal tribes had little or no contact with the Malay peasants or anyone else. Then the Communist guerrillas began to use them to gather food, as scouts and guides, and even trained and armed some as raiders against the British and local forces. Both sides used these primitive peoples during the long war, and brought some of them into direct contact with arms, bombs, mechanization, propaganda and counter-propaganda, and other delights of civilization.

The civil war began what history will decide was their total destruction or their assimilation, for with growing land pressures on a fast-increasing population, the chances of survival of a blowpipe people are slim. If the Malay peasantry are fourteenth century, then the Negritos and the Senoi are still B.C.

But the aboriginals of Malaya are not the only wild things facing the bewilderments of the twentieth century.

A generation ago tiger attacks on rubber tappers were fairly common and the appearance of elephant herds near settlements—even close to K.L.—was hardly news. But on returning to Malaya I was told that these animals had been reduced to a few hundreds and that they and others were facing extinction —until I asked Jim Hislop.

"Many years ago there were countless thousands of elephants in Malaya, but they were so heavily shot for their ivory that only a quarter of a century ago hunters were not allowed to shoot a bull whose tusks were less than thirty pounds. There are still many thousands of elephants left, especially east of the main range from the Thailand border to Johore. Estimates of a few hundreds are nonsense.

"It's true they will be wiped out unless their future is planned for them—unless major areas are set aside and policed. Most important of all, and not only for the elephants but also other animals, is that their vital salt licks are preserved. These are either places where the water contains the minerals they must have to survive or where the soil itself contains salt. Destroy these licks and the wild animals are doomed.

"The problem with Malayan elephants is that they live in family groups which keep to age-old areas and never move more than about fifty miles in any direction. This makes them vulnerable because the more land you open up for plantations or farming, the more the small family herds are disturbed."

Would the disturbed herds move to other areas? Jim shook his head.

"That's the problem. A herd won't leave its traditional country, even when part of that area has been occupied by man. But man reduces natural food and water, so the elephant herd begins to raid farmland and crops. The rest is obvious. Man retaliates. The elephants are killed off."

He talked about his elephants as though they were intimate family friends.

"They're the most intelligent, sensitive, wonderful animals I've ever had anything to do with. Their family life is an example to man in love and affection. They have an uncanny knowledge of the weather and the seasons and follow the fruit trees with an accuracy I could never fathom. Up in the wildest part of central Malaya, where Pahang, Kelantan, and Trengganu meet, a bull elephant, and an old friend of mine, returned every year to feed on one fruit tree. He was never more than a day or so early or late, and often he arrived on the same day. I know, because I watched for him and timed him. I always tried to get back to that fruit tree, even if I was miles away, to see if old faithful had kept his annual appointment."

Jim Hislop once had the unenviable task of killing a rogue. He hates killing, but this elephant had trampled three men and would kill others unless stopped.

"Following a rogue is living dangerously. You're dealing with an animal which thinks clearly and you must outthink him to stay alive. A rogue knows when he is being followed and will deliberately circle back and ambush you—just like a good guerrilla. I had tracked this killer for miles along a mountain ridge when something warned me that he had circled on his tracks and was waiting for me. It wasn't a pleasant feeling. I had no idea where he was, but I knew that I was no longer the hunter but the hunted. I heard nothing and saw nothing that could help me, but some instinct of self-preservation, perhaps even the jungle itself, told me that only my eyes and speed would keep me alive in the next five or ten minutes. I advanced feet at a time along the game trail, stopping every few yards, not to listen, because a waiting elephant makes no sound, but to watch. I was nearing a point along this trail where the track began to curve and the jungle thickened when I knew that, although I could not see the rogue, he was watching me with his alert little eyes. I can't explain this feeling. I just knew that if I reached that curve he would fell me with his trunk and trample me. Yet I could not see him. I froze, finger on the trigger, and examined every leaf ahead, watching for the one movement which gives an elephant in ambush away. I had to wait only a few seconds—perhaps ten. Then, as he twitched an ear, I saw leaves move to the right of the track. I flung up the rifle and fired. He came out like a tank and faster than the echoes of that shot, and galloped up the track, but I knew I'd hit him hard and knew also that he would come back. I got beside a tree and waited as he turned and charged. I fired again and saw him stumble to his knees and die."

I was sweating as he went on to talk of tiger, of rhinoceros, overhunted for his hormone-filled horns coveted by the Chinese as an aphrodisiac and for medicines, of the Malayan tapir, with its black forequarters, grey-white body, and black hind legs, of powerful seladang, the wild ox, which will charge like a race horse, of deer and honey bear and crocodiles.

"The aristocrat of all is rimau, the tiger, probably the most difficult animal to track, because he leaves so few trails. He is beautiful to look at and to watch move, but he hasn't the intelligence of gajah, the elephant. Tiger and elephant keep away from each other. They seem to have an ancient non-aggression pact based on mutual respect for their speed and power. They avoid each other as much as possible and clashes are extremely rare. The tiger lives mostly on deer and pig, yet his most dangerous enemy is the old experienced boar, who will attack to defend his family or if water is disputed.

"An old boar is so courageous that he will fight even the lord of the jungle if he has to—and will attack first. I've never seen a fight between these two—probably nobody has—but I've seen the next best thing. I noticed one day that the jungle beside a small stream had been disturbed, and pushed farther in to investigate. For yards the undergrowth had been flattened or bent and the damp earth and leaf mold plowed and scattered. Then I found them, lying together, and I realized what a dreadful snarling, squealing battle had taken place. The boar was bitten and ripped, and his neck was broken. The tiger's belly was slashed open and its guts had tumbled out. It had bled to death in a few minutes. I couldn't tell how long that terrible fight had lasted, but I do know that if a tiger fails to kill at its first spring, a boar will generally kill him with his sideways-slashing tusks. In this fight they both succeeded."

The only animal not on Jim Hislop's visiting list is the wild dog—red with pricked ears and a tail carried like a fox's. This he regards as the most dangerous and relentless of all the inhabitants of the jungle, because the red dog works in packs of up to forty, respects no other animal, and once he gets on a trail will never leave it, even days later, until he pulls down and kills.

We said good-by after that long lunch under the wide entrance portico of the old Great House.

"I wish I could take you north and show you the wild things," he said.

Watching as this good-looking man with clipped copper mustache walked to his car, I knew that the frontiers for the Jim Hislops of this world were disappearing—the earth-bound frontiers at least. But while they lasted they provided magic you and I could never fully understand.

Nostalgia to me is a house in Malaya I have never seen, on a hilltop in Selangor between Rawang and the sea, and it is called, as it has always been, the House of Palms.

It is a house for dreaming, with a curving Sumatran roof of deep-etched atap, its soaring Minangkabau ends reaching for the sky above magnificent rooms windowed to gardens along the winding Selangor River.

It is owned by Socfin, and in its grounds are the first oil palms brought to Malaya by this company half a century ago, but to me it is a house not of palms but of words, for in it was recorded the most haunting prose ever written in Malaya.

Nearly sixty years ago two young Frenchmen went to Malaya, planted three hundred acres with oil palm, and called their estate Rantau Panjang. One of these men was F. E. Posth. The other was Henri Fauconnier, and it was he who named their small thatched Malay house in the jungle clearing the House of Palms. . . .

"Soon, however, I became aware of a clearing just in front of us. The air moved more freely among the high branches and seemed to sweep them from the smooth surface of the sky, as a breeze dissolves a cloud. A snow-fall of light dappled the undergrowth. Rolain stepped aside to let me come up with him and said rather solemnly: 'Here is my House of Palms.'

"We stood at the edge of an open space, and I saw a Malayan house, quite small and completely overshadowed by two great trees: a kompas with a stem so straight and tall that it looked slender, and an ara spreading bastioned roots to the edge of the jungle as though to check its encroachments. All the rest of the vegetation had been cleared except the palms, and the place looked like a vast hot-house glistening with delicate blades of silver. Tufts of bertam shot up on all sides like firework bouquets beneath a leafy downpour of the slim nibongs.

"It was a house such as is still owned by the old fashioned rajahs, built of red varnished oak with a pierced balustrade to its veranda, the design of which was repeated over the doors and partitions: long low windows with curved uprights, and an overhanging roof broadening at the edge in a curve like the side of a tent. Within, no furniture nor ornaments, but a profusion of mats and cushions and gold-embroidered hangings."

That is what Henri Fauconnier wrote in *Malaisie*, his book about this house, and about Malaya and the Malays, which won him the Prix Goncourt in Paris and which the *Times Literary Supplement* called a "shimmering gem." Later still, *Malaisie* was to appear in its English translation as *The Soul of Malaya*, first published by Elkin Mathews and Marrot, London, in 1931, and by Penguin Books in 1948.

When Fauconnier left Malaya after World War I, his House of Palms was enlarged by Socfin's general manager, M. Robert Michaux, who even added a swimming pool. The Argyll and Sutherland Highlanders used this pool as a defense position during Japan's invasion of Malaya, and when they were forced to withdraw, the Japanese soldiers burned the House of Palms before they continued their advance.

But after the war it rose again, larger, grander, more beautiful, yet with its true character intact, under the direction of the company's managing director, H. A. ("Jock") Campbell, for everyone who has lived in the House of Palms, the old and the new, has known the enchantment of this hilltop dwelling in Selangor.

Henri Fauconnier died only last year, at eighty-four, but in 1958 he made one last journey back from France to stand on that hill, to see the palms he had planted, to sleep in his House of Palms, where everything was different but nothing had changed. . . .

"The silence round the house had turned to a quiet murmur like the sound of a moving river with far-off noises on its banks. I felt lulled and lost. It recalled my first night on the steamer that had brought me East. But the impression of launching into the unknown was now more marked. Then I passed gradually into a vague dream in which I seemed to recover the pleasure that man must have felt in bygone ages when he crouched in some hidden lair.

"And later on I heard the awakening of the jungle when the light of the rising moon began to filter through the foliage. It stirred with myriad rustlings that rose and fell like waves on sand. One feels that innumerable furtive creatures are everywhere in movement: a soundless tumult that sometimes grows more distinct. Thus, for a while, I heard a clear persistent signal, like a short sharp bark, and then an answering bark. It was a pair of panthers hunting, but that I did not know, and I tried vainly to decipher the strange music. . . ."

Malaysia III

16

The night flight from K.L. to Singapore was just long enough, before the light flashed Malaya's version of "Fasten your seat belt"—"Fasten your lap straps"—to share drinks with my seat companion, an English-educated Chinese university lecturer.

We had been discussing the creation of Greater Malaysia, and some of the problems which would have to be solved before union between Malaya, Singapore, and the three Borneo territories could be achieved, and as the Viscount began to let down, the Chinese said:

"Singapore, where the Communists are powerful and nearly all Chinese-speaking Chinese, is more important than many people realize to the future of Malaysia. It is an international danger spot which local and Indonesian Communism will try to use in any way it can to penetrate and dominate this area."

And just before we landed, he added:

"I agree with Lee Kuan Yew, who once said that the five territories must either get together, form Malaysia, and survive, or the Communists will hang us separately."

Back in my Chinese hotel, and months later, I was to think of those comments often.

Although May 27, 1961, is generally accepted as the genesis

of Greater Malaysia, for that was the day when Tunku Abdul Rahman first mentioned it at the Foreign Correspondents' Association luncheon in Singapore, the idea of Malaysia was not new. It had been discussed many times since World War II, and even before the Japanese changed the history of Asia. I remember arguments in Singapore before the war that the logical act for the British would be to join all their Southeast Asian colonies and protectorates and to govern them from their geographical center, Singapore.

Although the Tunku was not being original when he suggested Greater Malaysia—he has also called it Happy Malaysia and even Mighty Malaysia—the time and the setting were peculiarly right in that month of May, in the Chinese Year of the Ox, and within hours Malaysia became the most debated subject in Southeast Asia.

On that May 27, 1961, the Tunku said:

"Malaya today as a nation realizes that she cannot stand alone and in isolation. . . . Sooner or later she should have an understanding with Britain and the peoples of the territories of Singapore, Borneo, Brunei, and Sarawak. It is premature for me to say now how this closer understanding can be brought about, but it is inevitable that we should look ahead to this objective and think of a plan whereby these territories can be brought closer together in political and economic cooperation. This will not be possible if the Chinese start to think and talk of everything Chinese. The Malays will be made to feel nervous, if they do, of their presence as Chinese and not as Malayans. The Chinese are a practical people and as such must think clearly ahead. Above all Malaysia must be the sole object of their loyalty."

That statement was the announcement of a plan, the renunciation of an attitude, a combined warning and appeal to the Chinese populations, particularly of Singapore, an appeal to the Malays and other races, and the beginning of one of the most fascinating political and social experiments of our time.

Until the Tunku made that speech, he had always opposed

any merger between Malaya and Singapore, and he gave his reasons, which were well known, in a speech many months later:

"I was not in favor of the idea as I was of the opinion that integration would spell danger for the security of this country [Malaya]. The difference in outlook of the people of the Federation and Singapore was so pronounced that for me a merger was out of the question. The majority of the people here [Malaya] have accepted the idea of Kingship and Sultanate, of Malay as the national language, and of Islam as the official religion of the nation. I realized that it would be difficult to persuade the people of Singapore to accept these ideas because seventy per cent of the people of the Island are Chinese. . . . In the event of a merger of these two territories the different views of the people of the Federation and Singapore might clash and thus create problems which would be difficult to solve. However, times change and so must our outlook. Hence, what was not agreed to yesterday might be agreed to today when we give it a second thought, and so the idea of Malaysia took shape."

But what made the Tunku change his mind? The answer is one word—fear. Fear of Singapore, a Chinese city in a Malayan environment, was why the Tunku for so long opposed any form of federation between Malaya and Singapore. And increasing fear of Chinese Singapore, and suspicions about Indonesian intentions, particularly in Borneo, forced him to change his mind and propose not just merger with Singapore, but the even wider federation of Greater Malaysia.

It is said that the British first whispered the idea of Malaysia to the Tunku as a solution to their own economic, territorial, and defense problems. True or false, it doesn't matter. But the Tunku, with nearly forty per cent of his own Malaya population Chinese, and most of them urban Chinese, had always been suspicious of welcoming more than a million Singapore Chinese under a Malaya-Singapore merger until he realized that the Communists of Singapore, almost all Chinese, would eventually take over Singapore unless they were controlled, and he would wake up one morning with a Communist island—a Chinese Cuba—at his front door.

Singapore's Prime Minister, Lee Kuan Yew, who had always wanted merger with Malaya and who gladly supported the Tunku's plan for Greater Malaysia, also acted from fright— combined political and economic fright. Lee Kuan Yew knew that Singapore, with its large and rapidly increasing young population, few industries, declining trade, and serious unemployment, could not live a separate existence from rich and prosperous Malaya. He knew, too, that most of the Island's water came across the Causeway, from the Malaya mainland, and that Malaya could cut that supply, as the Japanese did. Whoever controls Johore controls Singapore. Lee also knew that Singapore lived on the British military bases and that without them the Island would almost starve.

When Lee's People's Action party was elected by a large majority in 1959 with the help of the Communists, Singapore's problems seemed secondary to the virtual end of colonial rule, the achievement of self-government, and the popular power of the P.A.P. But Lee was soon to learn a lesson of contemporary history, that the party which holds hands with dedicated, skillfully organized Communists will eventually get hurt. The Communists helped him to power, then deserted and undermined him, and with the help of political opportunists and Lee-haters, reduced his 1959 majority to almost nil, and forced him to govern with the support of the political right, who disliked him only a little less than they disliked the Communists.

Both the Tunku and Lee knew that while the British remained in self-governing but not independent Singapore, the power of the Communists could be checked through the Security Council and the defense forces. They also knew that constitutional talks planned with the British Government for mid-1963, could give Singapore her complete independence and that this could lead to a Communist take-over.

The Tunku and Lee knew that the one way to frustrate the Communists and control them in Singapore and the other territories was through the master federation of Malaysia, whose central government in Kuala Lumpur would control foreign affairs, defense, and internal security.

This was what Lim Chin Siong and his masters, the Central Committee of the Malayan Communist party, feared most, and it was why Communist parties everywhere, taking their lead from Peking, denounced the Tunku's Greater Malaysia from the start, branded it neo-colonialist and directed all their planning to frustrate it.

Lim Chin Siong knew that once the internal security of Singapore was controlled by the federal government of Greater Malaysia, Communist power on the Island would be clipped. This was why he and his Barisan Socialis, although they did not oppose merger, demanded it after—and "after" is the key word—Singapore had gained its independence. The reason was transparent, as the Tunku and Lee knew. Given independence before merger, and with control of the major unions, the Communists would be free of the security and defense restraints on the Island and would be in a position to create a revolutionary situation and take over Singapore. A take-over, or even the threat of it, would force the Tunku's Government to invade Singapore. Communist Singapore would call for aid. The result could easily be general war.

An American historian who visited Singapore not so long ago argued that there was a world-wide trend for small states to federate—to increase their strength, to pool their resources, to improve their standard of living.

"No small country on its own can hope to survive long today," he said, and the history of southern and eastern Asia in the past decade confirms this warning.

Tibet has been raped and slaughtered. India has been invaded and all the small Himalayan border states between China and India are in danger. Korea has been cut in half, though Russia started this. Much of the territory of old French Indochina is Communist. Laos, if we face facts, is already within the Communist heartland, for her international neutrality, which was proclaimed in July, 1962, is merely another step toward total Communist control as yet another satellite of Peking. What is left of Vietnam is surviving only with massive American aid. Cambodia's neutrality will eventually be squeezed. Thailand and Burma are threatened.

The only present check to further aggression into Southeast Asia from the north is the threat of a major war. But the dangers inside Southeast Asia are just as real and urgent as the dangers from outside.

Malaya (as also the Philippines) has already fought a long war with its own Communists—a war which failed because it was stupidly timed and strategically inept, and because of massive British, Australian, and New Zealand armed opposition. The Communists control the main trade-unions of Singapore. In Sarawak, North Borneo, and Brunei the Communists are extremely active. Given a revolutionary opportunity—and the death of Dr. Sukarno would certainly provide one—and the two-million-strong Indonesian Communist party could take over and hold a large section of Java—all western Java, some observers think.

Even the Communist civil war in Malaya, though officially over, is still being fought. Comrade Chin Peng, who led the war for twelve years, has not been cleared from his secret camps in the mountains along the Malaya-Thailand border. Estimates of his numbers vary from one to four hundred, but even if there are only a couple of hundred Communist remnants of the twelve thousand guerrillas who fought the civil war, they are still a significant force. Significant, not in numbers, but in dedication, in organization, in jungle experience, and, perhaps most important, in geography. They are exactly what any Communist guerrilla leader, even a defeated leader, needs —a trained nucleus on which to build. They are where any Communist guerrilla wants them—among hard-to-penetrate jungle mountains in what is known as the Betong Salient, where part of southern Thailand is like a fist striking into the Malayan State of Perak. Here they could be reinforced by party members in Malaya and Thailand and from outside the country and rebuilt into a dangerous striking force to menace Malaya to the south or Thailand to the north or both. Serious trouble in Thailand or Malaya-Singapore or Borneo or Indonesia would be Chin Peng's opportunity to restart the civil war and turn it into real war.

The Communists have been hunted for several years by police from both sides of the border and by troops on the Malayan side, but until SEATO forces moved into Thailand in mid-1962, co-operation from the Thais had always been limited and no real attempt had been made to clear the border area, even though clashes had occurred with well-armed groups of up to fifty jungle-green guerrillas, and men on both sides had been killed and wounded. Some of the jungle camps in the Betong Salient have been big enough to accommodate fifty guerrillas and have been well equipped. One camp even had table tennis and was well supplied with food and all the latest antibiotic drugs.

The Communist guerrillas in the Betong are not dangerous now, but so long as they remain, they are a threat—an organized officer corps for future trouble. The Communists, as history proves, can afford to wait.

Put some of the pieces together and the pattern of planned slow conquest of Southeast Asia—from outside and from within —becomes increasingly clear, and all by remote control, largely from Communist China, which does not have to move a man, while the Communist parties, at a dozen points, plan, undermine, and bleed for her. China can maintain the fiction that party work from Rangoon to Djakarta is not her work, that all she is concerned about is the direct protection of her borders, but when the blood of her foreign devotees is no longer necessary, then Peking control, not Moscow, would extend south to the Timor Sea and Peking would demand tribute as it did centuries ago when the Chinese Emperors claimed the barbarian lands of the south as their own and even sent emissaries and fleets to enforce that allegiance.

Put all the pieces together, from Indonesia to as far west as the Hindu Kush, and the internal and external pattern which emerges is the beginning of a battle which could take decades—a battle not just for Southeast Asia, but for Asia and the world.

Greater Malaysia is part of an enormous crescent which sweeps for more than two thousand miles south from Thailand through Malaya and Singapore, then east to Borneo and northeast to the Philippines. Bangkok is at its western horn, Manila at its eastern. South of the crescent is Indonesia and North Australia. Within its arc is the South China Sea and South Vietnam, Cambodia, and Laos, where one of the battles for Southeast Asia is now being fought. North is China.

Greater Malaysia is five territories not only different in shape and size but in political, economic, and social outlook and development. The largest of these "precious stones" mounted on the crescent is the independent Federation of Malaya. The smallest is its neighbor, the city-state of Singapore. But what of the others—the British Crown Colonies of Sarawak and North Borneo (or Sabah, as it is now called) and the British-protected Sultanate of Brunei?

These three fill the northern third of the island of Borneo, third-largest island in the world, after New Guinea and Greenland. The southern two thirds of the island is Indonesian Borneo, now known by the Indonesians as Kalimantan, the ancient name for Borneo.

The three, which have a combined area of about eighty thousand square miles, would fit tightly into Minnesota and loosely into Victoria or England-Wales-Scotland. But Sarawak, forty-eight thousand square miles, is about the same size as New York State, North Borneo (Sabah), twenty-nine thousand square miles, is a twin of South Carolina, and Brunei, a little more than two thousand square miles, is only twice as big as Rhode Island.

A total area, just north of the Equator, of low, steamy coastal strip fringed with casuarina trees and palms and backed by peat swamps and brackish waterways edged with nipah palm. Then low-timbered cultivated hills which reach south for jungle mountains and uninhabited plateau along the Kalimantan border.

A green land of drumming rain, broad brown-stained rivers, magnificent peaks, like Kinabalu in Sabah, more than thirteen thousand feet, sometimes snow-tipped, highest mountain in Southeast Asia. Kinabalu, marked on old charts as St. Peter's Mount, which looks down on the emerald shallows of the Sabah coastline, the blue China Sea. Mighty Kinabalu, worshipped by every native within its sight as the resting place of the dead.

A rich, undeveloped, backward land of timber and sago, rubber and pepper, oil palm and rice, bauxite and oil. Sarawak's oil field at Miri is declining, but the Seria field in Brunei, which has enabled the state to build up foreign investments of more than six hundred million Malayan dollars, is still highly productive though slowly declining.

Tiny Brunei is a small wedge between Sarawak and Sabah along the fifteen-hundred-mile coastline of northern Borneo which links the South China and Celebes Seas. The capital is Brunei Town, on the Brunei River, a hot damp Somerset Maugham settlement, where many of its twenty thousand people, Malays mostly, live in Kampong Ayer, or the Water Village—wooden houses built on stilts in the river and looking from the air like a vast collection of flooded chicken coops. Kampong Ayer, which has its own schools, clinics, shops, and meeting places, is not one marine village but about thirty, where most families have their own boats, powered by outboard motors, and where the Sultan's famous silversmiths and weavers live and work. Overlooking Kampong Ayer is the golden Mosque, Islam's most modern place of worship, with its two-hundred-foot minaret even equipped with a lift and tape-recorded prayers, and its great carpet, said to be among the oldest in the world. And nearby is the Istana Durel Hana, the not particularly distinguished palace of the ruler of this oil-rich principality.

Sultan Sir Omar Ali Saifuddin, twenty-eighth of his line, went to school at the Malay College at Kuala Kangsar, in the Malayan State of Perak, and succeeded his brother to the Brunei throne in 1950. Apart from making the hadj to Mecca, he has traveled widely and is the first of this royal Malay house to move about his minute kingdom with any interest in its progress. Thirty years ago, before oil was discovered at Seria, sixty miles by road from Brunei Town, Brunei's total annual revenue was less than four hundred thousand Malayan dollars. Today the state's revenue is one hundred and twenty million dollars, and all from oil.

The Sultan is wealthy, autocratic, cautious, and slow to realize that he lives in the twentieth century. Although his people, including the truculent forty-five thousand Brunei Malays who make up about half the population, are the only people in Asia to get a non-contributory old-age pension, and although education, which is poor, is free, and rural children get free lunches, Brunei is even further back in time than the Malay peasantry of Malaya. If Malaya is semi-feudal, Brunei is feudal, particularly in a political sense.

The Sultan's only comparatively recent extravagance was to build himself a palace in Ampang Road, Kuala Lumpur—a white Istana with a flat roof shaded by six gold domes not unlike flattened beach umbrellas. He has four boys and four girls, and two of his sons, including his heir, live at the Istana while attending school in K.L. The heir, who is nearly seventeen, is the Yang Teramat Mulia Duli Pengiram Muda Hassanal-Bolkiah.

In K.L. a popular story claims that the Sultan of Brunei built his Istana in the Malayan capital not primarily to house his school-age sons, but to have a private home available when the time came for him to be installed as the Yang di-Pertuan Agong, or King of Malaysia. The Sultan is believed to be ambitious for the crown and is said to have supported the Tunku's plan for Greater Malaysia, against fierce opposition from some of his Brunei Malays who demand a greater share in the running of the state, on the understanding that Brunei would become a state and that he would then be eligible for election as King. This story, if true, would be fascinating for the historian, particularly as the Sultan's ancestors were among the most powerful in Southeast Asia and once controlled much of the area washed by the South China Sea. It is certainly true that beside Sir Omar Ali Saifuddin, the twenty-eighth of his line, the Sultans of the Malayan states are almost parvenus.

The ancient Sultanate of Brunei once claimed much of Borneo, and even the name for that big island is said to be a corruption of "Brunei" itself. Chinese fleets, southwarding on the northeast monsoon, anchored off Brunei not long after the collapse of the Roman Empire to trade pottery and other goods for timber and camphor and monkeys' gallstones and rhinoceros's horns. The ancestors of the Brunei Sultan sent tribute to the Emperors of China more than a thousand years ago—a fact which modern China or local Chinese have not forgotten. Even in early Ming times, tribute was still being paid, though after that it ceased. The Chinese also remember the tradition that the second Muslim Sultan of Brunei—Islam reached Borneo late, in the fifteenth century—was a Chinese, Ong Sung Ping. Brunei was a power in Southeast Asia early in the sixteenth century, when the sea rover Sultan Bolkiah, the "Singing Captain," dominated the whole area and even captured Manila. One legend claims that he carried a bag of pepper seeds on one raiding voyage and refused to return until he had given to each seed the name of one of the thousands of islands he visited and claimed.

It was probably during this Sultan's reign that Ferdinand Magellan's fleet, after the death of Magellan in the Philippines, called at Brunei in 1521 and made what was, for the Western world, the discovery of the island of Borneo. Pigafetta, main chronicler of the first circumnavigation of the globe, vividly described the Sultan's capital—a city on stilts, a population of twenty-five thousand families, a splendid court, and a host who welcomed his strange visitors with gifts carried on the backs of elephants draped in cloth of gold.

But in Magellan's wake came the Europeans—Spanish, Portuguese, Dutch, English—seeking trade and finding it through conquest. By the end of the sixteenth century Brunei's power was already in decline, and by the early nineteenth century Brunei had been squeezed to little more than present-day Sarawak and part of Sabah. In 1841 Brunei ceded Sarawak to James Brooke, the island of Labuan was handed to Britain, and later part of Sabah went first to an American-Chinese commercial company, the American Trading Company of Borneo, which started a settlement which failed, and later still to the British North Borneo (Chartered) Company.

Well before the end of last century, once-mighty Brunei had been reduced to a minor British protectorate, but while Brunei was crumbling, Sarawak, the old southern province of the Brunei Sultanate, was rising under the first of the White Rajahs, adventurer James Brooke, who arrived in 1839, helped the Brunei Viceroy in what is now Sarawak's capital, Kuching, to settle a revolt of Malays and Dayaks, and, in return for his services, was made Rajah in 1841.

For twenty-three years Rajah Brooke chased head-hunters and pirates, often with the help of the Royal Navy, faced severe political criticism in England for his private empire building, grabbed more territory from Brunei, and lived to see the United States recognize Sarawak as an independent state in 1850, and Great Britain to appoint a Consul to Kuching in 1864.

James Brooke, a bachelor, was succeeded by his nephew, Charles Johnston, who changed his name to Brooke and, ruling as the second Rajah for fifty years, almost wiped out

piracy, reduced head-hunting, did not forget to expand his
territory, and started the modern development of his tropical
principality.

The third White Rajah, Sir Charles Vyner Brooke, succeeded
his father in 1917, and in 1941, the centenary of Brooke rule,
produced a new constitution which abolished his own absolute
powers and started his state on the way to self-government.

Five years later, after the Japanese occupation had left
Sarawak hungry and in chaos, the long rule of the White
Rajahs ended when Rajah Brooke handed Sarawak to the
British Crown as a Colony and presented with it thirteen
million Malayan dollars' worth of reserves, six million dollars
in cash, and a personal gift of about four hundred thousand
dollars for education.

In the history of cessions of territory Sarawak is probably
unique, for in return the third White Rajah, last of the auto-
crats who had ruled in Kuching for a century, received a pension until his death this year.

North Borneo was originally the northern province of the
Brunei Sultanate and was know as Sabah. Until late into
the nineteenth century it was a wild area controlled by coastal
chiefs, raided and plundered by sea rovers, and in a condition
of constant tribal warfare inland, where head-hunting was not
an occupation but a profession.

British colonial rule did not begin until 1882, forty-one years
after James Brooke became Rajah of Sarawak, and it started
in the old tradition of the "Company" with the establishment
of the British North Borneo (Chartered) Company, which
controlled the area for the next sixty years, until the Japanese
conquered all Borneo.

The Chartered Company died among the ruins of Jesselton,
the capital, and Sandakan, the commercial capital, and after
the war North Borneo, with the island of Labuan, which, like
Singapore, had been part of the Straits Settlements, became
a British Crown Colony.

It is only now that Sabah, North Borneo's ancient name,

which the Chartered Company abolished in 1882, is coming back and will be used from now on, just as the Indonesians have restored the name Kalimantan to their southern part of the island of Borneo.

In Sarawak, Brunei, and Sabah live about one million three hundred thousand people—eighty-five thousand in Brunei (capital Brunei Town, twenty thousand), seven hundred and fifty thousand in Sarawak (capital Kuching, fifty thousand), and four hundred and sixty thousand in Sabah (capital Jesselton, twenty-two thousand). But unlike Malaya-Singapore, where the three main racial groups are Malay, Chinese, and Indian, many different peoples, in varying stages of development, live in the three Borneo territories.

Of the total population of one million three hundred thousand, about two hundred thousand are Malay, and about a quarter of the population Muslim. About three hundred and fifty thousand are Chinese, some intermarried with local people. And the rest, more than half the total population, are many distinct peoples, who create for the layman an almost bewildering pattern of race, customs, language, and belief.

In Sarawak live the Ibans, Land Dayaks, Kayans and Kenyahs, Kelabits and Muruts, Punans and Pennans, Melanaus, Bisayas, Malays, and Chinese. In Brunei, Malays, Kedayans, Dayaks, Muruts, Tutong, Belait, Dusuns, and Chinese. In Sabah, Dusuns or Kadazans, Muruts, Bajaus, Suluks, Binadaus, Illanuns, and Chinese.

The Ibans of Sarawak are probably the original head-hunters of Borneo. Their attacks downriver and out to sea first brought them into violent contact with the early Europeans and earned them the name of Sea Dayaks. They are short, round-headed, with straight black hair and brown hairless skins. They live in longhouses inland and cultivate hill rice after burning and clearing the jungle. Up to sixty families may live in one longhouse, controlled by an elected headman, or Tuai Rumah, and a group of longhouses elect their chief, or Penghulu. The Ibans, like most Borneo people, are monogamous. They are noted for their love of argument, oratory, and Rabelasian wit. They believe in an after-life, in a place called Sebayan, where living is athletic and comfortable and free of disease and disaster. They last went on the warpath during and after the Japanese occupation and took a fine variety of heads, but unfortunately civilization has now stopped this satisfying social habit, which helped keep down the population in relation to the food supply. The Ibans number two hundred and fifty thousand, about the same population as the Sarawak Chinese.

The Land Dayaks, though related to the Ibans, are a milder and more conservative people. They also live in hill country, about sixty thousand in Sarawak but many more in the high across-border country of Indonesian Kalimantan. They resemble Malays, live in longhouses, and even today the most impressive building in their high villages is the "headhouse," where the captured heads of their neighbors were once ceremoniously preserved and stored. Land Dayak chiefs are known as Orang Kaya, literally "rich men."

Through the Malays, who play an important part in the life of the country, Islam has made many converts among the indigenous peoples. The most notable group of such converts are the Melanaus, a coastal people of about forty thousand and the main sago producers of Sarawak. They look like Malays, but are heavier, with broader shoulders, paler skins, and are generally more handsome. The Melanaus women, with a reputation for beauty, used to be regarded as more beautiful when their foreheads were bound in childhood and forced by pressure into a concave shape. The Melanaus are fine boat builders and catch fish by tossing a palm frond overboard, waiting until surface fish gather in its shade, then lowering a net while a member of the crew slips underwater and herds the fish into the mesh.

The Kayans and Kenyahs are a short, powerful upriver people who live by farming. The Kayans were once great rivals of the Ibans until the Brookes led fifteen thousand Ibans against them a century ago and broke their power. The Kayans particularly are fine craftsmen, skilled makers of canoes and weapons, great singers and dancers. They are extremely class conscious, with an inherited aristocracy which contrasts with the much more egalitarian social structure of the Ibans and the Land Dayaks. The doors of the chief are in the center of the longhouse, and doors become smaller on either side as rank declines. A distinguishing symbol of social status among the related Kayans and Kenyahs is the ownership of strings of ancient beads, some of them beautiful glass of fine workmanship and of ancient Mediterranean origin.

The Kelabits and Muruts, who are also closely related, live in the remote uplands, where they graze zebu cattle, buffalo, and goats. These energetic, intellectually gifted people, who have a most distinctive life and culture, are famous for their parties, which are guaranteed to keep guests drunk for a week. The Kelabits are ruled by aristocratic families whose class symbols are rare and ancient Chinese red earth jars, some of which date back for more than a thousand years to the T'ang Dynasty.

The Punans and Pennans are nomadic people with pale-parchment skins and gentle eyes. They are incredibly silent hunters, experts with the blowpipe, and use a poison which will kill a pig before it has run a few hundred yards. Their few social laws deal mainly with sexual offenses. If a man takes another's wife the injured husband must be paid a new spear and a parang, useful damages in a hunting economy. If a man finds another in bed with his wife he must by tribal law hold him down while he shouts for all in the village to come and witness his cuckolding. For allegedly primitive people this is a highly sophisticated law, and could well be adopted in white society. The shouts from our better suburbs would be socially instructive.

In Sabah, the Dusuns, or Kadazans, as they are known in some areas, are the largest and most progressive group of native people. There are one hundred and fifty thousand of them, who live mostly on the west coast and plains and grow most of Sabah's rice. They are intellectually bright, with their own distinctive language and culture, and are interested in education. Although mainly animists, many villages have been converted to Christianity.

The Muslim Bajaus of Sabah's east coast—they adopted Islam from the Brunei Malays—are today the fishermen descendants of the pirates who terrorized the Sulu and Celebes Seas deep into the nineteenth century and who even today use their old profession to make a fast buck. There are sixty thousand of them. The Muruts are another major group, but they are not related to the Muruts of Sarawak. They number about twenty-five thousand and occupy the high country inland, where they follow a seven-year cycle of cultivation and still use the spear, the blowpipe, and the hunting dog.

The Chinese story in the three Borneo territories starts with regular junk trade between China and Brunei more than a thousand years ago, ceases with the coming of the early Europeans (except in southern Borneo), and begins again in the nineteenth century.

From early times the Chinese played an important part in the life of Borneo. They were traders, they bred with the coastal people, they strongly influenced their art. And then, in modern times, they came to settle.

By the middle of last century many thousands of Chinese were in what is today Indonesian Kalimantan, and it was from there, not China, that the first migrations moved into Sarawak. About the time that James Brooke was becoming the first Rajah, in 1841, Chinese Hakka gold miners, in trouble with the Dutch in what was then Netherlands Borneo, overlanded to Sarawak and began to plant pepper and vegetables and to pan for gold. It wasn't long before Rajah Brooke punished some of these migrants for secret-society extortion and they replied by attempting to murder him. The Hakka

Revolt almost succeeded, but was smashed with the help of the Dayaks and a few Cantonese Chinese led by Lau Chek, who had come to Sarawak in 1830 and was the Rajah's steward.

The Chinese Hokkiens of Sarawak date from the first years of Rajah Brooke, when Ong Ewe Hai came from Singapore to Kuching to start trade between the two areas. Hokkien settlers who followed Ong spread all over Sarawak to become what they are today, mainly shopkeepers and traders. Other Chinese followed, from Singapore and China—Hakkas, Hylams, Teochews, Foo Chows—until in this century, boosted by steady migration and a high breeding rate, the Chinese population of Sarawak reached nearly thirty-one per cent of the population by 1960 and is today about to pass the largest local racial group, the Ibans.

In Sarawak the White Rajahs were careful to respect the customs of the different peoples of their country, including the Chinese, and in 1912 the second Rajah established a Chinese Court of seven leading Chinese in Kuching. These men handled all civil cases involving Chinese and all problems on Chinese marriage, divorce, and custom. The president of this Court was Ong Tiang Swee, who was known as the Kapitan China General over all the Chinese communities. The Court lasted for nine years, before its duties were taken over by the Civil Courts and the Protector of Chinese, but for years afterward, until the Japanese invasion in 1941, the Rajah still approved the firing of a seven-gun salute at Chinese New Year in recognition of the voluntary service of the members of the Chinese Court.

The Chinese population in Brunei is small, about twenty per cent, but in Sabah more than one hundred thousand Chinese, many of mixed Chinese-Dusun blood, form nearly a quarter of the population and are increasing.

Sabah's Chinese are much more recent in Borneo than the Chinese in Sarawak. They first began to settle in Sabah in the early years of the Chartered Company, after 1882, and came almost entirely from China through Hong Kong to work as traders and farmers, and to become powerful in the community as merchants and shopkeepers, clerks and technicians. Sabah Chinese have much closer links with China than the Chinese of Sarawak, who look more toward Singapore.

Political development in the Borneo territories is only a few years old, and when it began, spurred by Indonesia, more recently by Malaya's independence and Singapore's self-government, and more recently still by the idea of Greater Malaysia, it was organized along multi-racial lines. But this did not last, and parties today largely represent racial groups.

Sarawak is the most politically advanced of the three territories. The largest party, formed in 1959, is the Sarawak United People's party, commonly known as S.U.P.P. and modeled on Singapore's People's Action party. It began as a mildly socialist, multi-racial party and continued that way until its Chinese-educated Chinese members, led by leaders of the illegal Communist party, took control, and S.U.P.P. rapidly became a Communist-front organization. Its executive officers, including chairman Ong Kee Hui, a wealthy banker and grandson of the famous Kapitan China General under the last White Rajah, are anti-Communist but were unable to prevent Communist domination of the rank and file, and S.U.P.P. seriously splintered. This split was widened in 1962 when two Chinese executives of the party had their residence restricted in Sarawak and left for China, and the wife of one, and another executive, were deported to China.

The Communists behind S.U.P.P. have tried hard, by organizing among the Chinese population and other groups, to stir up opposition to Greater Malaysia. They even used Chinese school children—a popular method in Singapore—to take part in demonstrations against Malaysia when Tunku Abdul Rahman visited Sarawak in November, 1962. But since then first moves have been made by liberal groups to purge the party of its Communist control and to bring it into political

line with all other parties in Sarawak who support the formation of Malaysia—and these groups seem to be succeeding.

Backward Brunei, which is dominated by its Sultan and
Malay ruling families, has only one registered political group,
the Party Ra'ayat, or People's party, which is generally believed
to have political links with the Indonesian Communist party.
Party Ra'ayat, whose leader is Inche Ahmad Azahari, opposes
the Sultan and Malaysia, wants independence under a fully
representative government, and wants a union with Sarawak
and Sabah. Azahari has always been publicly careful, while
demanding political reform, economic development, and a
share for all in the oil royalties of Brunei, to praise his "beloved Sultan" and to criticize the Malay aristocracy who have
wickedly misled him.

Azahari, who is not yet forty, has worked for years among
the Brunei Malays and has played on their backwardness and
political inferiority to the Malays of Malaya. Although he calls
himself a Brunei Malay and was born in Brunei, he is an
Indonesian with some Arab ancestry, and looks more Arab
than Malay. He was in Indonesian Sumatra under the Japanese
in World War II and has advocated a union between Brunei
and Indonesia. He returned to Brunei in 1952 and helped
form Party Ra'ayat in 1956. In 1957 he went to London to
demand independence for Brunei. He is a dynamic speaker
with dreams of a "Greater Brunei" and bitterly opposes Malaysia, which would prevent his dream becoming reality. Reliable observers claim that his real ambition is to become
political dictator of all north Borneo, including Sarawak and
Sabah, and of welding this union to Indonesia. They also
claim that, even if he is not a member of the Communist
party, he has strong personal links with Indonesian and Singapore Communists. Others say he is a fanatical nationalist.
Whatever is true, he is a man to watch in this fermenting
little Sultanate, where political reform is urgently needed.

In Sabah, the most politically backward of the three territories, parties did not exist, at least officially, until after the

Tunku's Greater Malaysia speech. The first and largest to organize was the United National Kadazan Organization, or U.N.K.O., whose membership comes from the Kadazans around the capital, Jesselton, and from the Dusun people generally, who form about one third of the total population of Sabah. U.N.K.O. and other parties support Malaysia.

But of all the political leaders whom the Tunku's speech hatched in Sabah one man stands out. He is Donald Stephens, founder of the United National Kadazan Organization, editor-owner of the Sabah *Times*, the only English-language newspaper in the area, which also prints pages in Malay and Kadazan, and a member of the Executive and Legislative Councils of Sabah.

Stephens is, like Azahari, of mixed blood. He is part English, part Kadazan, and he claims, with pride, that his grandfather was a head-hunter. He is short and rotund, with the bespectacled face of a comedian, a relaxed manner, and a laugh which makes his face flame and which can be heard half a block away. He is seldom without a cigarette dribbling from his full lips, and he coughs and wheezes and snorts through the curling smoke as he answers questions, tells stories, and tells them well, or sings lustily at parties, which he prefers to attend wearing an open-neck batek shirt hung outside his trousers.

Donald Stephens, who is still in his early forties, and married, with two adopted children, worked before the war as a journalist on the *Straits Times*, Singapore, where one of his friends was a Malay journalist, Inche Yusof bin Ishak, now Singapore's Yang di-Pertuan Negara, or Head of State.

Stephens, on one of his visits to Singapore, was asked which hotel he was staying at. He laughingly replied: "At the Istana [Government House]. I like the publican."

During the war the Japanese in Sabah murdered Stephens' father in a reprisal for sabotage. They rounded up ten men at random and shot them. Stephens Senior was one of them—and it was an act his son is never likely to forget.

After the Tunku's Greater Malaysia speech and the formation of the United National Kadazan Organization, Donald Stephens played a leading role in discussions in the Borneo territories, Singapore, Malaya, and London on Malaysia and how it could best be achieved—discussions which led eventually to the five-man Commission under Lord Cobbold to study the views of the people of Sarawak and Sabah, and which in turn led to the announcement in London at the beginning of August, 1962, that Britain and Malaya had agreed to the establishment of Greater Malaysia by August 31, 1963.

Although the Borneo territories are about one and a half times the size of Malaya and Singapore, they hold only about fourteen per cent of their population. It was because of this, because of fears among the diverse races of Borneo that Malaysia would mean a form of "colonial" and "Islamic" subjection by the Malays, a flood of Chinese immigrants to Borneo, and a threat to the economy, languages, and cultures of Borneo, that the opinions of political leaders like Donald Stephens could not be ignored.

Both Tunku Abdul Rahman and Lee Kuan Yew were men in a hurry. They knew that, to defeat the Communists of Singapore, Malaysia had to be a geographical and political fact before the all-important constitutional question of independence for Singapore was raised in 1963. Their deadline for Malaysia, for Malaysian Merdeka, was mid-1963, and in public and behind the scenes, in Kuala Lumpur, Singapore, Kuching, Jesselton, London, they worked to make Malaysia a Southeast Asian reality as quickly as possible.

The political doubts of the Borneo peoples were only some of the problems of merger. There were wider and more involved questions of trade, foreign capital, the use of natural resources, the location of industries, even oil. Would wealthy little Brunei, for example, with a per-capita income of about twelve hundred Malayan dollars from oil alone, and about equal to the income per head from all sources in Malaya, share this wealth as a state with her poorer partners in Malaysia?

Problems like these were discussed by the Commonwealth Parliamentary Association, and from this regional meeting came the Malaysian Solidarity Consultative Committee, whose job was to study the Borneo territories, against the perspective of Malaysia, and test public opinion.

This Committee issued its report on February 3, 1962, and its main recommendations were far-reaching: Sarawak, Sabah, and Brunei to join a Federation of Malaysia, each state to retain some autonomy. The central government of Malaysia to control all-important foreign affairs, defense, and internal security. Islam the official religion, but freedom of worship to all, and Malay the national language, but English to continue as the language of instruction in schools. Less-dense areas to have more than proportional representation in the central government—a precaution against Chinese dominance. Special safeguards against uncontrolled migration—another precaution mainly against the Chinese. Gradual introduction of uniform Malaysia taxation and other revenue producers. Restraints against trade and businesses which might thrive at the expense of the less-developed Borneo territories.

This was a beginning. Then the British Government appointed a Commission of five members under Lord Cobbold, former Governor of the Bank of England, to assess public reaction in Sarawak and Sabah to Malaysia. This Commission, which included two Malayan members, Dato Wong Pow Nee and Enche Muhammad Ghazali bin Shafie, and Sir Anthony Abell and Sir David Watherston, studied more than two thousand letters and documents and interviewed four thousand people in many parts of Borneo.

The Commission did not go to the Sultanate of Brunei, because it was an independent territory under the protection of Britain—not a Colony.

The Cobbold Report, which was published on August 1, 1962, is one of the most lucid and objective in British colonial history. It is not only a piece of fine reporting and interpretation, but is also, as a study of multi-racial problems, a significant document for history.

The Cobbold Report unanimously recommended the creation of Malaysia and closely followed the suggestions of the Solidarity Consultative Committee. It found that about one third of the population of Sarawak and Sabah strongly favored Malaysia. That one third favored it but wanted special conditions and safeguards. That one third was divided between those who insisted on independence before joining Malaysia—the Communist party line—and those who wanted to see British rule continue for some years, though many of this last sub-group showed that they would almost certainly support Malaysia once it was established.

The "hard core, vocal and politically active" which opposed Malaysia "on any terms unless it is preceded by independence and self-government" amounted to less than twenty per cent of the population, or perhaps two hundred thousand of the one million two hundred thousand people in Sarawak and Sabah, and, significantly, many of these two hundred thousand were Chinese.

On the same day that the Cobbold recommendations were published, Prime Minister Macmillan and Prime Minister Tunku Abdul Rahman announced in London that the Federation of Malaysia would be established "by August 31, 1963," and that a formal agreement would be signed "within the next six months" after legal, constitutional, and technical problems had been worked out. They also announced that they "would welcome" the State of Brunei in the new Federation, and later the Sultan of Brunei agreed in principle to join, though he did not say outright that he would join. (See Postscript: Brunei and Afterward, page 291.)

"By August 31." That is a symbolic date for the Tunku and Malaysia, because that was the day in 1957, Merdeka Day, when the Federation of Malaya won its independence from Britain.

August 1, 1962, and the official agreement to create Malaysia, was only fifteen months after the Tunku's original Malaysia speech and a clear indication that the Tunku and Lee Kuan Yew were anxious to beat the Communists for the real prize, Singapore, and also anxious, with their eyes on Indonesia, to make sure of the Borneo territories.

Progress toward Malaysia had been so rapid and successful that the Tunku probably relaxed a little, but Lee did not even slow down. A month later, on September 1, 1962, he held a referendum in Singapore.

When, months before, he had first mentioned this referendum as a way to test opinion about joining Malaysia, he worried many people as far apart as Singapore and London. A heavy anti-Malaysia vote by the extreme left wing was certain, particularly as Communist parties everywhere had opposed Malaysia without "independence first" and Peking had called the proposed new federation "neo-colonialist."

But Lee remained confident, and September 1 showed why. His referendum, if it can be called one, did not give the electorate an opportunity to vote for or against Malaysia. All it did was clarify citizenship. Voters were merely asked to choose among three ways of federating: merger under the terms of a Singapore Government White Paper, making all Singapore citizens automatically citizens of Malaysia and giving Singapore as a state of Malaysia autonomy in labor and education; merger which would give Singapore the same status and citizenship provisions as the component states of the Federation of Malaya; merger on no less favorable terms than those given to the Borneo territories.

The first choice was the only one a voter could make that day because the second meant practically the same thing but in different words and the third had no appeal to a Singaporean. When the left wing told its supporters to record blank votes at the referendum, Lee passed the word around that blanks would be counted as votes for the Government. Of 417,482 marked ballots, 397,626 favored the Government's choice, but the discipline and size of the extreme left wing was shown by the 144,077 blank votes counted. Although seventy per cent of the voters supported the Government by voting for the first choice, this was so much a shotgun referendum that even the Communists must have secretly admired the way Lee Kuan Yew used their own methods.

The referendum solved the final problem of Singapore and Malaysia, and as a guide to how to win a referendum, September 1 was a classic if you believe that the end justifies the means, but it could hardly be described as a triumph for democracy.

While roadblocks were being cleared on the trail to Malaysia, an attempt was made to build another, and probably not the last.

A press and political campaign had begun earlier in the Philippines "to recover North Borneo"—a campaign based on the argument that the Sultan of Sulu—the Sulu Islands are between Borneo and the Philippines—leased and did not cede this territory to the British Chartered Company in 1878.

The claim—it was supported by the Philippines House of Representatives and reached the United Nations General Assembly in November, 1962—came at an embarrassing time and from an unexpected quarter, for the Philippine Government is an ally of Britain in SEATO and, with the Federation of Malaya and Thailand, is a member of the Malaya-sponsored Association of Southeast Asian States. A.S.A., the letters optimistically spell "hope" in all three languages, seeks closer economic and cultural links between the three countries.

Both the Spanish and American former owners of the Philippines recognized Britain's control of North Borneo, and in 1946, when the United States granted independence to the Philippines, there was specific reference to North Borneo being under British protection.

Fortunately for the British, they hold a picturesque little document dated January 22, 1878, which supports the old business practice of keeping copies of all letters and documents. This scrap of paper says: "We, Sri Paduka Maulana Al Sultan Mohamet Jamal Al Alam, Sultan of Sulu and the dependencies thereof, on behalf of ourselves, our heirs and successors . . . grant and cede of our own free and sovereign will to Baron de Overbeck of Hong Kong and Alfred Dent of London . . . their heirs, associates, successors and assigns forever and in perpetuity all the rights and powers belonging to us over all the territories and lands being tributory to us on the mainland of the island of Borneo. . . ."

Under the agreement the Sultan of Sulu, who was overlord of northeast Borneo, not all North Borneo, "grants and cedes" the territory not only to Overbeck and Dent, but to their "successors and assigns forever and in perpetuity" on the condition that these pay the Sultan's heirs five thousand dollars a year.

The claim that the Sultan—Manila ceased to recognize the Sultanate after 1936—only leased his lands and that Overbeck and Dent had no authority to assign them, is refuted by this agreement—though we live at a time when many pacts and agreements have not been honored.

Baron de Overbeck, who was Austrian Consul-General in Hong Kong, sold his share in the North Borneo Company to Dent, and around Dent's enterprise was built the British North Borneo Company, which was granted a Royal Charter by Queen Victoria. The territory became a British protectorate in 1888, and in 1946 was ceded to the British Crown as a Colony, which continues to pay the five thousand dollars to the Sultan's heirs.

Although the real purpose of the Philippines' claim, which Britain and Malaya reject, and which Donald Stephens of North Borneo has called "silly and without legal backing," appears to some to demonstrate, mainly for internal political purposes, the Philippine Government's new foreign policy of being completely independent of the United States, there seems to be a deeper purpose behind the move—fear of Indonesian expansion into northern Borneo, fear of Indonesian Communist infiltration from that area into the Philippines.

Tunku Abdul Rahman dismissed the Philippines' claim, but reacted much more strongly to a statement from Djakarta that Indonesia "would not remain indifferent" to the formation of Greater Malaysia. To this country he distrusts, he said, "Keep your hands out of our affairs."

The history of the next year or so should tell us whether they took any notice of that statement.

17

In official discussions on Malaysia, the Singapore Base has been used by all sides as a bargaining point. By the British, as a condition to agreeing to the inclusion of Sarawak and Sabah and as a guarantee for British investments. By the Tunku, who needed it for protection but who, because of Malaya's policy of non-alignment, had to keep up the public fiction as long as possible that the Base could not be used as part of the SEATO alliance. And by Lee Kuan Yew, who also needed it for security and because the Base, which covers about one third of the Island and employs about forty thousand workers at a cost of about one hundred million pounds a year to the British taxpayer—a sum which accounts for nearly one quarter of the Island's economy—is vital to the stability of Singapore.

In the early stages of this horse-trading the Tunku repeatedly said that he would not agree to Singapore being used as a base for SEATO, but even then it was obvious that as he wanted Malaysia, and wanted it quickly, he would have to compromise. And compromise he did in November, 1961, when, following a visit to Saigon, where the military realities of South Vietnam frightened him, he agreed that the Singapore Base should continue to function without restriction under the proposed Federation of Malaysia.

This London agreement allowed Singapore to be used for the defense of Malaysia and for Commonwealth defense and also for "the preservation of peace in Southeast Asia," a clause which, although deliberately vague, meant that Singapore could be used for SEATO, as it is now.

But look at the Base and its geography and you wonder as a layman whether it has a future. Is it, as an English writer once said, at worst a liability, at best a wasting asset?

The Singapore Base—Naval, Air bases, Army establishments and workshops—is on a small island. One atomic rocket, two, at the most, would atomize it and all Singapore Island. Singapore is a static base in a world where military survival, so the experts insist, depends on dispersal and the use of highly mobile forces.

Singapore exists on the water which comes across the Causeway from the Malaya mainland, and whoever controls that water controls Singapore.

The Tunku's successors may not share his views about the Base when it is on Malaysian, not British, soil.

The Base is literally next door to Indonesia, the strongest resident military power in Southeast Asia, with the third-largest Communist party in the world.

The British Government spends one hundred million pounds a year on Singapore. This was understandable when Britain owned territory in Southeast Asia, but when Malaysia is established, her sole possession in Asia will be Hong Kong, which remains British through the grace and favor of Communist China.

Britain, in agreeing to Malaysia, virtually severed her long connection with Southeast Asia and reversed her centuries-old strategic policy.

My interpretation of this is that she is abandoning Asia to concentrate on Europe, that in the future her share in SEATO will be token only, that she would be unable to play any major part in Southeast Asia in time of war or to reinforce any forces she had there, and that Australia and New Zealand must be prepared to look after themselves and to play a much more positive part militarily, economically, and all other ways to help their friends in Southeast Asia.

The implications of Britain's withdrawal—and all signs suggest withdrawal once Malaysia is firmly established—are immense for Australians and New Zealanders, the only white people in all Asia from Japan to the Mediterranean.

This new psychological isolation, for physical isolation ceased with the jet and the rocket, is something Australians have never faced before and, happy in their ignorance and indifference, still hardly realize is almost an established fact.

Australians are still as ignorant about Southeast Asia, and Asia generally, as they were a quarter of a century ago, and, except for a few diplomats, businessmen, students, and others, almost as uninterested. They look at television pictures of India or Malaya or Indonesia, but still think of those places as being far away and not part of their world and urgently close. If you asked ten Australians where Kuching was, seven wouldn't know, three would guess China, and none would care.

Australians still teach their school children about the "Far East," still use the term in everyday writing and conversation, and continue to build up an unreal impression of distance and remoteness. They still concentrate on the history of England and Europe when they are no longer Europeans and when the history they should know, and don't, is just north of them.

In what is a continental extension of Asia—North Australia is only a few hundred miles from Indonesia and Australian Papua now has a common border with Indonesian West Irian —this Victorian myopia toward Asia is perhaps best illustrated by many of Australia's political leaders, whose knowledge of Asia is vague, as Parliamentary debates will prove, and whose thinking on Asia, like Australia's so-called foreign policy, is fumbling and without conviction.

To her own people, and to people outside, Australia gives the impression that she waits until events happen, then tries desperately to decide what should be done about them. If she moves, she moves after somebody else has taken the initiative. Australia has for so long been a carbon copy of others that she appears to have ceased to have a mind of her own.

These are weaknesses, even for a minor country, which Asians notice. As one political leader in Malaya said: "You were a British colony once. So were we. This is a bond. You have a democracy which works. This is also our aim, though in time our democracy may take a different form from yours. We appreciate your part in the Colombo Plan. You are a training ground for our students. You are a natural supplier of many of the things we need to help raise our standard of living. But you should be playing a much more important role in this part of the world. Your heads of state should be on the most intimate terms with Asian leaders. They are not. Infrequent visits by Ministers can be not a help but an irritant. You worry us at times with your lack of elementary knowledge of Asia and its peoples. You are close neighbors physically. But you are not close in your minds."

Yet Australia's diplomatic representation in Southeast Asia, in Asia, is first class. Her diplomats are the best—able, well-informed men capable of making decisions with accuracy and conviction if their political leaders in Canberra, whose mental and emotional orientation is still toward Europe, showed real knowledge and critical appreciation of the tidal forces of history moving north of the Timor Sea.

For the tenth-anniversary meeting of Colombo Plan countries in Kuala Lumpur, all countries except Australia were represented by their Foreign Ministers. This may seem unimportant, but not in Asia. In K.L. the absence not only of a Foreign Minister, but of at least a Minister, created critical comment at top level against Australia. This absence was not

just bad manners. It was an example of political ignorance—
and not by Australian diplomats—which Asians are quick to
notice and to remember.

Australia had a fine opportunity after World War II to
create an impression of herself as a dynamic, liberal, humanitarian country with a mind of its own—above all a country
which was not only sympathetic toward Asia but also understood that she was part of the Southeast Asian world.

A share in the Colombo Plan was a gesture, not an embrace
of friendship. One man, Lord Casey, did his lone best to relate
Australia to Asia, and Asians responded to his warmth and
concern. In many areas he was the only Australian Asians
could name. But one man of good will, followed after a
lapse of many years by another, Australia's present Minister for
External Affairs, Sir Garfield Barwick, who is trying hard to
patch the errors of official indifference and be Attorney-Gen-
eral at the same time—a ridiculous situation—cannot hope to
balance generations of political and historical ignorance and
neglect by Australia. Over the years Australians have ignored
the warnings of rare individuals in their political life and
have drifted more and more into well-fed isolation until today
they have few firm friends and are gathering enemies.

This is a criticism, but it is more a plea. This is Australia's
world and she has to survive here, if she can. And Australians
will have a better chance of survival if they cease to be the
strangers they are, and show, through their interest, help, conviction that they are close, well-informed, understanding neighbors. Australians must stop bluffing themselves that they are
fine, friendly, outgiving fellows. They're insular and smug and
not overgenerous, and so content with the high standard of
living they love to praise that a Malay or an Indonesian peasant
living on a dollar a day if he is lucky doesn't move them because they never give him a thought.

Australians (the West generally) have a significant part to
play in the Southeast Asia of which they are a part—as university, workshop, training college, laboratory, as a place with

everything from sophisticated industry to a fine legal system, as a crucible of ideas, as a military ally, as a society of example and compassion. But only if they realize that the problems north of them are compellingly urgent, only if they make up their minds that as the most industrially and socially advanced country in Southeast Asia they have a responsibility to help their less-fortunate, less-advanced friends and neighbors.

I would like to see an Australian Ministry for Southeast Asia; a Canberra Plan, based on a special tax, which would shame Australia's pathetic Colombo aid; scientific and technical help of all kinds on a massive scale and directed at the peasantry; a major exchange of teachers and students and a major increase in scholarships for clever poor students and not the sons and daughters of the wealthy or the well-to-do middle class; the teaching of a much wider range of Asian history, geography, religion, and languages in Australian schools, particularly secondary schools and universities; many more resident correspondents in Asia for newspapers, radio, and television—specialists on Asia to keep Australians expertly informed; a quota system for Asians.

This last would at least be a gesture to Asia and to the multi-racial British Commonwealth that Australia no longer excludes because of race or color. But even a quota system would be too late if Australians think of it as a form of protection or appeasement. The only value of a quota system today would be as part of a completely altered relationship between Australia and Asia, and it is not too late for that. This implies much more than gestures. It means a change in heart, a change in perspective, the evolution of a new type of Australian, who is no longer European in his thinking but Southeast Asian.

The struggle for Asia is much more ideological than military. Lack of food is a weapon more deadly than bullets. The threat from within is just as dangerous as battles along the perimeter. Australia must be ready to give and help on a grand scale—on a scale she hasn't imagined before. Australians must discard their prejudices and apathy. They must become, as part of Southeast Asia, friendly and sympathetic with its peoples, personally concerned with their problems, ready not only to help them raise their living standards but also to share their dangers.

And there is little time, for the pressure is on Southeast Asia, from without and within.

18

The birth of Greater Malaysia will, with three small exceptions —Portuguese Timor in Indonesia, Portuguese Macao, and British Hong Kong in China—mark the end of European colonialism and authority in Southeast and Eastern Asia. And of these frail three, Timor is likely to disappear first, since its chances of surviving Indonesian occupation, either from without or within, are slim.

The old struggle by white-ruled people for independence will cease, but the new struggle, which has already been going on for years, will continue. As one collective imperialism dies it is being replaced by another (and possibly two), and one which is fighting not just for territory and trade but, brown skin against brown, yellow against yellow, brother against brother, for the conquest of this section of the world.

The issue in Southeast Asia, the one spot where the advance of Communism is not being held, is no longer Asian nationalism against white colonialism, but Asian nationalism against Asian Communism, for this is the close of one era, which began with Ferdinand Magellan four centuries ago and ended with the Japanese war and Mao Tse-tung's capture of China, and the beginning of another.

Greater Malaysia will be a fragmented place—a country joined by a Causeway and four hundred miles of sea. It will have the highest living standard in Southeast Asia, the most stable currency, the best health and education services, the finest ports, the only industry, riches in rubber, tin, oil, timber, rice. It will have the most stable and efficient government. It will be anti-Communist. It will disrupt the piecemeal conquest of Southeast Asia. Yet it will lie in a geographically and strategically dangerous position, clamped between Indonesia, with its third-strongest Communist party in the world, and the mainland of Asia, where Chinese and Chinese-aided Communism is slowly taking over.

Greater Malaysia will also be one of the world's strangest families—a collection of more than twenty different peoples at widely different stages of social and political development. These people will vary from highly sophisticated groups to blow-pipe tribesmen millennia behind the times—a tropical mixture of color, language, custom, and thought living in mountains and marsh and cities no more than two degrees north of the Equator.

Can this cocktail federation of university graduates and latent head-hunters, of millionaires and peasants, of simple fishermen and near-feudal Sultans, of hungry coolies and secret-society gangsters, survive? Can this racial and religious mixture with divided loyalties, few traditions of government, no common language or culture, and in an area where people and education and thinking have always been splintered, achieve a common understanding, a common identity, a common purpose?

In Malaya-Singapore, which will hold about two thirds of the ten million people of Greater Malaysia, Chinese, Malays, Indians, and others have lived together for generations in reasonable amity. There have been racial and religious clashes, though many of these have been more economic than anything else, but generally serious friction in this multi-racial and religious society has been rare. Rare, largely because the British kept the

racial peace, with clubs when necessary; and religious toleration was also helped by two important facts—the presence of
the Islamic religion and the scarcity of Christians in the population.

But racial harmony, however admirable, has always been
negative. All races were subservient to the British. Real unity
did not exist. Malays and Chinese and Indians appeared to
be united, but like marbles in a bag, they ran in all directions
when spilled on the floor. Now the situation has changed
radically for the population of Greater Malaysia; although it
will be a bagful of different peoples, it won't have the British
to keep the peace between two main and almost numerically
equal racial groups—the Malays and those native peoples of the
Borneo territories who are Muslims, and the Chinese.

The Malays suspect the Chinese and have within their own
society fanatical political sections whose retrogressive thinking
is tied to the Islam of the past. The Malays, who will dominate
the Government at the start, will therefore need immense tolerance to face with wisdom and tact the multitude of responsibilities and dangers of Greater Malaysia.

But what of the non-native Chinese, immigrants or descendants of immigrants who came directly and indirectly from the
China heartland?

Some see the Chinese of Malaysia, and particularly the Chinese of Singapore, as a huge fifth column. This is an exaggeration—at least at present. The majority of the Chinese want to
continue to live in Malaysia and to help make it work. They
have nowhere else to go. They are good citizens, by geography
and choice. Few, except the Communists and their supporters,
seek to destroy Malaysia and re-create it in the image of Peking.

But this is too simple, and for an important reason. Since the
defeat of Chiang Kai-shek and the rise of Mao Tse-tung, the
Chinese of Southeast Asia have become a schizophrenic people.
Their conflict is between where they live and their emotional
attitude to where they used to live or where their fathers lived,
for many have never seen China. Their intelligence—and no

more intelligent people exist—tells them that the realities of life, a much better life than they or their fathers ever enjoyed in China, or could enjoy, are where they live and prosper now —along the Equator. But their emotions, fed by their earth-deep superiority as a people, by a nostalgic idealized love for ancestral China, tug, tug, tug at them. Even anti-Communist Chinese, or Chinese bitterly disillusioned because of the treatment of relatives or friends in China, or Chinese who resent China's regime because they have to spend hard-earned dollars—millions a year—on food parcels and remittances to keep relatives in Communist China alive—even these Chinese still feel the pull of the ancestral soil while opposing the politics of those who rule that soil. But it is not only the soil. Even they have also received something indirectly from today's China —something they had never known before as overseas Chinese. That something is Face—pride, integrity, whatever you like to call it—and Face is the handmaiden of interest, sympathy, perhaps even of ultimate conversion. The Chinese-educated feel closer to China than the English-educated, and they are generally closer in time. And it is these Chinese-educated, who speak little or no English, perhaps no Malay, on whom the Communist party is working with success. The emotional pressure on all overseas Chinese is strong, for the air is jammed with propaganda flooding in from Peking, Korea, North Vietnam, a collective portrait of a resurgent fatherland, powerful, tolerant, just, and opposed by a wicked reactionary world. This endless tale of success and glory is not easy to resist indefinitely if you are Chinese, if you are an immigrant or the son of an immigrant, if you speak only your own dialect, if you are young, if you know even dimly that the Chinese Empire was once great and will be great again, if you remember that the white imperialisms of Southeast Asia, now departed into history, were built up largely by the sweat of your own people, the Chinese.

The Chinese know that the one great unsolved problem of Malaysia, of Southeast Asia, is simply themselves. They are the key people in Malaysia, and especially in Singapore, which some of them have already turned into a dangerous island. The Chinese are on trial—and they know it.

But the Chinese are not the only people who have to revolutionize their thinking, who have to start feeling Malaysians. How does a Murut from the Sabah highlands, who has probably never seen the sea or heard of Kuala Lumpur, begin to think as a citizen of Malaysia? How does this strange idea of a sea-separated federation look from the longhouse of a Sarawak Land Dayak a few years removed from his favorite hobby, lopping heads? How, indeed, can a Hindu rubber tapper or an Arab shopkeeper or a Pakistani taxi driver or a Malay peasant or a Punan blowpipe hunter come to feel a Malaysian?

As citizens of a manufactured Malaysia all face this problem of national identity, yet it is still the Chinese, because of their numbers, economic power, political awareness, apartness, arrogance, who have to prove, more than any other people, that they can become Asian, Malaysian, in a tropical sense. They have to prove that they can resolve their schizophrenia, harness the emotional Han chauvinism which is bedeviling them. They have to start thinking of themselves as Malaysians first, to submerge themselves in a new concept that is so alien to their thinking. And never did the Chinese face a more difficult task.

Becoming Malaysian does not mean changing their dress, eating different food, accepting the Muslim religion, altering their traditional customs and way of life. But it does mean that, although Chinese by birth and inheritors of an ancient and great cultural tradition, they can be Chinese first no longer, but citizens of Malaysia with a common loyalty, along with Malays and Ibans and two dozen others, to Malaysia.

Many Chinese, particularly the English-educated who have lived in Malaya or Singapore or the Borneo territories for generations, will merge into the mental and emotional environment of the new Malaysia. They are part of it already.

Their home is not China, but where they live. But some, especially among the Chinese-educated, and primarily the young, will not merge, and it is they who will make the formative years of Malaysia a testing time for all Chinese. If the Chinese as a community fail to adjust, to learn to belong, then apprehension will grow among their fellow citizens and fear will lead to repression and conflict.

But the testing place for the Chinese, the real danger point for Malaysia—though there are others—will be Singapore, for Singapore, unlike any other part of Malaysia, is a Chinese city and island in the geographical center of Malaysia.

In education the British failed the Chinese, who were forced, with their own money, to educate their children and even to start their own University of Nanyang, near the western end of Singapore Island.

This planned and landscaped Little China of cream buildings, hostels, bungalows, and flats grouped around the green curving Chinese roofs of its central Library and the red pavilions and miniature bridges and pagodas of its traditional Chinese garden, cost the local Chinese twenty million dollars to build and costs about two million dollars a year to run.

Nanyang University's Library holds more than one hundred thousand books, about seventy thousand of them Chinese. Its student body of two thousand, ninety per cent of whom live at the University, comes from Singapore, Malaya, Borneo, and Thailand. Nearly all its instruction is in Mandarin. Its academic standard is low and the quality of its degrees poor.

This physically attractive University, in its five-hundred-acre rural setting of forest and palms and kampongs, is a tragically mixed-up place. It was started by Kuomintang Chinese—wealthy merchants and others whose allegiance was to Formosa, and its direction is still by "Formosa" Chinese. But many of its students and ex-students and some of its staff have no sympathy toward the Chiang Kai-shek regime or the ideals and aims of Malaysia. They look to Communist China, some ideologically, some with a high degree of emotional attachment.

When Nanyang was opened in 1956 its first Chancellor was Lin Yutang, the noted Chinese philosopher and writer. But he stayed only six months or so, and the most common explanation in Singapore is that the student body virtually forced his resignation. As a Formosa Chinese he found it impossible to direct a University where many of the students looked to Peking.

Nanyang, which turns out many teachers and government servants, began with sound motives, but now it is helping to fan Chinese chauvinism and to split the Chinese community in language, background, and allegiance. A Chinese university has no place in a multi-racial society where the aim is to break down racial separateness. It is a danger spot for Singapore, for Malaya, for Malaysia. Nanyang should be taken over by the Government of Singapore and made "international"—Malaysian—for education, including tertiary education, has provided an ideal recruiting ground for the Communist party. The Communists, by accentuating the apartness of the Chinese-educated stream, and by playing on the emotionalism of that apartness, are winning converts among the splintered Chinese.

Malaysia is of course the last thing the Communists and their supporters want, because it will help break the developing pattern of conquest of Southeast Asia from within, will destroy or damage the carefully constructed Communist organization, fronts, and cells.

But it is impossible to consider Malaysia without looking south at Indonesia. One of the most ominous portents is how closely Malaysian Communists are working with the two-million-strong Indonesian Communist party, the P.K.I., which has denounced the creation of Malaysia. Singapore front organizations have even suggested that Singapore should merge with Indonesia. Malaysian party members train in Indonesian Communist schools—schools which concentrate on the indoctrination and conversion of the workers and the peasantry and the tribal groups in Borneo.

A Communist Indonesia would mean the beginning of the end of Malaysia, because, short of a major war to defend Malaysia, the Indonesians would squeeze the new federation and the Philippines from the south against the Chinese Communist–aided pressure from the north.

An expansionist, nationalist Indonesia could do the same. Although there are sane groups in Indonesia who want to consolidate and develop internally, there are others who see Indonesia controlling Southeast Asia, New Guinea, and the Western Pacific, and the Indian Ocean as far west as Madagascar.

With the creation of Malaysia, Indonesian Kalimantan will continue to have a common land border with Sarawak and Sabah. If the Philippines, a member of SEATO and A.S.A., the Association of Southeast Asian States, can claim part of North Borneo, then a claim to Sabah or Brunei or Sarawak or all three by Indonesia, or the support of anti-Malaysia groups within those territories, is possible.

Since Malaysia was first suggested, Indonesia has shown clearly that she does not want to see it created, and particularly as part of it will be the northern third of the island of Borneo.

Indonesia, with foreign arms, particularly Russian, is already the major military power in Southeast Asia. If Indonesia were friendly to her neighbors this arms build-up would not worry them. In a precarious world she has a right to be strong. It would be just as silly to suggest that Australia has expansionist aims because she has a small Navy, Army, and Air Force as to suggest that Indonesia has territorial ambitions because she wants to be able to defend herself.

But Indonesia has never been on the best terms with Malaya; she opposes the creation of Malaysia, and she used her Army to force the delivery of West Irian. Though West Irian, or Dutch New Guinea, as it used to be called, was part of the original Netherlands Indies, it should have been handed over to Indonesia after the Pacific war, and Australia a dozen years ago should have supported Indonesia in this as part of a realistic and friendly approach, as a Southeast Asian state, to her nearest neighbor.

It is understandable that the Indonesian leaders are still suspicious of colonialism, and find it hard to appreciate that colonial territories like Sarawak and Sabah will cease to be colonies with the creation of Malaysia. Anti-colonialism is a genuine deep-felt emotion which cannot be minimized or dismissed. It is part of the Indonesian revolution which the West, and particularly Australia, must try to understand.

It is no surprise that revolutionaries like Dr. Sukarno, beset with grave internal economic and political problems, including a massive Communist movement, should not talk publicly like a gentle Sunday-school teacher, although his fiercely worded truculence is more often directed to his own splintered Indonesians than to people outside.

You cannot hope to understand the Indonesians, who lived for three centuries under colonial rule, Dutch rule, if you think exclusively with a Western mind. Their logic, like the logic of the Japanese, has no white in it. That is why the greatest tolerance must be exercised before judgments are made, why understanding of thought processes and motives and needs is more important than criticism at this stage of the Indonesian revolution, and why Australia, the West generally, must give Indonesia its friendship and help.

It is, however, true that Indonesia, with one hundred million people, is beginning to see herself as the power of Southeast Asia, and because of the tensions this has created, especially between Indonesia and Malaya, and also with the Philippines, Indonesia's smaller and weaker neighbors can perhaps be excused for asking not why she is arming on a major scale, but what she is arming for.

Is it to put down the Sulu pirates, who every few months grab a boatload of food or island supplies? Is it her own Communists? Is it Malaya or Malaysia? Or somebody else? And who is encouraging this arms build-up? Her own expansionists? Russia, to outflank the United States and SEATO, or perhaps at long range even China herself? Her own Communists, who have infiltrated the Indonesian Army and seriously infiltrated the Air Force, so that they will have the military organization and arms for a take-over?

Indonesia is not entirely blameless if many people in the Southeast Asia of which Australia is a part are worried about her intentions, for rockets and atomic bombers in Indonesia, whoever controls them, would dictate the future of Southeast Asians from Hobart to Bangkok, from Manila to Rangoon.

The tourist, standing on Singapore's water front, does not realize that the islands he sees through the morning mist are Indonesian, that Singapore's common border with Indonesia runs through Main Strait, which separates Singapore from the "Thousand Islands" of the Rhio Archipelago. He does not realize that that border is not much more than a mile or so from Raffles Hotel.

19

For Han Suyin, mainland Asia ends almost at the bottom of her garden, where the red earth slopes to the Straits of Johore. The Straits are pewter or jade by day, copper-pink at dusk, an almost mile-wide span between the most southerly point of the world's largest land mass and the back door to Singapore.

Han Suyin does not see Singapore Island as the tourist sees it, from the rail of a liner threading the islands along Main Strait or from the window of a jet wing-dipped to Paya Lebar. She sees it as Chinese sailors saw it two millennia ago from junks bound for India and the Red Sea, for this was the passage they used to avoid the offshore reefs, or as the Johore Sultans saw it, a useless island clothed in jungle, sodden with swamp, the home of pirates and tigers and malaria. She sees it as Yamashita's weary soldiers saw it twenty years ago when, at the end of the Malaya campaign, they peered across the Straits, across the dynamited Causeway, to the island they would capture in a week.

From the workroom of her white stilted bungalow in the Johore capital, Johore Bahru, I could just see the water, and Singapore Island beyond, under the veranda rail draped with a Persian rug and two saris, one edged with gold. Airing, too, in the scalding sun, which destroys the tropical mildew sprouting in a night, were ten pairs of satin evening shoes—duck egg, tangarine, crimson, black, violet, emerald—lying with their high heels in the air like the legs of can-can dancers.

Her workroom had lilac walls and grey floor tiles and chairs and lounges upholstered in the color of strawberries. Her table was teak with metal legs, but her typewriter was closed and covered. Close by was a carved wood Ch'ing screen, a couple of centuries old perhaps, and on one wall a classical scroll and on another a swirl of mustards and greens.

I was still admiring the abstract, Chinese and local, when Dr. Elizabeth Comber, as the novelist is known in private life, came up the stairs from her ground-floor surgery, her arms full of parcels. She offered me her only free finger, a little one, and a smile so friendly that I was still holding that finger when she said, "If I depended on my medicine, I would starve," which is true, because these days she sees only her old patients and never even charges them except for medicines.

Her voice is quick and rich and decorated with that accent of the Asian to whom English is an alien. Her face is sharpened, her nose strong and un-Chinese, yet she looks far more Chinese than Eurasian. Her eyes are the color of raisins, not the black-brown of Asia, her teeth are unfashionably irregular, her hair is black, cropped almost like a boy's, and she brushes it off her forehead with impatient hands lean and strong enough to dig a ditch. She has two vertical lines etched between her eyebrows, which give her an artificial frown, and the lines narrow when she laughs, but in repose her face smiles secretly and only she knows why.

She is so slim that an Australian would say she needs a good feed. And her clothes—tight slacks of light-brown patterned batek and a Chinese coat—accentuate this skinniness. As she curled on a sofa, tucked her bare feet under her, and lit the first of many cigarettes, she was without a curve, without an angle, just for a moment a small hungry Chinese girl I remember in a cold doorway in war-torn Shanghai.

"Han Suyin means the small quiet voice," she said, smiling across the room.

"Of reason?"

Her European eyes widened. She came alive.

"No, of protest."

I had come to talk to her about the Chinese of Malaysia, and I did eventually. But for most of that morning I was much more interested in Han Suyin—her alertness and concentration, her way of pouncing on fact or opinion and shaking it, her exhausting energy, her warming charm, her sudden moments of almost frightening seriousness. She dominated with her vitality, her cerebration. Women would probably loathe her. Men—not every man's cup of tea. A brilliant, dynamic, delightful, unpredictable, and at times, I suspect, impossible woman. Under certain circumstances, about as emotional as a small cyclone. But there was a tenseness about her which puzzled me. She broadcast a wave—a strained searching for something she had never discovered and probably never would, an aloneness which set her apart. I had been told by Singapore Mems whom I suspected had never met her except at some impersonal party that I would discover a strong masculine streak, but watching her on the sofa, her feet tucked under her, her laughter as warm as the colors of the Persian rug over the railings, I found her alarmingly feminine.

She called for coffee, in Chinese, and pointed to cigarettes in a Cambodian silver box shaped like a leaf.

"I am a Eurasian, but I feel Asian—not international."

You know that she means Chinese, for she is more Chinese than anything else. Her European blood has been diluted by the strong Han. But she feels deeply for people, all people, and that is one reason, apart from her love of heat, why she prefers to live among many races and to use their intermingled problems and color and customs in her novels. She may even see herself as an Asian Lawrence Durrell, for she thinks that his ability to convey in his work the feeling and thought of the racial streams of the Mediterranean is the secret of his vivid success.

Han Suyin is forty-four and was born in Peking, where her family were aristocratic and wealthy. Her scholar father was Chinese, her mother Belgian, and she was brought up a Christian, a Catholic, but is now agnostic.

"My students [at Nanyang University, where she lectures] ask me if God exists. I say I don't know. It is just as silly for me to say there is no God as to say there is a God. Everything, the universe of rockets and radio-astronomers, is so immense that if God exists I can't feel that He would be interested in small me. All I can do is try to be truthful, try to live decently."

This novelist who always wanted to be a doctor and who in a serious and yet almost dilettantish way sees a few old patients at morning surgery, now earns a formidable income as a writer, a craft she does not particularly like. Yet she loves words and has an instinctive feeling for them, which she showed from the beginning with her first book, her *Destination Chungking*, written in Chungking between Japanese bombing raids.

For ten years after its publication she never wrote a line. She was busy, true, studying medicine, being a wife, having a baby, but if the desire to write had existed, she would have written. She is being honest when she says she doesn't like writing.

Her first husband, and father of her only daughter, Yung Mei, was Chinese Military Attaché in London during World War II. But Han Suyin was not designed for diplomacy. At a dinner party, when three of her guests were senior Generals, she suggested that the best way to stop the war would be to send all Generals over fifty to fight. The dinner was not a success.

After World War II, and after the death of her husband in the Chinese civil war, she returned to England and, while working to support herself and her daugher, finished her medical course at London University, and finished it with honors.

Only when she returned to Asia did she write again, and then it was A *Many-Splendoured Thing*, the novel which made her name—her own love story in Hong Kong with "Mark Elliott," an Australian-born English newspaperman with a China background, a man of great personal charm and sensitivity and a colleague of mine whom I served with in Burma and who was later to die on a land mine in Korea.

Other novels have followed, *And the Rain My Drink*, *The Mountain Is Young*, but although she still loves words, she still dislikes writing, and writes generally in frenetic bursts between periods which stretch sometimes for weeks of silence. Perhaps this is because she is caught between two worlds, between two languages she loves, between the words of her Chinese classical past and the words of her two classical English favorites, Chaucer and Shakespeare.

Like Joseph Conrad, who first thought in Polish, translated mentally into French, then wrote in English, Han Suyin first has to think in Mandarin before she can record her thoughts in English, and even after writing for years she still feels that she has never mastered English construction and never knows how to put speech into English mouths.

She thinks that one of these days her writing problems will be solved when she learns to think and write only in Chinese, but perhaps by then she will have switched to some other craft or reverted to her first love, medicine, to solve her unrequited restlessness.

The lives of most people flicker aimlessly. She burns. Her average day, when she is not traveling or interviewing some world personality or dropping in on Khatmandu or working on a film in Cambodia, is patients, writing, reading, studying, lecturing, a day which begins before dawn, when the Straits below her home trail mist, and ends at two or three o'clock the next morning.

"None of this, except writing, is work to me. It is being a functioning human being. It is living every minute. I am fortunate that I have always been able to do exactly as I liked."

In that statement is much of her real self, and her relationships with others must have suffered because of this consuming inward-directed energy, which seldom sleeps.

Han Suyin is a singular mixture of the practical and the fey, with an addition of something that might add up to fanaticism. She won't keep copies of her own novels in her house because she claims they inhibit her. And there isn't a Han Suyin manuscript in existence because she loses interest and destroys them. Her bungalow is one of three identical buildings on a couple of acres of land. One she rents to an English family, one to a Chinese. A sound business proposition in the best real-estate tradition—a conventional investment. Yet she refuses to see her banker more than twice a year—a fortunate arrangement few can share—people who keep strict accounts and pay their bills at the end of the month bewilder her, and she admits she is probably the easiest person in the world to cheat. While she was describing how she had been badly cheated only that morning, she began to quote her favorite author, and only later was I able to check the quotation and find that it was Iago's: "Who steals my purse steals trash. . . . But he that filches from me my good name/Robs me of that which not enriches him/And makes me poor indeed."

When we at last began to discuss the Chinese, she sat forward, serious, tense, smoking cigarette after cigarette, speaking rapidly.

"I am critical of many things in China today. Tibet, for example. But the influence of China will be felt here in the years to come. Ten years from now—who knows?"

I watched her closely, for Han Suyin suffers the same disease as many of the overseas Chinese. She is split in blood between two worlds, split geographically, split emotionally, as so many intelligent Chinese are. She is part of the bewildering conflict between desire to be associated with her father's people and dislike for the excesses of the regime which rules her homeland, between admiration for the good things in the Chinese revolution and dismay at the evil.

"The Chinese here have one great problem they must solve. They must learn tolerance. It is the key to the future of this part of the world. They must learn to regard this area where they live as home, to feel part of it with all others who live here. But understanding is not fully possible without communication, and half the battle not only of this area but also of the world is semantic."

I interrupted. "But communication here gets lost in words. If a politician has a simple statement to make, he uses a thousand words of double talk."

She smiled. "Asians are not inhibited like you Europeans. They express themselves freely. In Europe you feel that people are talking from behind huge defense works. They don't seem to be able to express what they feel. They are tight inside, constipated. A Malay said to me only yesterday, 'If you boil a stone it doesn't soften it.' That was perfect. It fitted our conversation beautifully. Ordinary Asians, peasants, talk freely, using classical allusions from the remote past. They don't know they are doing this, and that is the beauty of it. There is a freedom and a color in their talk you never get in the West. The Chinese do this all the time. I think it is only the intellectual, of any country, who loses his real freedom of communication, whose language becomes polished and lifeless because it has no blood left in it."

She smiled again. "I think I have said enough."

I smiled back. "Plenty. But what's the answer to this problem of communication—here?"

"The Malay language—the language of the area. The Tunku and Lee Kuan Yew are right in insisting on Malay as the national language. Malay is the only language which will give national cohesion, because it will open doors between all races. English is also important. It is an international language, and that is why there is tremendous concentration on it in China today. But you can't get that idea accepted here.

"Malay, not Chinese, should be the main language at Nanyang University, but the Chinese who support Nanyang are

for Formosa, and won't think of it, while the students are for
China. Chinese students from the English stream of education
should study in Malay and English, and Chinese students from
the Chinese stream, especially those at Nanyang, should study
in Malay and Chinese. Then both student groups would have
a common language, a national language, and would have a
common meeting ground which they do not have now."

I wondered whether she would agree that Nanyang was
started by wealthy Kuomintang Chinese because of the failure
of the British to give the Chinese higher education and that this
had accentuated the split between the English- and Chinese-
educated Chinese.

"That is not only true. It is also perceptive. Few here will
admit it. But when will many people realize that this problem
is not in black and white, or should I say yellow and white. It
is still true that if a Chinese speaks English he is not necessarily
anti-Communist, and if he speaks only Chinese he is not necessarily pro-Communist.

"The most intelligent thing for the Government to do would
be to support Nanyang. If it fails to do this it will drive the
student body toward China. It is not too late. But to ignore
this problem in a Chinese city like Singapore, where most
Chinese are anti-Formosa or indifferent to Formosa, and where
the student body at Nanyang is chauvinistically pro-China, is
to push those students into the Communist camp."

Culture is the most-used word in Malaysia. It is also the most
meaningless. Politicians speak monotonously of the need to
develop a "Malayan culture" as a solution to national identity
and unity. Some talk as if a culture can be manufactured like
shirts. Others take the artie-craftie attitude that a national culture will flower from Indian dancers, Malay pantuns, and
Chinese jugglers.

There is no such thing as a Malayan or Malaysian culture.
Nor could a common culture hope to develop among the
racial fragmentation of colonialism. But today, although no-

body can identify it, a Malaysian culture is at least an ideal, vague and unformed, something to think about and stumble toward, a flickering mirage on the rise at the end of the road.

Malaysia at its beginning will be a clash of cultures which can begin to blend into something tangible only through a common language, common citizenship, education, intermarriage, living together for a long time, through the sifting of ideas, the breaking down of racial prejudices, the acknowledgment that your neighbor is not Chinese or Indian or Iban but your neighbor, the slow, painful, destructive, creative, exasperating evolution of a common identity.

For most of its adults Malaysia will be too late, but not for its children, if they are given time, and time, in the world we live in, is a doubtful question mark, and Malaysia will desperately need time.

I was sitting one evening in a bar in Singapore's Orchard Road talking with an English academic.

"The peoples of Malaysia may achieve some racial and cultural integration in a century," he said, "but long before that China will rule most of the world."

Few people think that much can be achieved under a generation, but the population of Malaysia is among the world's youngest, and it should be possible, largely through this youth, to achieve the beginnings of Malaysian awareness and cohesion in less than twenty years.

What stands out most about Malaysia is not the federation of the five territories but the attempted integration of so many widely different peoples, and again and again, as I talked and thought about this, I had an almost uncanny feeling that I was at the start of what could prove to be one of the most important experiments in the history of man.

Malaysia at least assumes that Malays and Chinese and Ibans, that Hindus and Muslims and Confucians, that black and brown and yellow, can, in the sharing of a common language and citizenship, in the toleration of different customs and colors and gods, become a new society united not by nationalism but, for the first time, by their blended internationalism.

Malaysia could, if given time to succeed, be man's social pattern for the future, for, as someone once said, it is only one step from toleration to forgiveness.

In my last hours in Singapore I joined the pilgrims who go to Kusu in the Chinese Ninth Moon in sampans which wear scarlet and green and apricot flags on their bows.

Kusu, off Singapore's dockland, is little more than two large rocks joined by a sandspit at low tide. On one island is a Chinese temple roofed with bleached-green tiles. On the other, at the top of steep winding foot-worn steps, is a Muslim shrine.

The pilgrims of many races bring sticky yellow rice wrapped in banana leaves, eggs painted blood red, fruit and flowers, plucked chickens and curry, and even tiny figurines of dolls and warriors, and offer them in the smoke of joss, under crimson banners, to the golden god in his alcove of red lacquer.

They pray and ask for favors and learn their fate and fortune by shaking marked bamboo sticks before the god, and then those who want children go outside and hang stones on the weary branches of a lone tree.

As more sampans arrive and the temple overflows, pilgrims, pimps, prostitutes, and pickpockets cross the sandspit to climb the steps lined with pleading spitting beggars to the Muslim shrine, fifty feet above an apple-green sea brushed with cloud.

There, under Dali trees hung with more stones, and in drifting sandalwood smoke, they pray and make offerings and eat their lunch and drop banana skins and wander down the steps again to their waiting sampans.

But Tua Pekong, god of Kusu, is not a god of the China pantheon, but a local god, exclusive to Kusu and to Singapore, a Chinese god who, through generations, has evolved in a Malayan environment, a Chinese god who has become Asian, Malaysian, in a tropical sense.

Equally important, the pilgrims of all races who pray to him offer the same prayers at the shrine of Fatima, daughter of the Prophet Mahomet, at the top of the stairs, and ask from her the same favors of health and fortune and children.

As I stood on Kusu, looking back at Singapore Island in the heat haze, watching a white liner move toward the docks, thinking of Malaysia and the problems its different people will face, I felt that, if Tua Pekong and Fatima can be worshipped side by side on Kusu, then nothing was impossible.

Postscript: Brunei and Afterward

This book was almost finished when, in December, 1962, the Azahari revolt began in the British protectorate of Brunei.

I therefore decided, because of time and the merchanics of book production, not to incorporate Brunei and other developments into the general story, which would remain unaltered, but to add a postscript to bring the book as up to date as possible in basic detail before publication.

The Brunei revolt, which was to bring Malaysia to world attention, began early on the morning of December 8, 1962, when Inche Ahmad Azahari, from the safety of Manila, proclaimed himself "Prime Minister" of the rebel "Government" of Brunei and ordered his secretly organized Tentera Nasional Kalimantan Utara—the North Borneo National Army, which he optimistically claimed numbered twenty thousand men—to take over Brunei and the other Borneo territories of Sarawak and Sabah.

The British put five thousand troops into Brunei from Singapore and, although the rebels had occupied the Seria oil field, most of Brunei Town, and other small towns, and had spilled into Sarawak and Sabah, the revolt was over in about a week.

When I read of rebellion in Brunei I was not surprised. I had expected serious trouble within Greater Malaysia before August, 1963, because of the organized opposition to the new Federation from within—particularly from the Communist party —and from without, since all Communist parties in Southeast Asia and Indonesian political leaders had never hidden their opposition to Malaysia. Some attempt, I was convinced, would be made to smash Malaysia and to use "colonialism" as the tired excuse, even though, with Malaysia a fact, colonial control would end in British territories in Southeast Asia and an independent Federation would take its place.

This is what happened. The revolt was only hours old when Indonesian spokesmen were talking of "colonialism," "imperialism," and the "struggle for freedom" by the Brunei rebels, and it was only days old when President Sukarno pledged Indonesian moral support for Inche Azahari's forces. Tunku Abdul Rahman, Prime Minister of Malaya, claimed that these forces were encouraged by political parties in Indonesia who had aided the rebels with arms and given them military training in Indonesian Kalimantan and other parts of Indonesia.

On December 17, Britain's Commissioner General for Southeast Asia, Lord Selkirk, told correspondents on Labuan Island, North Borneo, that the British Government had no evidence of outside support for the Brunei revolt. There apparently was "moral support from unofficial organizations outside Borneo territories," but no concrete evidence of men or material being sent to Borneo territories from outside. He was not aware of official support by any outside Government for the rebels.

This diplomatically worded statement looked even less convincing two days later, when President Sukarno told a mass meeting in Djakarta that Indonesians who did not support the Borneo rebels were "traitors to their own souls." The Indonesian people were born in fire and had fought and suffered for their independence, he said. It was only natural for them to sympathize with any nation fighting for independence.

The Brunei revolt had major results. It drew attention to the political backwardness of the Sultanate of Brunei, to the genuine demand for reform from the Brunei Malays, and to the urgent need to reconstruct the little fourteenth-century principality, socially and politically, from top to bottom. History will probably, though indirectly, thank Inche Azahari for his revolt, even though his real objectives were far more dangerous than political reconstruction.

Although the revolt was largely among the Brunei Malays, who rightly wanted a greater share in the governing of their little state, "Malay" is not an accurate description. Some of these "Malays" trace their ancestry to the Malays of Malaya, many have Javanese blood, and some are of mixed blood, including Chinese. The one thing they have in common is that they are Muslims, so that a better description for them is Brunei Muslims, not Malays.

The revolt showed clearly that Brunei, which had dithered for months about joining Malaysia, would have to be part of Malaysia to make the new Federation work, because, if left outside the Federation, it would be a political menace, a rallying point for anti-Malaysia forces, a potential fifth-column area to threaten its next-door neighbors, Sarawak and Sabah, and even the Philippines.

The revolt strengthened support for Malaysia within the Borneo territories, but brought directly into the open Indonesian opposition to Malaysia, and Philippine opposition due to security fears that Indonesia might grab part or all of northern Borneo and link it with Indonesian Kalimantan.

It also demonstrated, if any demonstration was needed, the Communist plan to prevent the federation of Sarawak, Sabah, and Brunei with Malaya and Singapore.

But Brunei was only the beginning of acute tension and near cold war in Southeast Asia, a time of threats, foolish statements, personal abuse, wild accusations, distortion, arrests. It also started frenetic diplomatic scurryings and negotiations.

On Saturday, February 2, 1963, the Security Council in

Singapore ordered the arrest of more than a hundred members of the Communist-controlled Barisan Socialis, including the Secretary-General of the party, baby-face Lim Chin Siong, whom I had interviewed at Barisan Socialis headquarters, and other members of the "Lunatic Left"—Fong Swee Suan, Dominic Puthucheary, Sandra Woodhull.

The official statement of the Security arrests said that Lim Chin Siong and another arrested man, Said Sahari, had met the Brunei rebel leader, Inche Azahari, in Singapore only four days before the Brunei revolt.

Singapore's Prime Minister, Lee Kuan Yew, who had given Lim Chin Siong and his friends their freedom in 1959 when Singapore became a city-state, said that those arrested were all only open-front leaders and that eighteen important Communists had escaped the Security net. These included the "Plen"—the real Communist power in Singapore-Malaya. This is the same man the Prime Minister described in his 1961 radio talks on Communist organization in Singapore and the man the Prime Minister has always refused to denounce.

Lee Kuan Yew said: "We believe that Communist leadership is concentrated in Singapore and southern Malaya. Their closest link with other Communist parties is with the Partai Kommunist Indonesia. We believe that they use the Rhio Islands for meetings of cadres from Singapore and their equivalents in the P.K.I. It is very easy to get in and out of Singapore to the Rhio Islands by boat, and neither our patrols nor those of the Indonesian Government can keep a complete check on all small-boat movements."

After the Security roundup, propaganda against Malaysia became intense.

February 6: An Indonesian Foreign Ministry spokesman accused Malaya of being a "police state."

February 7: The Sultan of Brunei, who last year agreed in principle to join Malaysia, announced in Kuala Lumpur that Brunei would now join. Brunei's treaty of protection with

Britain expires on August 31, 1963, final target date for the foundation of Malaysia.

February 11: Indonesia's Foreign Minister, Dr. Subandrio, warned of armed conflict if Malaya's "present hostility to Indonesia spread to the Borneo territories." He declared Indonesia's official opposition to the proposed Malaysia Federation and attacked Tunku Abdul Rahman for "hostility toward Indonesia."

February 13: President Sukarno of Indonesia described the Malaysia plan as an attempt to save rubber, tin, and oil for the imperialists. He said: "Indonesia's opposition to Malaysia is not because of Communist influence but because Malaysia represents the forces of neo-colonialism," and added: "Nations who will become strong and famous should be ready to face moments of danger. We are still facing challenges. We are being besieged because we are standing on the principle of anti-colonialism and anti-imperialism. We will support all nations struggling for independence. What is the reason for our opposition to Malaya? Malaysia is neo-colonialism and we do not agree with this. If the Malayan leadership continues its present policy Indonesia will have no choice but to face it with political and economic confrontation. We must live in a sphere of confrontation—confrontation in all fields."

In the next fortnight: Malaya talked of reintroducing national service. Donald Stephens of Sabah, at a meeting of pro-Malaysia political parties, said the conference should prove to the world that the largest parties of the five territories were solidly behind the creation of Greater Malaysia. Britain's Chief of the Imperial General Staff, General Sir Richard Hull, said in Kuala Lumpur, "We will honor our defense treaty with Malaya." Tunku Abdul Rahman implied in a speech that Malaya, if attacked by Indonesia, would seek SEATO aid. Four United States Senators, led by Senator Mike Mansfield, recommended that the U.S. maintain a policy of "non-involved cordiality" toward Malaysia, a fence-sitting statement which encouraged the Indonesian Government to make more threats, and also encouraged the Indonesian Communist party. The inter-Governmental Committee on Malaysia's constitution, which had been studying problems of federation in the Borneo territories, issued its report on February 27. This Committee, headed by Lord Lansdowne, Britain's Minister of State for Colonial Affairs, and Tun Abdul Razak, Malaya's Deputy Prime Minister, recommended most important constitutional safeguards for the smaller states of Malaysia.

March opened with lively diplomatic comings and goings. Sir Arthur Tange, head of Australia's External Affairs Department, had conferred on Malaysia with the State Department in Washington. Australia's High Commissioner in Malaya, Mr. T. K. Critchley, and one of the best-informed diplomats in Southeast Asia, flew to Canberra from Kuala Lumpur with a stopover in Djakarta to talk to Indonesia's leaders. Britain's Commissioner General for Southeast Asia, Lord Selkirk, told the Australian Cabinet in Canberra of Britain's irrevocable support for the Malaysia Federation.

Then, on March 5, the Australian Government, with the support of the Australian Labour leader, backed Malaysia. This was the most momentous decision in Australia's one-hundred-and-seventy-five-year-old history. For the first time it recognized that Australia was part of Southeast Asia and therefore irrevocably linked with the countries of that region. As Australia's Minister for External Affairs, Sir Garfield Barwick, said on March 7, on the eve of his mission to Manila to seek and to achieve admission to the Economic Commission for Asia and the Far East (ECAFE), and to try to improve Malaya-Indonesia relations over Malaysia, Australia was making a positive attempt to play its part "as an Asian nation, not just a country outside."

These were revolutionary words from insular Australia—but words which should have been spoken many years before. Only history will show whether they are already too late. Unfortunately, those words, and the decision to support Malaysia, did not come from long-held conviction about Australia's place in Southeast Asia. They did not stem from Australian initiative, but were forced from Australian leaders by the tensions and pressures of immediate events. So that, as always in the past, Australia followed others lamely instead of proving early in the Malaysia squabble that even a small country can have a mind of its own and a foreign policy, a Southeast Asian policy, good or bad, that she is prepared to back.

At least Australia has at last faced the realities of geography and history. Never again can she be a "country outside." Australia has supported the formation of Malaysia—and rightly. She would have committed a "Munich" and been discredited had she failed Malaysia. She had obligations she had to honor. This does not mean that she is anti-Indonesian or anti-Philippine. She disagrees on this issue, but is friendly with both. But if she is to play a positive role in Southeast Asia, there will be other issues when she will have to side with Indonesia or somebody else—perhaps even against Malaysia.

In March and April, while comparatively minor officials of Malaya, the Philippines, and Indonesia were agreeing in Manila to hold a Foreign Ministers conference on Malaysia which would ultimately lead to a summit meeting between Prime Minister Tunku Abdul Rahman, President Diosdado Macapagal; and President Sukarno, Russia's Defense Minister, Marshal Rodion Malinovsky, visited Indonesia, followed almost immediately by China's Premier, Mr. Liu Shao-chi. Both, while conveniently forgetting places like Hungary and Tibet, damned Malaysia as neo-colonialist and supported the "revolutionary struggle of the people of North Borneo." But Mr. Liu went further. He said that Communist China would "forever remain reliable comrades-in-arms," not of President Sukarno or the Indonesian Government or Army, but of the "Indonesian people." They were words to remember.

Mr. Liu was well aware when he spoke that forty-eight hours before, sixty men in jungle-green uniforms and armed with automatic weapons and carbines had raided Tebutu village, only three miles inside Sarawak's border with Indonesian Kalimantan, and had then withdrawn to the jungle with all the arms from the local police station, where a constable lay with a bullet in his head. The raiders were from Kalimantan.

It was still too early to know, as British troops moved into the area where Communist indoctrination and weapons-training camps were believed to have been established, where raids like this would end, but the pattern was clear and typical; the lessons from the Malayan civil war were there. Tebutu and an attack on a British commando patrol which followed on April 23 in the same area were warnings of a Communist guerrilla war—warnings that the battle for northern Borneo, for Malaysia, for Southeast Asia was moving into another stage.

Almost at the same time, history of great significance in the Pacific was being made, for on May 1 at Kota Bahru (Hollandia), and more than two thousand miles east of Djakarta, Indonesia took over Irian Barat—West Irian (formerly Dutch New Guinea)—from the United Nations administration, and for the first time Australian territory, in Papua-New Guinea, had a common land frontier with an Asian country.

By mid-May Indonesian opposition to Malaysia had hardened into what was called almost "national dogma," with President Sukarno warning that his policy of confrontation would continue even after Malaysia was formed.

Why? Why also have both Muslim Indonesia and the Christian Philippines, countries which have never been close politically, so bitterly opposed Malaysia?

The primary concern of the Filipinos is security. They, too, have already fought their own Communist civil war. They are afraid of Indonesian and Malaysian-Chinese Communism and also of the possibility of Indonesian expansion. They feel that Indonesian occupation of any part of northern Borneo would open a direct route for the P.K.I. across the Sulu Archipelago into the southern Philippines. But their longer-range fear is the Chinese—fear that Chinese Communism in Malaysia, or some part of it, might take over, fear that through this China herself could eventually extend her power deep into the South China Sea. The Filipinos are an island people who look suspiciously at mainland Asia and at steppingstones, like Borneo, which reach out toward themselves. They don't like what they see.

There is no one explanation for Indonesian official hatred of Malaysia. The Indonesian leaders face grave pressures from within and from without, and much of their verbal opposition to Malaysia is intended for their own people as a diversion from internal problems. The great mass of Indonesians are peasants whose life has changed little in centuries. Opposition to Malaysia has never been a popular issue in Indonesia, as the West New Guinea issue undoubtedly was, and anti-Malaysia feeling has been difficult to arouse. The Indonesian economy is seriously lame and largely through lack of experience, shortage of skilled people, mismanagement, heavy spending on arms which can't even be properly maintained. Internal political and religious groups oppose Djakarta control and don't like taking orders from Sukarno. The Communist party is a large and dangerously permanent internal threat, especially as the defense forces are heavily infiltrated by the Communist party of Indonesia, the P.K.I. The Indonesian leaders are envious of Malaya's wealth and progress as an independent country, and with this envy is mingled the contempt of the revolutionary because Malaya was given her freedom and did not have to fight for it. They are also envious of Tunku Abdul Rahman's good record and prestige. Sour grapes undoubtedly play a part. President Sukarno was once invited to make a state visit to Kuala Lumpur. He replied that as he was the leader of Southeast Asia, Malaya's King, the Yang di-Pertuan Agong should visit him. The Malayan leaders haven't forgotten this insult. On the other hand, the Indonesians haven't forgotten that Malayans, many of whom have Sumatran blood, were openly sympathetic to the Sumatra rebellion of 1958. The Indonesians, even many Indonesian Communists, are also afraid of Chinese Communism in Malaya, Singapore, and the Borneo territories.

It is also impossible to ignore the genuine concern Indonesians feel, after more than three centuries of colonial rule, about any suggestion of colonialism. Men who took part in the Indonesian revolution can hardly be expected to be tolerant of any plan proposed by a Western-educated and oriented leader like Tunku Abdul Rahman, or any plan which the British are supporting, and supporting with arms. Indonesian support for Inche Azahari, the Brunei revolutionary of Indonesian blood, is also understandable. Official approval, and not just Communist approval, was inevitable for Azahari's rebellion in Brunei.

Indonesian leaders also see their country, which has more people than Japan had when she started the Pacific war, as a new Asian and Pacific power, and a power whose future greatness could perhaps be retarded by others. It is this sense of power-destiny, only yet in its infancy, but again and again stressed by President Sukarno, who has recently been made President for life, which will need to be watched by all her neighbors. The Indonesian leaders know that tiny Malaysia, with only ten million people, can be no threat to them, but a prosperous stable federation next door would be a constant example and reminder of their own failures. They also face intense pressure from their expansionists and from the Communist party, whose instructions are to destroy Malaysia now, and if that fails, to destroy it later and take over its territories one by one.

Remember, it was Lee Kuan Yew, the outstanding socialist leader of Singapore, who once said that the five territories of Malaya, Singapore, Sarawak, Sabah, and Brunei must get together, form Malaysia, and survive, or the Communists "will hang us separately."

Finally, in late May, as the Indonesian Communist party showed signs of becoming more and more pro-Peking, the whole Malaysia situation dramatically changed. The Indone-

sian propaganda campaign faltered. President Sukarno, holiday-
ing in Japan, invited Tunku Abdul Rahman to see him. The
two leaders met in Tokyo from May 31 to June 1 and agreed to
"settle their differences" peacefully. Later the Foreign Ministers of Malaya, Indonesia, and the Philippines met in Manila,
and on June 10 approved Malaysia as a first step to a meeting
of their leaders and the possible formation in the future of a
confederation of their three countries, which hold one hundred
and forty million people. Only history will show whether this
sudden change of attitude will be sustained.

One month later, on July 9, the official agreement to create
Malaysia, as a member of the British Commonwealth, on
August 31, 1963, was signed in London by Tunku Abdul
Rahman, Lee Kuan Yew, and the British Government. Brunei
refused to unite with Malaya, Singapore, Sarawak, and Sabah,
but may join in the future. If she finally decides not to join
Malaysia, she will become a real danger to the Federation,
because those forces which oppose Malaysia will do everything
they can to use her in the much wider struggle for supremacy
in Southeast Asia.

July 10, 1963

Index